THE EXILED HEART

Also by Kelly Cherry

FICTION
Sick and Full of Burning
Augusta Played
In the Wink of an Eye
The Lost Traveller's Dream
My Life and Dr. Joyce Brothers

POETRY
Lovers and Agnostics
Relativity: A Point of View
Natural Theology

LIMITED EDITIONS
Conversion, a story
Songs for a Soviet Composer, poems

THE EXILED HEART
A Meditative Autobiography

Kelly Cherry

LOUISIANA STATE UNIVERSITY PRESS
Baton Rouge and London

Designer: Rebecca Lloyd Lemna
Typeface: Bembo
Typesetter: G & S Typesetters, Inc.
Printer and binder: Thomson-Shore, Inc.

Library of Congress Cataloging-in-Publication Data

Cherry, Kelly.
    The exiled heart : a meditative autobiography / Kelly Cherry.
      p.   cm.
    ISBN 0-8071-1620-3 (alk. paper)
    I. Cherry, Kelly—Biography.   2. Authors, American—20th century—
Biography.   I. Title.
PS3553.H357Z467   1991
818'.5409—dc20
    [B]   90-13332
                                                            CIP

The author is grateful to the editors of the following journals, in which the essays
noted first appeared: "An Underground Hotel in Leningrad," in *Witness*
(Spring–Summer, 1990); "Love," in the *Southern Review*, n.s., XXVI (April, 1990),
254–65; "Nightwork," in the *Gettysburg Review* (Winter, 1991). She is also grateful
to the editor of the *Virginia Quarterly Review* for permission to reprint "Justice,"
which originally appeared in Vol. XLVII (January, 1991) of that journal.

The paper in this book meets the guidelines for permanence and
durability of the Committee on Production Guidelines for Book Longevity
of the Council on Library Resources. ∞

for Imant

If only we could go back to Moscow! Sell the house, finish with our life here, and go back to Moscow.

—Chekhov, *The Three Sisters*

Author's Note

The events in this book are true. Conversations are abbreviated but true to life. I am not a journalist, and I don't carry a cassette or notebook, but because the conversations I quote were so vital to me—they would determine my future—I was able to record many of the sentences word for word. I kept close notes of events as they happened.

These events happened, of course, in the context of what is now seen as history (though it is useful to remember that, as Janusz Glowacki has put it, "Socialism is a system in which the past cannot be predicted"), and, further, I wrote this book about them over a period of fifteen years, many of which are now known as "the period of stagnation" or "the Brezhnev Era." Rather than convert the present tense to the past, I have retained it as a record of my struggle—and the struggle also of thousands of other people—to understand the events of our time.

The names of officials are their real names, but I have changed the names of most of my friends, to shelter them from reprisals and embarrassment, which, though impressive reforms appear to be taking place in the Soviet Union and the Baltic States, are still not out of the question. Latvian names are declined, like Latin names, with endings to indicate their grammatical function in the sentence. I have dropped the diacritical markings, and generally the endings, from proper names, for the sake of simplicity. Imant, for example, is Imants Kalniņš in the nominative, but here he is Imant Kalnin in every case.

I had planned to change his name, too, but he asked me not to. "Would not be honest," he said. "You must say our story to the world, please." As the KGB already know who he is, I agreed.

Theoretically, of course, Imant should never have been in any danger at all. He was "guilty" only of wanting to marry me—and a citizen's right to marry whom he pleases has, since Stalin's death, been protected by Soviet law; it is reaffirmed by the Final Act of the Helsinki Accords. So I have written our story, as he asked me to, and if the Soviet Union objects—well, it was they who dictated it.

Contents

In Indra's garden

CHAPTER 1

Arrivals and Departures

I

I was waiting in the car, and it was plain at once from the look on Imant's face, when he came out of the building, what had happened. He had been warned to stop seeing me. The Latvian Central Committee had made the threat and Imant's chief at the Union of Composers had relayed it. Without saying a word, Imant and I shot out from the center of town, along the near bank of the beautiful Daugava and across the bridge; finally he pulled over to the curb. Imant had a little yellow Soviet Fiat. A couple of days earlier I had asked him if it might be bugged, and he said he thought not—he thought that the only microphones we had to worry about were in the hotel and at Karl's. I therefore felt at liberty to burst into tears, confident that the one piece of information the KGB still lacked about us was that they could make me cry.

According to Imant's chief, the informant complained particularly about the way we had greeted each other at Rumbula Airport: "Kissing in public! Hugging!" To me, this sounded less like the Politburo and more like a vengeful wife, especially since we'd neither kissed nor hugged—at the airport; that came later. Were somebody's spies slipping? After ten years apart, Imant and I could at first only dumbly grip each other's hand, while Karl did the talking for both of us. "I was so excited," Imant told me later, in careful English, "that I forgot to be happy." He admitted that he hadn't really remembered what I looked like, only how he had responded to me. I had been afraid he'd be disappointed with how I looked. I was wearing a brick-red dress with pink and green embroidery and a cowboy hat, and I had checked my makeup compulsively all the way from Moscow to Riga, but what if he'd touched up the picture in his mind until it was no longer me? I'm medium height, small-boned, brown-haired, and brown-eyed.

For my part, I had made him taller and darker than he is in fact, but I would never mistake the light in his eyes for anyone else's. I *had* forgotten how thin he was. I knew from snapshots he'd sent that his hair was thinning—at the forehead—and the hair he had left he wore longish. Long hair was still a social statement in the Soviet Union. He also had a close-cut beard, and his eyebrows and the beard were much darker than his hair, almost black. His eyes are deep-set but light gray, like light at the far end of a cave. Whenever he agreed with something somebody'd said, he made a small, precise nod; he had these East European gestures and manners, and they sometimes seemed at odds with his attempt to dress like an American.

We had had to put all this together to find each other in the crowd at the airport in Riga. I heard a voice behind me and whirled around. It was Imant.

Bear in mind, please, that we had seen each other only for four days, less than two hours a day, ten years before this reunion. Now it was 1975.

II

1965: Imant and I first met in a lobby of the Metropol Hotel in Moscow. It was January: Khrushchev had been ousted a few months back, with the coming of winter. But my arrival had nothing to do with Khrushchev's departure; truthfully, until a

Swedish girl staying in the same youth hostel in Amsterdam told me about her tour of Russia, I thought it existed only in nineteenth-century novels. I was in love with Tolstoy, Dostoevsky, Turgenev, Gogol, the rueful Chekhov. Turning the pages of a book, I caught the scent of the trees of Yasnaya Polyana. I knew what the leaves smelled like when it rained. The Swedish girl clarified for me what Tolstoy well knew, that Russia is made of earth and not paper. She didn't tell me how *much* earth: you can put the whole of the United States and China inside the Soviet Union and still have space to spare. I rented a room on the outskirts of Amsterdam, making it my headquarters for the year I planned to spend abroad, and three months later boarded a train for Moscow.

The train you step onto in Amsterdam is electric, as sleek and clean as a cat. A funny thing happened on the way to the Workers' Paradise: every time the train stopped, it exchanged a new car for an old one, or two. This was progress? In East Germany, in a more sinister, Circean transformation, our conductors became armed soldiers. Then at Brest, a respite and hope: the border guard patrolling the station outside my window kept glancing surreptitiously in my direction. Just as the train pulled out, I waved; he grinned and waved back, running alongside the train, and we waved each other out of sight.

Here, then, was a good omen, and when the door of my compartment opened, I was cheerful as could be, though the compartment was cold. And it isn't every day that the companion who presents himself at your door is the son of the former Polish ambassador to Brazil. He carried a sword and a briefcase; I guess the sword was for duels. He was going to enter the university at Krakow, but he said he would be in Warsaw two weeks from now to show me around during my stopover there. We stayed up all night, talking, though not, I'm afraid, in Polish, and when it was time for breakfast, he excused himself to join his parents. I was hungry too. After a while I screwed up my courage and went in search of the dining car. We were in Russia, all right. The doors between cars were more or less locked in ice. I pushed like crazy and fought my way into the adjoining car. Once, between cars, the wind nearly blew me off the train; the metal under my feet was coated with a thin sheet of ice.

The boy and his parents were sitting at a nearby table, and I smiled at them, but they didn't speak to me. I didn't know what I'd done wrong. I stood there awkwardly, in my one skirt. I had one skirt, one dress, and one pair of jeans. Why was I being ostracized? I would have gone to Siberia to be somewhere other than where I was, but all I could do was sit down. The fabled Russian winter was knocking at my window—there was snow on the ground now—and I sat at my table, morosely self-conscious. The boy and his parents left; I got up to leave. "Nyet," the cashier said. Was something wrong with my *money* too? "Nyet," he said again, "nyet."

"No?" I asked.

"Da!" He held up my tab, shook it, and pointed at the door, where the ambassador and his family had just exited. They had paid for me. I had plenty of time in my compartment that afternoon to wonder why it was that an ambassador who was glad for his son to take me sightseeing, as two weeks later his son did, couldn't be seen saying hello in person. Maybe it had to do with his being so suddenly recalled. Recalled. Recalled. The train had a lot of territory to cover. I settled back, feeling as if I finally had room to breathe in, after three months in the most densely populated city in the world, Amsterdam. I didn't miss the electric trains; I'm fond of old things. In my expansive mood, I even felt great affection for the little old women energetically sweeping snow off the tracks as we chugged into the last station, slowly, many, many hours later.

I didn't know, in 1965, where that train was taking me: to Moscow, I thought, but equally to my heart and my conscience. This book is a kind of log, a moral travelogue if you will, of a course that was set then and there, deep into heartland.

In the eighteenth century, a *Maggid,* or preacher, was an itinerant storyteller. The *Maggid* would wander purposefully from town to town, village to village, every so often gathering around him a group of eager listeners. Like any performer, he always waited until everyone had settled down. The coughing died down, the foot-shuffling gradually ceased. Then when the room was so quiet you could sense your neighbors' unspoken words just below the surface of silence like heated bricks under a blanket, the *Maggid* opened his lesson with an illustrative parable. One man especially was renowned for his skill at this method of preaching, Jakob Kranz, the Dubner *Maggid*. His fame reached even Elijah, *Gaon* of Vilna.

Now the *Gaon* of Vilna was no slouch himself, but he recognized in the *Maggid's* method a simplicity more effective even than his own analytic approach. So he invited the Dubner *Maggid* to visit him and after dinner asked the *Maggid* how it was that he always managed to find the precisely appropriate parable for a particular text or proverb.

"*Gaon,*" the *Maggid* said, "I will let you in on a little secret. Just as the archer may shoot his arrow first and outline the target after, I likewise cheat a little. I find a story first, and sooner or later the moral of the story turns up too."

I didn't "find" my story; it found me, as autobiography always does: finds you out in your deepest, most private places. But I *tell* my story in this book because, like Jakob Kranz, I believe that in the end the right truth will make itself known.

Okay: what I write here is autobiography. Elsewhere, in a short story ambitiously titled "Where the Winged Horses Take Off into the Wild Blue Yonder From," I made fiction out of some of the events of that first visit to Russia. For the sake of literary consistency, I gave my narrator a somewhat more sanguine character than I possess and rendered Imant more compulsive than he is. I made us both more pragmatic than we are. Actually, Imant is quiet and easygoing, though his moods can swing wildly. He does not like to draw attention to himself.

In the Metropol, I was aware that Imant was watching me. I was sitting on a couch in an upstairs lounge, waiting for the coffee shop to open. My chance came when we got into line. I leaned across Imant and asked the girl with him if she spoke English; I was going to ask her to tell me how to order a cup of coffee. Probably it would have been sufficient to say to the waitress, "Coffee," but then I wouldn't have met Indra— or Imant.

Indra had long, wavy hair, the color of Russian red-gold (a natural resource), and she had intelligent eyes and wore no makeup, but she couldn't speak English. Only German, Russian, sign language, and Latvian. Imant spoke for her, introducing himself. (You say: Ĭ'mahnt, accent on the first syllable.) *He* knew French, Russian, a little English, a little Estonian, and Latvian. And he knew I was American by the way I had lit my cigarette in the lounge. Europeans strike a match in toward the body. They were both Latvian; she studied theatrical production and direction in Moscow, he was a composer come to the city to listen to rehearsals. And what was I doing here, and why was my vocabulary so limited? I promised to speak my one tongue slowly.

I asked Imant if he had learned English in school.

"From *žurnāli,*" he said. "*Time* magazine."

This interested me, because it helped to explain the young man from Ghana I had met on my first night in Moscow. At loose ends until the next day when the rest of my tour group was supposed to materialize, I had wandered out into the street in front of the hotel, amazed to find that not only did Russia exist, it was populated as well. It had never occurred to me that there were so many Communists in Moscow, or that they all bought evening papers and hurried home after work. Then I looked more closely and realized that surprisingly few bought papers; what's the point, when you know what the papers are going to say before you read them? If I sound provincial, remember that in 1965 Russia was not exactly the resort most frequented by Americans. My home was Richmond, Virginia. I had been born in Baton Rouge, Louisiana. And here on this first night in Moscow I had been approached by a young man from Ghana. He asked if I'd go with him for coffee, and, considering how soft-spoken he was, I said sure.

The cold was incredible, at least to somebody from Virginia. It tickled the inside of your nose; it froze the hairs there, and you felt like you were breathing glass. I was happy to get on a warm bus with the boy from Ghana. But then we rode, and rode, and rode. "Do you like it here?" I asked him, meaning Russia. He was a student at the Patrice Lumumba University. "Oh, yes," he said.

"Which do you like better," I went on, seeking a commitment, "Russia or Ghana?"

"One always loves the Motherland," he answered. He was either a good student or a clever one. In any case he was certainly eager for information. The first thing he did when we were seated in the café was ask me if I had brought any *Time* magazines to Moscow. And as it happened, I did have one or two European editions in my suitcase. "Please," he said, "may I have them? I will pay you." His glance kept flickering around the room and only rarely lighted on me. I don't know how he could tell if anyone was watching us: the room was jammed with workers in wet overcoats, and a heavy odor of Russian cigarettes, lemon tea, and sweat seemed to lie over the concrete floor like a pall. I had the impression that nobody wanted to be seen—or even to see—but Intourist warned travelers against buying or selling on the black market, and I wasn't about to risk Siberia for the sake of a *Time* magazine. I stalled. We finished our coffee, and then the student took me back to my hotel. But every day he called, to inquire whether I had found my *Time* magazines yet.

Now here was Imant, telling me that *Time* was available in libraries, for people who only wanted to read it. "But look," Imant said, "we can talk better if we go some *else* place." So once again I was riding across town, this time in a taxi with Imant and Indra. We went to a bar, all three trading bits of our lives the way strangers do in transit, but I already knew, perched on a stool at the counter, that I was home, next to Imant.

"Having coffee," I learned, was often an elaborate business, involving vodka, wine, cognac, chocolate, ice cream, apples, and quite possibly coffee. Sometimes Imant ordered steaks for everybody, but he stuck to vodka for himself. Of course, drinking is the patriotic thing to do. The State earns twenty-three percent of its annual revenue from the sale of alcohol, which more or less means the country is either drunk and solvent or sober and bankrupt. There *is* a third alternative: to teach Soviet citizens to put it down slowly and on a full stomach . . . and the State's working on this now, but in 1965 Imant was knocking his drinks back in the best tradition, neat.

The free time I was allowed was limited, though not so much as it would have been if the rest of my tour group had shown up. I'd been joined by an American named Bryce who was in computers; Intourist wouldn't tell us what had happened to the other twenty: they might have canceled, they might have been canceled. Anyone who deals with Intourist, and that's everyone who visits the Union of Soviet Socialist Republics, quickly learns that it is not a travel agency. It is a branch of the government and shares with other branches the pervasive Soviet paranoia. What is most secret is most real! If the problem cannot be identified, we cannot be charged with the responsibility for solving it! Applications are ignored, tickets appear and disappear, tour groups vanish—and Intourist won't even say if it's merely because the flight was grounded and the group rescheduled.

I wasn't complaining. Because we were the only two, Bryce and I were given first-class treatment for cut-rate prices, and we had a lot more time on our own. Assuming we were on our own: the guides are supposed to report regularly. (Like every American tourist I've talked with since, I searched my hotel room for bugs, giving it up in disgust when I realized that I wouldn't recognize a bug if I saw one.) But we were still expected to stick to our sightseeing schedule. Imant and Indra saw me to the hotel and returned later when I was back from a concert. We followed the same pattern the next day. It seemed to me that Bryce and I ought to repay both Imant and Indra, so we asked them to come with us to the foreign currency bar in the National Hotel, mecca for journalists.

Imant and Indra were reluctant. We thought this was because they didn't want us to feel we had to spend money entertaining them, and naturally we urged them to let us. Finally they agreed, and we climbed the stairs to the bar. It was crowded, full of smoke and noise: talkier than the other places we'd been. We managed to get a table, and Bryce went for the drinks. Imant and I had difficulty understanding each other's accent under any circumstances, but conversation was practically out of the question here. Indra and I communicated by doodling on a paper napkin. I could tell Imant was uncomfortable with something in the situation, but I couldn't tell if it was the noise, or Bryce, or if he simply felt conspicuous in a bar for foreigners. All at once Bryce returned with a man who said he was a man without a country. "Wait till you hear my story," the man said, still standing, and declaiming like an actor. Thinking of Nathan Hale, I said I already had. "You think it's a laughing matter?" he asked. "Do you know what it's like not to have a passport?" By this time he had pulled up a chair. We assumed Bryce had invited him over, but even Bryce seemed agitated.

I was dazed by the atmosphere, the confusion. I sensed something was transpiring, an event was taking place precisely in front of me, and yet I couldn't locate it. On the other hand, maybe I was a little overexcited, and maybe a little drunk. But why was Bryce shuffling and scuffling? Was he trying to get the man to leave, or stay? At one point, Bryce offered to fight somebody, but I think it was somebody on the other side of the table. Imant stopped him. Meanwhile, the man without a country was sitting between Indra and me, telling his story. Forget its finer points: the gist was that he had been in one place for a while, and then in another, and somehow his right to a passport had been sacrificed in being too long between the two. It didn't make sense. I knew very little about the law, but in an idle moment I had read the data printed in my own passport, and they didn't jibe with what this man was telling me about his.

I had also noticed that while Imant was occupied with Bryce, trying to pacify him or at least get him to shut up, the man had pocketed a box of matches which we had left out on the table. Imant, Indra, and I were all smokers then. The man palmed the matches perfectly. Running his hands over the table in the course of his monologue, as if looking for his glass or some other item too incidental to stop talking for, he plucked the little box from the table like an egg from an ear and made it disappear into his pocket. At the crucial moment he happened to be looking in Indra's direction, since he wasn't wizard enough to keep an eye on both of us at the same time. I suppose he figured I wouldn't think about what I saw, or that if I did, I was inconsequential anyway.

Some small time later, Indra took out a cigarette and was getting ready to light it when she realized there were no matches on the table. I said to the man, "You have them," but apparently he couldn't hear me over the noise, so I said it again, louder. He was snapping his fingers, signaling someone at the bar, and he ignored me. Without knowing quite why, I was incensed by his pretending not to have the matches, and the third time, I spoke up loud and clear enough for Imant to understand. "He has the matches," I said. The man patted his pockets and shrugged. "He took them—" I insisted, starting to explain; Imant cut me off and then said something to Indra in Latvian. All this happened very swiftly. But the man from the bar had come over to our table, flashing a cigarette lighter. He bent down to touch the flame to Indra's cigarette. There was a point, as she half-turned toward him, paused, and leveled her gaze, when all of the energies at the table seemed suspended, a point of great preparation, pose and focus. Then suddenly the incident was over.

We left almost immediately afterward. Out on the street, I asked Imant what had happened. He said, "They took her picture."

"With the lighter?"

"Yes, with the lighter."

It was late, and the street was nearly deserted. A drunk fell out of an alley, but he was a silent drunk and stumbled off into the night soundlessly, like W. C. Fields leaving a darkened studio after the day's rushes. In *My Country and the World*, Andrei Sakharov says that, counting only in the Russian Republic, ten thousand drunks pass out "and freeze on the streets" each year. (You keep an eye out for the lurching shadow, the icy body.) Starlight glittered on the sidewalk; everything seemed eerie, alien, but at least the constellations were familiar. East and West shared a planet, after all, and a heaven. Why not a bar? "What will they do with it?" I asked, thinking of the photograph.

"They will put it in a file."

"Why? What does it mean?"

"It simply means, if someday she asks for a visa, it will be more difficult for to get."

I felt it was my fault, for taking them where they hadn't really wanted to go. Worse, we now had to separate for a few days, while Bryce and I went to Leningrad. We were to fly there in the morning. The third place on our tour was Riga, and Imant and Indra would meet us there, but I didn't like leaving even temporarily on this note of perplexity and despair. Imant saved the day. Just before we were to leave for the airport, he arrived at the Metropol with a going-away present, a gigantic pineapple.

I didn't know very much about Imant other than that he gave me, in addition to the pineapple, a sense of peace. Looking back, I think this feeling derived from his willingness to accept me for what and who I was. He never tried to change me or deny my perceptions.

What I knew: he was a composer. He was twenty-three. He wore a black turtleneck. And he wore a wedding band. In the Soviet Union you wear your ring on the right hand, and if you divorce, you may decide to move it to the left. Later I learned he'd already been married *twice* before we met—twice before he was twenty-three.

I didn't know that then.

When both parties agree—and if the KGB doesn't interfere—divorce in the Soviet Union is a simple matter. It's a frequent matter, too. As I write this, the national divorce rate is one in five, and in certain cities, it's running close to one in two. The sociological reasons for all those divorces are the same ones that prompted all the marriages in the first place: though the housing shortage isn't as severe as it used to be, families are still jam-packed into tiny apartments, and the first obstacle to having an affair is the lack of a place to have it in.

Nor can the Soviet citizen take a hotel room with any name but his own. To sign in, he has to show his passport. The hallways are watched day and night by key-ladies, and the rules permit visitors after 9 P.M. only with the permission of the hotel manager, and then only until 11 P.M. They're laxer about these rules for some foreign visitors, but at first glance it would seem that for the Soviet citizen there are only two answers to all this: celibacy and marriage.

Marriage, however, does not mean mere sex; it means procreation. During the Great Patriotic War, known to the rest of us as World War II, the Soviet Union lost twenty million men and women. They are understandably eager to restore the population, but even here their stratagem is the usual one of secrecy. Information about birth control is deliberately withheld, and contraceptives are difficult to obtain. The pill, at least for now, is unavailable. A married woman may be told about nonartificial methods—if she asks. Other methods are not prescribed until the doctor feels the woman has had enough children. If she has ten, she will receive a medal and the title "Mother-Heroine of the Soviet Union." I don't know whether you can qualify for your title without being married, but it's a relevant question. One in every ten children is born out of wedlock.

In fact, the illegitimacy rate is an indicator of a third widely practiced life-style, living together—permanently enough to set up housekeeping in a shared apartment but without the bother of going through what is, after all, in the Soviet Union only a bureaucratic process.

But of course there are yet other, hidden alternatives, such as parks and friends' flats, and love in the afternoon. "It means," said Imant, "that in Russia we are doing by day what other countries do at night."

Composers aren't, by and large, a puritanical group of people. I wasn't surprised to learn Imant had had two wives so early on (though I was shaken; I worried that his commitment to me might be just as unserious as it had been to them).

I knew about composers in general because I come from a family of musicians and know that musicians tend toward extremes. Music is an internal art, the study of structure, like mathematics; both musicians and mathematicians forget that the actual world is made up of contingencies. Only a musician or mathematician would avow, as César Thomson did to Ysaye while walking along the riverside in Brussels one afternoon, that anyone with a competent technique could walk on water. And so saying, he stepped onto the river and sank.

Imant met me in the hotel in Riga. Bryce said, "I think the guy's glad to see you."

With him were Indra, Rudolf, and two other friends, all Latvians. Rudolf wanted to be a film director but couldn't attend the institute in Moscow because there was a quota system for the minorities, of which Latvians are one. Opportunities and advantages of all sorts are reserved for Russians; minorities, like minorities everywhere, receive short shrift. The Western minorities, including the ethnic populations of the Baltic States, are rapidly being assimilated out of existence; for instance, the best housing in Riga, Latvia's capital city, goes to Russians. It's a deliberate policy, one intended to eliminate any hope of secession. Riga is now seventy percent Russian, and Rudolf has had to give up his first ambition. Happily, he likes his work, restoring a palace. He will spend his life on this project, for the work is painstaking and time-consuming. The palace was designed by the architect of the Winter Palace in Leningrad and will one day be very beautiful again.

One day, someday, a lifetime. But we had only forty-eight hours in Riga, and much to talk about—or to try to talk about, with Imant acting as interpreter for all of us. Once he seemed unwilling to translate. We were trying to get into the Luna Restaurant. The restaurants in the Soviet Union don't have enough food to feed everybody who would like to eat in them, so getting in becomes a business of who-you-know and who-you-bribe; the Russians call it having *blat,* connections. Imant had *blat* here but the woman nevertheless refused to let us in. A man appeared—I assumed Imant had asked to speak to the manager. The manager was shaking his head. "Tell him from where you are coming," Imant said to me. Secretly pleased at having passed for Russian, I said, "I'm from America." I must have sounded authentic, because we were abruptly ushered in and given one of the better tables for our coffee, and also for our cognac, wine, vodka, chocolate, apples, and steaks. I kept pestering Imant about the conversation at the door, wanting to know what the problem had been. Imant didn't exactly blush, but color rose in his face, and he began to fiddle with his fork, drawing the tines across the tabletop as if he were clearing it with a miniature rake. Did they have rakes in Latvia? Tripping over my own pun, *I* blushed. "What calls what you are wearing on your legs?" Imant asked. Startled, I said, "Tights."

"Yes, tights. This the problem is, which you are asking about."

I still didn't understand.

"Here there are many Russian whores who wear these black tights for standing in the cold. At first, they think you are one."

I had passed for Russian, all right—a Russian prostitute. Imant started to smile in spite of himself, but just then a suspicious-looking man asked me to dance. He really did look as if he'd emerged from behind a potted plant and I started to say no, but Imant whispered to me to say nothing. My would-be dance partner went away. I still don't know if Imant thought the man was KGB, or if he just didn't want us to lose time while I explained my nationality to someone else. Or maybe he thought the man was going to offer me a couple of rubles.

It had snowed when I was in Leningrad, a whirling windfall of white flakes straight out of everyone's childhood. Descending, each snowflake said, History, and stuck to the courtyard gates, or Mystery, and melted on your head. Winter or summer, Leningrad must be, I think, the most beautiful city on earth— but Riga is the prettiest, even lacking sufficient paint and asphalt, or downy snow. Seven hours' drive south of Leningrad, warmed by the Gulf Stream, it's much more temperate, though the Gulf of Riga freezes over from December to February. The ground was packed hard as ice, our steps rang in the night, but the air was Windex clear.

Imant was going to play me a tape of his First Symphony;

we all went, in a line like a snake, through the narrow streets of the Old City—past Hanseatic warehouses and cathedrals with gilded cocks atop their spires. The silence was overwhelming, a presence—not an absence of sound but a physical presence of silence—that dominated the dark streets like an invisible dictator. (Sure, if you hang around Red Square at night there's plenty of activity to be seen and heard: tourists mill, the guards in front of the tomb change, lovers stroll, and somebody is bound to try to buy the clothes off your back. But elsewhere in Moscow, and in Leningrad and Riga, nighttime elbows people off the streets.) No one said anything. I was cold, even in black tights. I pulled my wool scarf farther over my face, like a *babushka,* and shoved my hands down into my pockets. I kept close to Imant's side and away from alleys and still felt, when after this long, silent journey we arrived at the door of a building, that I would gladly have followed him for another three thousand miles—but preferably west.

Imant knocked softly. Someone I hadn't met before let us in and ushered us into a medical lab. There was a blackboard, so I knew we were in a school. There was a skull on the table at the front of the room, but there was also a tape recorder on the table, and that was what we had come for; but the skull seemed to be saying, *Et in Latvia ego: And I am even in Latvia.* Imant put the tape on the machine, and we sat on straight-backed wooden chairs, like a miniature audience, facing that *memento mori.* Imant sat slightly behind me and to the side, the better to observe the expression on my face.

I don't know what he saw on my face, but I know what I heard, and what I felt in my heart. Granted, it happens that my heart is easily pierced by sound, as easily as by any arrow, and given my family, it's clear why. But Shostakovich, for one, was probably not so Oedipally predisposed, and when he heard it, he thought just as highly of Imant's work as I did. I didn't know then what other people thought or would think of Imant's work, and when I first grasped his reputation, I was quite proud. The irony is that if Imant were not so well known or respected, we might have been better placed to live together privately.

"When I am not writing music," Imant said, "I do not exist."

Years later I wrote a long song sequence for Imant, which he scored for chamber orchestra, chamber choir, soprano, and rock set. The text for one of the songs goes, *Trees are the clear bass line; their leaves, the complication. Deer are grace notes. And so forth, if I define creation as bringing into view what was previously only heard, God's word. On the seventh day, he listened to a little night music.*

The final night. We went to the cemetery where the dead of World War II are buried, the cemetery with two willows. One willow symbolizes strength; the weeping willow stands for sorrow. The trees are at the far end. They were too far away for us to see them; it was midnight. Out here, the pavement was still slick with ice, and a crust of snow lay undisturbed on the graves. It felt like the end of the world, the last stop just before you drop off into space. We huddled around the eternal torch, a flame in the center of a large square concrete block. This is the stone beginning and stone end. The flame's warmth, like the willows, was also symbolic, too modest to hold our hands up to, but its light silhouetted my friends' sad faces all too clearly. I could hardly bear to look at them, not knowing if I'd ever see them again. They gave us presents: cufflinks for Bryce, a necklace for me. Both were amber, the exquisite geological idiosyncrasy of the Baltic Sea. We said our thanks and then faltered. I felt—but I didn't even know what I felt. You find out your feelings from a kind of running commentary the heart keeps up. The pulse quickens or it lags. But I simply felt—as if my heart had stopped. Where do you go, when you start from the end of the world? I thought we would begin by walking back to the hotel, but instead Imant raised his arm as if hailing a cab. Surely there weren't any cabs in the middle of a cemetery at midnight?

Imant had on a black leather jacket, a black turtleneck and trousers, black boots, and black Astrakhan hat. He stood out sharply against the snow or disappeared into the black sky, and somehow, when the taxi materialized around the bend, from behind a clump of trees, I wasn't surprised. He opened the door for me, and we were both inside before Bryce caught on. I looked back; Rudolf and Indra waved.

Imant was laughing—or smiling, I should say, which was usually the closest he came to laughter. This was the first moment we'd had alone, and we used it as might be expected: to kiss. The cemetery was falling away behind us, and time was running out. "Will you wait for me?" he asked. I didn't know what he meant; in this country, I didn't even know if it was all right to ask what he meant, but I said yes.

"Five years?" he asked.

"Yes," I said.

"Ten years?"

I said it again.

"Fifteen?"

I nodded, a little hesitant about fifteen, and here Imant really did start to laugh, but he was laughing just because he felt good, and because waiting fifteen years seemed a ridiculous thing to do, something nobody would ever have to be asked to do. As for the KGB, they were probably laughing their heads off, or at least snickering. In front of the hotel, Imant paid the taxi, and we stood out in the cold, talking. He took off his watch and put it on my wrist, telling me to wear it until we were together again. I said I was afraid Customs wouldn't let me take it out; he said he thought they would. So I promised I would keep it, little guessing how long it would have to tick before we were together again.

The others showed up at that point, and we went in, but the night manager wouldn't let them stay, and we said good night, and good-bye. I should have said good night to the KGB too: they must have been at least as tired as we were. But I hadn't realized we were being followed. When Imant mentioned it, ten years later, he said he'd assumed that I had. "Didn't you see the white Volga?" he asked.

"No," I said. "What white Volga?"

And that was another time when he laughed, almost.

Zhores Medvedev, in his completely devastating little book *Ten Years After Ivan Denisovich,* writes that "'operational' cars of this kind have extremely powerful engines and can reach higher speeds than ordinary Volgas. Also, operational cars can ignore traffic regulations, go through red lights, etc. A transistorized transmitter, so small as to be quite inconspicuous, is installed inside the car of the person who is being shadowed, and its signals enable the car to be easily traced if the driver succeeds in temporarily evading his pursuers." Furthermore, the method's international. "Thus the signals of a transistorized radio transmitter concealed in the victim's car enable its position to be pinpointed anywhere in the city with the help of the listening devices available to police and security agencies in most of the world's capital cities. An operational car following its victim closely will not use the same number plate all the time. It always has a collection of different number plates in the boot."

Very early the next morning, Bryce and I flew back to Moscow. I had let myself half-hope that Imant might be at the airport, but he wasn't. Despite its being morning, it was still dark as night. Moscow, when we got to it, was a letdown. The same buildings that only a few days ago had seemed surpassingly strange and exotic now were thick lumps of gray clay, unimaginatively pressed against a gray horizon. Even the Kremlin had faded. I thought of the dead man in Red Square, his waxen face literally drained of color.

Bryce was flying out; I was taking the train back, first to Warsaw, then Berlin and Amsterdam. I had Imant's watch on my wrist, the tape of his symphony in my suitcase, and in my handbag a clutch of Communist newspapers and journals I'd picked up gratis at the Metropol. I planned to use the papers as a decoy, sidetracking the customs officials at Brest from the watch and tape. At Brest, a no-nonsense woman who talked a mile a minute in Russian and never once looked me in the eye burst into my compartment and went through everything I owned, including my handbag. Every scrap of paper—except the Communist newspapers and journals, which were ignored utterly—was taken out and photographed, including a tiny note at the bottom of my bag, on which a Dutch acquaintance had printed in capital letters the sinister word COLDREX. (It's

the name of a cold remedy he advised me to buy.) The train
was delayed for an hour while officials in the station played the
tape. But I thought I was clever, boldly waving my left hand
about. Don't people say the best hiding place is the most obvious one? Later on, I learned that regulations allow every
tourist to take home a Soviet watch. It's good business.

It was night when I got into Amsterdam. I lugged my suitcase
up the steep, narrow stairs and turned the key in the lock as
stealthily as possible. I rented a rectangle—you couldn't really
call it a room—in a private apartment; it had four walls and
a door but hardly any space in the middle, and now, under
the door, I found a note: "We have learn there is epidemic of
Span. flu in USSR. Please to leave so soon as possible."

"Come on," I said to my landlord—in the morning, when
everyone had gotten up—"I don't have the flu. I don't even
have a cold, in spite of the fact that there's no heat in my room.
What is this all about?" (I had spent the night rehearsing what I
was going to say.)

He hung his head. "My wife does not like the noise."

I stared at him. I had no radio, no phonograph, no television, and no Dutch friends. I didn't usually talk to myself.

"So soon as possible," he insisted. "It is my wife's wish."

I had been on good terms with his wife; one of my sou-
venirs was for her, a *matreshka orbabushka* doll, actually five
wooden dolls nesting one inside the other.

Baffled, I went to my rectangle and began packing. And
slowly I began to notice that things were missing from there.
A silk nightgown, a charm bracelet, several books. Maybe my
landlady was a part-time pilferer. Maybe she had thought that
if I left in a hurry I wouldn't find her out. On the other hand, I
reflected, she neither read nor spoke English, so what was she
going to do with books by Joyce Cary? I chalked the unpleas-
antness up to experience, and when, moving out, I bumped
into an American guy moving in, I thought I had solved the
riddle: they simply had come across someone willing to fork
over more rent. Any room in Amsterdam, even this rectangle,
was at a premium. "How much are you paying?" I asked him.

"Eighty gulden."

That shot my theory; it was exactly what I had been giving them. Feeling unwanted and socially misfit, I went on down the steep, narrow stairs. I was moving to London.

III

What had happened was that while I was in the Soviet Union someone visited my landlord and his wife, asking about my political allegiance and personal habits. (They learned I liked silk nightgowns and the novels of Joyce Cary.) The someone—someones, rather—weren't very cordial; they intimidated the hell out of my landlord and his wife, and they seem to have been U.S. Army Intelligence men, who, we now know, were given to doing that kind of thing in Europe then. Corroboration came from a couple I knew—slightly—who were in Brussels doing research for the Presbyterian church. The visit *they* received was short but to the point. Two strangers had called on them, making similar inquiries about one Kelly Cherry.

It seems that just making a trip to the Soviet Union in 1965 was enough to distress Army Intelligence. Then, too, while in the Soviet Union, I had mailed postcards to my parents in Virginia, commenting with deliberate enthusiasm on the ballet, the ceremony of the changing of the guard at Lenin's tomb, the Hermitage. I thought I was being shrewd—no Russian censor could object to anything I wrote. It had never occurred to me that an *American* censor might.

As I write this I am back in England, and with my morning orange juice I can read that, between 1953 and 1973, the CIA illegally opened and photographed 215,000 pieces of American mail. (The FBI, in good American decentralized fashion, had its own mail-opening operations, which are supposed to have ceased in 1966.) Then there's the NSA. *Time* tells me—and perhaps Imant too—that the National Security Agency, headquartered in a three-story building outside Washington, is the "ultimate bug." Like a cockroach, it feeds on paper: coded messages intercepted by ship, plane, satellite, and even person.

Read on; I do. "At its Fort Meade, Md., headquarters, variously known as 'Disneyland' and 'the Puzzle Palace,' the NSA . . . is reputed to employ everything from the world's largest bank of computers to blind people whose acute hearing can pick up signals on tapes that sighted people might miss." From 1967 to 1973 the NSA intercepted international calls or cables transmitted by 1,680 American citizens and groups and by 5,925 foreign nationals and groups, routinely monitoring U.S. citizens whose names appeared on various governmental agencies' "watch lists."

So much for figures. We can and must read them, and wonder whether other figures remain hidden, but presumably neither the CIA nor the NSA read a letter that finally caught up with me in *England* in the spring of 1965. "It seems me, that the world has grown so big I should not to be surprised if I never hear from you again." Imant said he loved me, something he'd neglected to mention before. Then in the next letter he said it embarrassed him to have been so candid. And in the letter after that, becoming bitter again about the earth's size and divisive borders, he wrote, "I did not mean for you to forget what I said. I never meant you should forget. I did think, to say such a thing by letter is the same as to say it by words. But you are so terribly far, there is no need for such illusion." I won't record my reply here, inasmuch as it is probably already on file with the KGB.

IV

And so Imant and I began our correspondence. I daydreamed about the day we'd meet again but wondered whether that day would dawn in Russia or America. Imant never said he wanted to leave; his work and his children were over there. I was back in the States, and the money I'd saved for a return trip was rapidly running out.

I wrote to Imant by lamplight in summer, moths dancing around the bulb, their winged shadows swollen and mysterious on the netherside of the white shade. I remember wondering what light he read the same letters by. He lived alone, near the Baltic Sea. Was the air there soft, as here? Was there prickly salt on the wind? Did he know, could he guess, that where I was living in North Carolina I said his name silently to myself a hundred times a day? (It was a charm, an amulet, a prayer, the kind you say in secret.) I wrote him my ideas about poetry, my dissatisfaction with both conventional and contemporary poetic structures, which by and large disregard the logic of association, mistakenly imagining that metaphor is merely image, when it is also transition. Imant wrote about his work. "I should like," he said, "to hear already a little of the last music I will write. For I dare to say, it will be a little of what I would call, *real* music."

I had made my parents listen to his First Symphony. We had to cut the tape in half and wind it on two reels before it would fit on our machine. After that, my parents wanted to meet him, and we went to the Soviet embassy in Washington to see if we could sponsor him for a visit. We were summarily dismissed.

Since Imant couldn't visit me in America, I hoped to go back and toward that end hung on to the remainder of my savings account as if it were a lifeline. I still didn't know what "wait for me" meant; maybe he didn't know himself. I was afraid to ask in case a censor might read my letter and clap Imant in jail. Not that I knew whether such things occurred still; few Americans at that time could have such knowledge. Today we can speak with the precision of scholarship of the people that perished in Stalin's slave camps. At the height of the purges, the Gulag Archipelago held at a *rock bottom* estimate twelve million prisoners. Solzhenitsyn counted them for us.

For three months I didn't hear from Imant; I thought he had forgotten me. I thought, *It was implausible, a romance; we were playing hands-across-the-sea.* I thought, to tell the whole truth, that I was never really going to be loved by anybody; people kept telling me I was a loner. I fitted into no established social role—wife, mother, girlfriend. It would have been clever of me to liberate myself before the Women's Movement began, but I didn't think of that.

When a visiting lecturer in art history arrived on campus from New York, unmarried, musically alert, and argumentative, I decided he was going to ask me to marry him. I was that sure because David—I'll call him David—plainly needed me to display to the people around him, just as I (mistakenly) felt I needed a man. I could see him adding two and two together and coming up with His Idea of a Wife: independent, tough-minded, *spunky,* for God's sake. (It's a word he would use.)

Women's lives were so proscribed then, especially in the South. I had ambitions but no understanding of how they might be spelled out in a professional life and very little encouragement and *no* guidance. Only retrospectively do I realize that, in fact, I stood right on the edge of being able to see where I wanted to go, professionally, and I blew it, traded it all for a chance to say, See, I too have a husband. Because I knew, knew just beyond reach on the rim of consciousness, that something was bad wrong. If I was "in" love with David, I didn't love him; and how could he love me? He had made his love of me conditional upon his approval of me. That was exactly the reverse of how Imant felt about me. I could love Imant freely, but David only with emotions he thought were admirable. The felt difference was this: with Imant, there was peace; with David, anger. Once, he refused to speak to me for six hours on a bus. Try riding a bus sometime for six hours sitting next to someone who's deliberately not speaking to you. It's winter, you're sweating inside your heavy coat, the bus smells of gasoline, melted snow, rubber, and wet wool, the teenager up front holds a transistor to his head like a compress but you're the one with a headache. But of course I believed David had a good reason for not speaking to me, and on other days he spoke terrifically, a blue streak, irresistibly. Best of all, he came South carrying history in his suitcase, and now my family-inculcated sense of alarm had company, and facts to back it up as what had been a tenacious but dimly defined perception developed into a clearer picture of the world's whole

23

appalling past. That *was* seductive. He wasn't Imant—but Imant was in the USSR, and it looked like I'd never hear from him again.

That still didn't stop me from hoping, and when I wrote to Imant and told him about David, I was still hoping he'd write back and tell me to keep waiting. I wanted him to clarify our situation so I'd know why I had been waiting, or at least what for. I wanted—you know, a letter that said, "I love you." It came—

Too late. The letter I wanted came two days before the wedding.

Here is where the modern curtain drops, not over the marriage bed but over the marriage.

I believed David and I were in it together, for the long haul, period. So if my marriage to him was a disaster, it wasn't because of Imant; there were more than enough other reasons, two of them being David and me. As for Imant, he wrote, "I am afraid that my letters may interfere somehow with your marriage"—and for the next two years that was it, no letters, nothing. I thought I would never hear from him again, and grieved, but I also thought I had to respect his feelings—and David's.

We were living in New York City, David's hometown. It's supposed to be a big city, but if you've ever been in a failing marriage there, you know how claustrophobic the whole scene can become. The tears, recriminations, insights, analyses, and apologies all take place in Loew's in Brooklyn or the Thalia (now gone!) on the upper West Side, your shrink's office or your spouse's shrink's office, and Central Park. With my life thus bounded on all sides, the Soviet Union simply didn't exist. It was a memory, not a possibility, and the remainder of the money I had saved for a trip back went toward rent. But it was a very special memory.

David, proposing, had said that he didn't want a "housewife." He said he wanted me to put writing first, even before him. The trouble was that now that we were married, I *couldn't* write. I tried, but whatever I wrote, I found out quickly, would be at once subjected to interpretation by David. I had married my very own live-in censor. He was a believer in Freud and expected my fictional characters to behave in ways that made a Freudian kind of sense. But my characters, perhaps feeling their lack of freedom, went on strike and refused to behave any way at all. Writing began to be a memory, like Imant. It may even have been true that to write would have been to remember Imant—and I didn't dare do that.

Since I felt I'd been excused from housewifing, I took up Greek and Latin. I was studying fourteen hours a day and felt fine but the apartment was a wreck and we ate out a lot, which was hard on our budget inasmuch as David had an aversion to work, and after a year had gone by like this, David blew up. He was standing in the middle of the room and simply exploded, like a land mine somebody'd left lying around.

One day, shortly before the marriage ground to its halt, I was in the living room, going through some mail forwarded from my parents, when I discovered—a letter from Imant. Cool, a trifle formal, but a letter. "Write, please, even if it takes two years to make up your mind. In case you answer, I will have more to say you. . . . My regards to David," he added, signing off. I ran into the kitchen and gave his regards to David. Even David seemed gratified; after all, by this time Imant had become only a kind of mental color slide of his wife's trip to Russia, a souvenir.

A few weeks later, David and I were getting a divorce.

The worst thing was that he sprang it on me without warning, the same way he got angry. It was like going to work one morning and finding a pink slip in your pay envelope. I wasn't only being rejected; I was being fired. I could only assume I hadn't done a decent job; I was a failure. A failure at everything, because I had no other position to retreat to, having essentially stopped writing.

Feeling superfluous and worthless—"'Self-pity,'" Renata Adler says, "is just sadness . . . in the pejorative"—I took the first job I could get. What I did didn't really matter anyway, I thought: it was just a way to pay the bills until I located a bridge to jump off of. There was only one life I felt I might hope for. I wrote to Imant, asking him if he still wanted me. First I enumerated all the things that were wrong with me, and then I promised to be a good wife.

"I sat with this letter for many nights," he told me years later. "And I could not think what to do." For, as he finally answered that summer, the more he had to say me was that he was living with a woman and they had a child. "I would give all I possess if I could have in return the winter you were in Moscow," he wrote. "I dare not say more."

I could not butt in any further. Imant had done me that favor when I was married to David; now I owed as much to him. Besides, the situation suited my sense of poetic justice, if not my sense of justice. This irony, I felt, was well deserved. I didn't write again for some weeks. When Imant and I did resume our correspondence, it was on a professional basis. He was setting some lyrics of mine to music. Old lyrics, because I still wasn't writing and wouldn't for a year or so, but one way and another I was recovering . . . recovering my footing in the world. You walk down a street in August, feeling the sun's heat on your scalp like a massage, the pavement's hard smack against the soles of your shoes, and you know you're halfway there.

I moved, and moved again, and again.

In 1971 my one room was on upper Fifth Avenue. The telephone in it rang one night at 3 A.M. "Come to Russia," Imant said, "or I die."

He was drunk, though cheerful, and I joked with him; later I found out that he had called because he was trying to decide whether to marry the woman he lived with. They had three children now, the eldest and twins. The way he told it to me, she'd been perfectly willing to have all three out of wedlock. She was an actress, capable of supporting herself, and the kids, if she wished to, but of course he didn't want to give them up. He said—I realized this might be a distorted point of view or an excuse—she didn't love him but just enjoyed the prestige of being associated with him. After the birth of twins, they needed a larger apartment. To qualify for one, they had to legitimize their children, and every day she pressed this point home.

He made it sound as if he were under siege. "Come to Russia,"
he said again, "or I kill myself." But I, extrapolating from my
own experience and sympathizing with jilted wives everywhere, chided him for being drunk. I told him he shouldn't say
such things, and I thought I was being virtuous, but I was
really only being shortsighted.

Imant telephoned on a number of occasions, usually drinking
occasions. He didn't always say he couldn't live without me;
once, instead of saying anything at all, he sang. The operator
said, "I have Moscow on the line," and Moscow burst into
song. It was 3 A.M. again, but as a matter of fact, that time
Imant wasn't drunk.

Halfway through, I realized Imant was singing me my own
poem, from the cycle he was setting for solo. (He sang like a
composer, off-key.) Then a couple of weeks later he called
again, having completed the cycle, and later still, he used the
cycle as the unvoiced text for the last movement of the Fourth
Symphony, a sort of secret message transmitted by music, a
code to which only I knew the key. I wished I could sit in a
train in Brest waiting while customs officials checked for illicit
communications in *this*. The record of the Fourth Symphony
reached me in Richmond in the fall, a few months before I was
to return to Minnesota, where, after finishing a novel, I'd
taken a job as writer-in-residence in a state college. At about
the same time, I also learned, from Karl, that Imant was in the
hospital. Karl is Imant's brother.

I've skipped through several years as if they didn't exist because, as far as this book is concerned, they didn't. I was living
in North Carolina, New York, Virginia, Minnesota, but the
touchstone by which I judged my life's reality was in the Soviet Union. Imant agreed. "It is strange," he wrote, "but you
are for me the only felt centre, like the Sun for the Earth." In
another letter he said, "It seems, the only real life I have is that
which I live in our letters." Thousands of miles away, Imant
was my most constant companion.

When Karl informed me that Imant was in the hospital—

"Nothing serious, of course"—I tried for the first time to imagine a world without him. The center wouldn't hold. In my *mappa mundi*, Imant was the place from which all other places were farther: 0,0. I felt like a compass with no north.

V

Other people's love affairs, like their pain, never seem quite real. What's all the fuss about? we want to know.

The fuss here is first of all about the right to marry. The Final Act of the Conference on Security and Cooperation in Europe, the Helsinki Pact, to which the U.S. and USSR, among others, are signatories, considers marriage one of the basic human rights. "The participating States will examine favorably and on the basis of humanitarian considerations requests for exit or entry permits from persons who have decided to marry a citizen from another participating State."

Second, it's about love itself—or, in *other* words—or, in *another* word, a word not synonymous but analogous—pain.

Here I sit, at my desk, trying to figure this out. At four in the afternoon, the sky is the color of stone. It is November, and for the past few weeks the oak outside my window has been losing its leaves. Now it's an X-ray tree. I can look right between its bare bones to the pines across Auclum Close.

It occurs to me that I could follow my gaze east, identifying every tree and rock along the way, and never find the hill or river that says, Here is where one country stops and another begins. Our earth, cooling into land and sea, didn't also harden into communist and capitalist sectors. Grass signs no pledge of allegiance; in fact, it will scarcely grow, unless it's crabgrass. And the Iron Curtain isn't iron or any natural element; it's barbed wire.

You are a prisoner in a camp. The barbed wire surrounds you like a moat; you live on a man-made island, and freedom is as far away as the mainland. For three days you have subsisted on bread and water, or rice and water, or salted herring and no water. You are in Russia, Germany, Vietnam, Greece, Chile, China, Iran. America? It's now, or it's then—the year is irrelevant. You hurt. Your arms are stiff. Your legs feel like crutches; maybe they are crutches. Your eyes itch: you think maybe someone has sneaked in during the night and planted fleas under your eyelids. But no, it's impossible. Nobody could have done that because you were awake all night; the interrogator saw to that. You have been awake since time began, and your only hope is to evolve toward sleep, or death.

You are a parent. Your child, for whom you would gladly give your life, is bawling its head off. Classmates have taunted it or refused to play with it. Try to teach your child history: go ahead, take out chalk and a blackboard and explain that unhappiness is what happened yesterday, and that yesterday is what today will become tomorrow. (The child who stops crying is a mystic.)

You are a new parent, of a baby born without a brain. Anencephaly means that if you stick a flashlight in the back of the head, the light comes out through the pupils.

You are a child in Bangladesh or Biafra. Or you are the infant the Buddhist priest tried to save at My Lai. "No Viet," the priest cried, "no Viet." According to William Manchester, court testimony swore that Lieutenant William L. Calley, Jr., having shoved the butt of his rifle, an M-16, into the priest's mouth like a battering ram, swung the gun around "and pulled the trigger in the priest's face. Half his head was blown off." And how was the infant comforted? "Lieutenant Calley grabbed it by the arm and threw it into the ditch and fired."

Dying, you are Christ on the cross, with a mouth full of vinegar and gall. Over the heads of soldiers, you can see friends, family; on the horizon, dark clouds stuffed with rain like a quilt with rags. You spit. The wind smells wet and you stick out your tongue, striving to sip a single drop. The soldiers roar. You could put on a truly spectacular show, of course: you could climb down from your cross and walk away. But now one of the soldiers is bringing you a sponge soaked in vinegar, and by this time you have grown positively fond of the taste.

29

Why walk, when the world comes to you? Better to stay close to wood and take a nap; you will just rest your eyes for a moment. Miniature faces, places appear on the inside of your eyelids like muscae volitantes, stars. *You remember voices, words, snatches of psalms. In particular, you remember a psalm of David: "I am poured out like water, and all my bones are out of joint: my heart is like wax; it is melted in the midst of my bowels."*

You *know* that pain is as real as your hand; you have to *believe* that it's as real as *my* hand.

Call it moral imagination, the faculty that lifts you out of your body and sets you down in somebody else's skin. And if you stretch your arms, and if you try out this strange body . . . look: you see with new eyes; new images, new thoughts present themselves to you, there are new stirrings, new synapses; you speak in a new language. But your new lungs pump old air, and your heart sings the same song as before, Love.

A second leap of the imagination, therefore: love is as real as pain. It is not you but your sister's husband who has been taken prisoner; they are your friends who are fathers, who are mothers; it is your neighbor's child who lies half buried face down in a muddy ditch. (But it is your mother's one and only child who is, as you have always suspected, brainless.) Christ is *your* only begotten son.

VI

I discovered the less-than-romantic reason for which Imant was in the hospital: alcoholism.

In Russia, the cure for alcoholism is an admixture of hypnosis, humiliation, and drying out. At sobering-up centers, a drunk's incoherent speeches are recorded for playback when he's clearer-headed; photographs may be taken. In Riga, Imant, when I saw him again, would bring out for me photographs friends had made of him when he was drunk. The photographs had had the desired effect on him—"Ai-yai-yai," he said, slapping his face and then shaking his head with his hand still on his cheek, "is terrible!"—and yet he was just a little bit tickled by them, too. Quoted in the *Guardian* in October, 1975, Professor George Voronkov, head of the Kiev Medical Institute's psychiatric department (*sic*), informed me: "Some seventy-five per cent of offenders are aged between twenty and twenty-five and they come from the better-off families. Parents give their children money and they do not attempt to control how it is spent. These parents want to give their children everything; they want them to have a better time than they had. They say, 'We suffered so much during the war, we want to make sure you have everything.'

"As a psychiatrist, I can say that I do not think people drink because of a disaster or because of family or money worries. There is no unemployment in this country, and all social problems have been solved. . . ."

By the time I found out why Imant was in the hospital, our correspondence had escalated, even if he wasn't in mortal danger. I had finally quit hiding my feelings and that was all he needed; he told his wife that he wanted to marry me. "She said"—he wrote—"she was knowing for years, that ours was not merely an amicable relationship." She consented immediately to a divorce. I was still in Minnesota when Imant wrote asking me to marry him. "You were my wife before you were born," he said. A Maoist might resist that, but not me.

I took a week to decide how to reply to Imant's proposal, never doubting that I wanted to marry him. I *did* wonder whether I could emotionally survive that bleak political climate, but roughly 250,000,000 people currently do, and I felt I had every right and reason to swell the population to 250,000,001, or, with luck, 250,000,002. "I wish," Imant wrote once, "we were two only people on the earth. And then raise up a new mankind, with no evil in it." Our brave new world would be a bit more crowded than Imant wished, but paradise always comes with a wrinkle or two: a snake in the grass, and in Arcadia, death.

In Minneapolis I bought a wedding dress—a long, tiered, sashed skirt with red and white stripes and a white blouse with eyelet edging.

In August I went to the writers' conference in Bread Loaf.

Evenings, I drank gin with writers in the gathering house. People tried to caution me against my plans. The plight of the writer in a police state. . . . Yes, but—I explained—a life which leaves out love is like a story with no people in it. But love "happens" in different places for different people; you go where you have to, to live. You shape the walls of your house out of mud and thatch your roof with care: love lives there.

VII

"In the Beginning," a philosopher said, "all the world was America."

America used to be referred to as the "new Jerusalem." Some people went further: Mircea Eliade states that "the most popular religious doctrine in the Colonies was that America had been chosen among all the nations of the earth as the place of the Second Coming of Christ." But the CIA decided the Second Coming should occur off the coast of Cuba: according to what I read, they were going to set off an eschatological display of fireworks; this was actually supposed to convince the island's inhabitants of Christ's approach, and Castro would find himself, charismatically speaking, nowhere.

Now, when the CIA plots to poison Castro's cigars, or devises a scheme to destroy his image by causing his beard to fall out, we know that something is rotten not only in Denmark and Cuba. But do we recall that, in the beginning, "Americans who spoke against the rebellion were deprived of civil rights and left at the mercy of mob violence"? One hundred thousand fled to Canada or Britain. What fine start could we think of, that didn't contain its own destruction, a kind of moral code like a genetic code programmed for self-destruct? Is creation itself set to go off, like a bomb under a car, and are we all assassins of time, accomplices after the fact? This is a political question.

Flying out, I wondered if I'd ever see America again. So I said good-bye to all the states.

Good-bye. To Virginia and New York. To Louisiana and North Carolina. To Minnesota and New Mexico. And bid a fond farewell to Tennessee.

The sky on my left was blue, becoming deep blue. Below us, a field of clouds stretched into infinity, furrowed as if someone had tilled it. I wondered if any pilot had ever left his controls to walk on that white bank; it exerted a fascination like an open window in a high rise. Later, the horizon began to blush; streaks of rose, peach, yellow stained the sky, spreading into pools of flame. I could walk—don't run—down that cloud bank to the far edge, poise, and dive into a lake of liquid fire. Then quite suddenly my vista cooled, as we flew into night.

CHAPTER 2

Riga

I

Imant's English seemed to have improved, but since he used it only to say, "A miracle, a miracle," I couldn't be sure. He urged me to eat—"Some substantial meat, yes?"—but I had to eat with one hand, as he was still holding the other. He wouldn't eat, and, since he was on the wagon, couldn't drink. When he let go of my hand, it was to light a cigarette. "A miracle," he muttered. He was looking across the table, at the floor or the ceiling—everywhere but at me. It was just as well: his shyness gave me a chance to sneak glances at him. Who, after all, was this man, this man I was sitting next to in a high-backed booth in a quiet dining room at the top of a winding staircase above a cobblestone street in Riga, Latvia?

Indra had been immediately recognizable, with her strongly modeled face marked by three small moles above the lip, her wavy red-gold hair pulled back from the high forehead, and the most unflinching gaze I'd ever met in any woman on any continent. She was wearing an aqua knit dress with a split seam under one arm, white heels, and no stockings on her unshaven legs—and she was a knockout.

Karl was tall and lean. He had unruly light brown hair, a goatee, and high cheekbones and a slightly snub nose which

34

gave his face a Slavic cast, but his tennis shoes were American, and he spoke English fluently, with an Oxbridge accent. He was thirty-six or -seven. He talked to me and to Indra by turns, covering for Imant until he could calm down.

Later, at Karl's place, after all the albums had been gone through and we'd reached photographs dating back to the war, I found an opportunity to ask Indra, with the aid of a dictionary, if Imant was happy; having just kissed him in the kitchen, I felt reasonably sure that he was, and her answer startled me: "No." When I asked why, she pointed to the words *excessive* and *emotion*. But I was too sleepy even to think much about this; jet lag had made me foggy. When Imant drove Indra and Karl to their respective destinations—Karl had turned his apartment over to us—I took a nap. The couch in Karl's room was also the bed, and by now it was early evening. I fell sound asleep, waking with a start half an hour later. The apartment was as silent as if it had been underwater. Outside, the failing light meshed with blue shadows until it became difficult to make out the edges of things, like reading a book with no paragraphs. Small children played in the dirt square out front; the girls all wore huge white gauze bows in their hair, like displaced angels' wings. (Another day, I asked Karl if these bows signified anything special. "Well," he said, seeming surprised, "I believe it is a whim of the parents.")

The apartment complex was partly under construction, and bits of wood and metal lay scattered on the dirt square like seeds. What they would flower into was a block of gray boxes, all alike, and each one with a climbing hallway twenty years old the day it was finished. But apartments are scarce: you take what you can get. If you can get it. Seventy percent of these particular apartments were occupied by Russians.

As for Latvians, five—six, with the new baby—lived in Karl's three-rooms-and-a-kitchen, although no one was there now. The father's room was the living room; I didn't see the mother's room. Karl and his wife and their two children normally shared the room I had napped in. The kitchen was small and drab, though to tell the truth, no smaller than some I'd had in New York—but a lot drabber. I thought they could paint the refrigerator red, drape colorful dishtowels from a rack on the wall, buy some potted plants for the windowsill. I didn't know that paints and fabrics just aren't to be had.

An hour went by, an hour and a half. The kids disappeared indoors, reeled in on invisible lines, and the blue darkened to black. I was cold and wrapped myself up in one of the sheets I found folded at the foot of the bed. I couldn't call anybody: there was no telephone. I couldn't walk anywhere: I was somewhere in the suburbs. I could knock on a neighbor's door, but suppose he spoke only Russian? Or for that matter, Latvian?

To keep myself company, I started to talk to myself; in this hushed room it seemed a natural thing to do. Then I remembered the microphones Imant had mentioned, and shut up. I thought maybe Imant had been picked up already, that I had seen all of him I was going to be allowed to see. I said to myself, "This is ridiculous." But I had recently read that the ridiculous happens. Alexander Dolgun, I read, stepped out for lunch one day in 1948 and spent the next eight years in prisons and labor camps and the following fifteen under surveillance in Moscow. And he was an American citizen.

But that was under Stalin—at least the *worst* part of it was. These things don't happen anymore, I told myself (not out loud).

When Imant got back at nine, I shrugged off my worry; that's the first thing you learn to do in the Soviet Union. The anxiety comes with the territory, it's part of the package. You don't think: Fear, when you put on your shoes in the morning; you couldn't live that way. Nobody can. But Fear is where you walk when you leave the house: it's the ground under your feet. And it's the air you breathe, but you breathe.

Imant began to tease me: maybe *I* was a spy? "Have they sent me the real Kelly Cherry?" he wanted to know. The question tickled him, and he took to muttering it at odd moments.

But now I knew who he was, this man; in a way, he was my soul. I think of the soul as a shaping principle, as the passion which determines the outlines of one's character, making one's self an integrated whole by registering the rest of the world and differentiating itself from it. To find oneself is, then, in every sense, to define oneself; and in the act of definition, we create our souls—or they create us, breathe life into us, set our arms and legs in motion toward some daily dreamed or dimly sensed purpose or goal.

This was the first time Imant and I had ever been alone together. He ushered me back into the room and sat me on the couch, and saying, "I have something to show you," he reached under the crib and brought out a scrapbook. The leaves were large and heavy. I opened the book—and read the fragment of a poem I'd tried to remember for him on a bar napkin ten years ago. Then I turned to my parents' old telephone number, jotted down on a scrap of paper during an interval at a ballet in Moscow. Then the first letter I had ever mailed him, and then the second. I held ten years of my life in my hands; Imant had saved them for me, rescued them from the hole in the existential pocket out of which the past is always falling, lost. I couldn't think. My brain blurred, and so did my eyes. When I came to the formal announcement of my first marriage, I stopped turning pages. "Why did you keep that?" I asked. "I kept everything," he said.

Much later, toward midnight, we went to a party.

At parties, Latvians sing. There is a song for life's every occasion, minute or grand, solitary or shared. By one count, the *Dainas,* or collected folksongs, number over 36,000; variations swell the total to 650,000. The *Dainas* say that the progenitor of all the Latvians was the sun. But scientists and philologists are inclined to concur, at least in part, with the Latvian layman, who firmly believes his earliest ancestors left India, for whatever reason (the Flood is legendarily adduced), forging north to the Baltic shore via the Black Sea Basin.

The Latvian of today cherishes—and uses—the old songs. "The work that I do praises me," he may sing, if he feels justified; or in an altogether different mood: "Cold as ice, sweet as honey, what a fine little ale!"

Riga's Opera is right across from the old Hotel Riga. And then there's rock music. For a time, Imant wrote some rock music and played electric organ in a traveling band. After a particularly triumphant concert, Imant and the other members of the band placed on Lenin's grave an armload of roses their audience had given them. "The greatest hippie in the world," Imant called Lenin, perfectly deadpan.

That was the highlight of his rock career, and also, more or less, the culmination of it. The band was becoming too popular. Shortly afterward, at the close of another concert, two teenaged girls presented Imant and his band with a religious icon. The KGB called Imant in for grilling: was he promoting, God forbid, religion? Why did he *consent* to receive a religious icon? "What was I supposed to do," he countered, "tell them the gift was unacceptable?" "Precisely," they said. So much for good manners. The group performed one more time and then they were "advised" to disband. "We never knew," Imant told me, "whether the girls had been told by KGB to present us with this icon, for to make a pretext."

Imant gave up the rock group, but not rock. He was interested in the classical disposition of a rock idiom, and as a result the Fourth Symphony employs a percussion solo, which, in the opening and closing movements, contributes a dynamically sexual thrust to a massively tragic mood. At one point there is even a burst of big-band sound. And then the drums die into their own beginning.

Imant settled down to a respectable routine. Sort of. It's true that, learning he'd been short-listed for a Komsomol prize, he called up the chairman of the awards committee and told him exactly what he could do with his prize. ("In Russian, which has very many words for to make the meaning plain.") If he couldn't accept non-Communist gifts, he wouldn't accept Communist ones.

Imant told me that Indra and Rudolf had also been called in for KGB questioning—because they were Roman Catholics. (Indra was also a mystic, "a great pessimist," and a vegetarian.) But Imant and all of his friends seemed to take the KGB as a given, as a volatile but inevitable element in the Soviet molecule, like carbon. They expected to be hassled, even harassed, and they complained only in jokes. Yet how do you laugh at a joke whose punch line is a prison sentence—even if the prison yard extends over eight and a half million square miles? If you took the KGB less than seriously, you could find yourself serving a six-year sentence in a labor camp in Siberia, like another friend. So you opted for the private life, and did what you could to beat the system. Indra could sew a chiffon blouse and an ankle-length skirt and look as funky as any foxy lady. Rudolf carried an olive-drab book bag made by a private tailor, visualizing himself as a student at Harvard or the Sorbonne.

But neither Indra nor Rudolf ever really pulled off the look they sought, a laissez-faire look. It was their faces that defeated them.

No matter how hard the Soviet government tries to keep tourists from seeing anything that might be read as a mark against their system, they can't dictate the look on people's faces or slap masks over 250,000,000 residents. I saw that look on the face of every passenger in the tram. It stared back at me in the Metro stations of sculptured marble underneath Moscow. It's not the outward sign of the inward slump that you see on the faces of homeward-bound secretaries on the Seventh Avenue Express. It's not even the dramatic deadness of the faces in Dust Bowl photographs: no, the features might go blank with impassive resignation, but something at the back of the eyes stays wary, alert, on the lookout—for the instant queue that means soap or apples, but also for the white Volga in the rearview mirror. I've seen the look on Imant's face. Oh, but I have also seen Imant's face in the faint glow of a bright night, pleased and shy and quiet.

We stayed the night in a little room at the back of the apartment where the party was going on. There was the sheen of moonlight on the floor, a flat, hard patina like clear ice on the surface of a still pool, but the August night was warm. I took off my T-shirt and pitched it across the room; it landed on top of my travel alarm, muffling the ring in the morning.

II

Theoretically, I was in Riga for the tour sponsored by my American travel agency, but in fact, hardly anybody on the tour was there for the tour. I had come to see Imant; similarly, the others were there to see friends or relatives, or just their hometown, for the first time in thirty-five years. The last time they'd seen Riga, it was "the Paris of the North." That was before the Communists had decided to improve the economy by lowering the living standard. These "tourists" were really exiles: they or their parents had escaped, maybe on the boats that had plied between Latvia and nearby, affianced Sweden during the war, and now they came back, some to see a brother or sister they knew they'd never see again. Intourist knows why Latvians visit Latvia, why Lithuanians visit Lithuania, why Estonians visit Estonia, but they pick up more hard currency by pretending it's tourism, and besides, they can keep closer tabs on everyone this way. So, playing our parts, we all went to at least one or two of the expeditions we were ostensibly there for, and in the perfect summer weather our Intourist bus was ventilated by vents: flaps in the bus roof could be opened and propped up on poles, and the air poured in, with a rushing sound like a waterfall. The bus was cool, but we were not, and if anybody had thrown a match at us, we would have ignited instantaneously, like northern California.

My travel agent had arranged for me to share a room with an English-speaking Latvian-American I'll call Vera. But as I spent my nights as well as my days with Imant, it was Vera who was in when the calls started coming to the hotel. Sometimes the caller would whisper my name, sometimes not, and then Vera would hear the click of the unknown party hanging up. Vera had offered to translate for me, but how do you translate a click?

And who knew me, yet knew not where I was but only where I was supposed to be? I arrived in Riga on a Saturday, but the calls began with the work week. They began the day after I walked across the street from the hotel to meet Imant at our special spot in front of the Opera—and found him not there. Hello, hello; shake hands with thin air.

I was with Karl, who had come into the lobby to get me. Just ten minutes before, he had left his wife and Imant in the car; we were all going to Rigas Jurmala, the seashore, for the afternoon. "Well," he said as we stood at the curb where the car should have been, "I do not understand."

"Maybe he went into one of the shops?" High noon made a traffic map out of Karl's face; his golden goatee glittered. He was pacing the sidewalk, scanning the street. Where was Imant?

Karl leaned out over the curb. "Very many young people," he said, sotto voce, "have simply vanished."

"Not in broad daylight!"

"Yes, certainly. In broad daylight."

"Why would anything happen to Imant?" I asked. I can still hear my voice, squeezed tight as if someone had wrapped a belt around my throat.

"Did Imant tell you what his wife said?"

I shook my head.

"A week before you came, she said that if you came she would make trouble."

"I don't understand," I protested, growing panicky. "Why?"

But one possible answer had already been suggested to me. Digging up all the information I could about marrying a Soviet citizen, I had been warned months ago by a specialist in East European and Soviet studies that a typical KGB scenario involved placing obstacles in the way of marriage; they frequently cajoled or coerced parents or spouses into withholding relevant signatures. But if, as Imant and I always assumed, the KGB had always *known* our intentions, why had they let me come here? Clearly, Imant's wife had to be the cause of any trouble. But Imant's wife had said she *wanted* the divorce; clearly, the KGB had to be the cause of any trouble. My head was spinning. "Why would Imant's wife want to make trouble?" I asked again.

Karl shrugged. "She is— Well! She is rather queer." The way he said the word carried for me the message: formidable, cunning, mean. These were extreme adjectives to apply to someone I knew nothing about, and when the little yellow Fiat suddenly drove up, manna on wheels, I felt duly ashamed. Getting in, I was only glad that Imant wasn't in a labor camp. There is one not far from Riga.

"What happened?" Karl asked, climbing in back with his wife.

"We saw Frederika," Imant said. "I drove off so she would not to see us."

After a while he said: "She was coming out of hotel. I think, Kelly, that she has been to ask if you are here."

We sat on a sandy bench, eating berries from a twig. The sea was as tranquil as if Christ had that very morning calmed it; with our backs to the water, we might not have known it was there. The Gulf Stream warms the Baltic Sea so successfully that Riga is a vacation haven for all Russia. Rigas Jurmala— literally, "Riga's seashore"—is a white fling of beach and a resort suburb roughly fifteen kilometers from the city.

The highway connecting the shore to the city is impressively streamlined; the people refer to it as "ten minutes along the U.S.A." The government would like foreign tourists to think this stretch is representative of the entire Soviet road system, but it is not. Russia remains, despite hydraulic dams and bureaucratic entropy, essentially rural; in the city, any city, and certainly in Riga, you can turn a corner and find the country— not parks but country, dirt roads, laundry on the line, and the irrepressible, shy grins of the *laucinieki,* country people, packed into an open-end truck in front of you. To say they have good faces—as Imant did—is to make not an aesthetic judgment but a moral one. Or rather, it is not to make the dichotomy between aesthetic and moral concerns that Western thinkers do.

In fact, one of the engagingly upside-down features of Soviet technology is the way their cars are built to withstand the shock of the terrain: cobblestone streets, dirt lanes, ditches, and the incredible, unpredictable, maddening delays caused by erratic red NO ENTRY signs which proliferate overnight and vanish in the bright sunshine like fairy rings. (But out in the countryside there are signs that stay in the same place, and the people say that if you traced on a map the path of these stable signs you would have a fair indication of the missile sites Latvia is mined with.)

If there's no NO ENTRY to block your way, you can ride your car over the curb and into the weeds: it will go. And back on the street you can drive like a bat out of hell. Or at least you could before the new speed limit. A higher standard of living has begun to make itself felt—in the rising roadway death toll.

Until recently, automobiles have been very scarce; right now, as I write this, the cheapest model costs 5,500 rubles, or about $7,000 at the official exchange rate, and there's no installment plan. But when Imant had written me that he was buying a car and I wrote back expressing my surprise, he said, "In the USSR there are a great plenty of people having cars." It must have seemed so to him. There were something like 2.5 million cars for 250,000,000 inhabitants. (But if American towns grew up around gas stations, in the USSR the gas stations were tucked out of sight like classified documents, and in an unfamiliar city you could burn up a tank of gas before you found one.)

Finally, there are at any rate a few people with a great plenty of cars. Somewhere among my clippings I have a newspaper article that tells me that "the country's number one auto enthusiast is Communist Party leader Leonid Brezhnev, who owns, among others, a Rolls-Royce, a Citroën-Maserati speedster, a Mercedes, a Cadillac and two Zils, the sleek limousines reserved for the top Soviet leadership."

In the Soviet Union, according to Sakharov, "The real masters are those who, morning and evening, speed through the deserted, closed-off streets in their armored limousines." Fighting your way crosstown at rush hour, you catch the gleam of the late afternoon sun reflected from the polished chrome of a back bumper as it flashes out of sight down a street you can't enter, ever—or until the red sign mysteriously disappears and reappears at the mouth of some other harmless-looking street. But it was nothing to me. Just so long as they didn't come after

Imant and me. They could; and I began to wonder what else they could do, if they wanted to. "Suppose, after I leave, they stop our mail?" Would the Soviet Union do such a thing?

"No," Imant said, "is impossible." Then he considered the possibility and then dismissed it again. "No. They would not do that. . . . How could they do that?"

"They could refuse to let me come in again."

Imant was writing my name in the sand with his big toe. "Then we will get married in Bulgaria," he said.

"Bulgaria!"

"Yes. I have an invitation to write music for a movie. Maybe I go in January or February, and you meet me there."

"In Bulgaria!"

"Why do you laugh?"

"I never thought I might someday be getting married in Bulgaria." For that matter, I don't believe I ever thought Bulgarians might get married in Bulgaria.

"But of course, is better to marry here, in Riga, with our friends."

"We can't get married anywhere," I pointed out, "until you're divorced."

"All will be okay, Kelly. I think that Frederika give it right away. If not, there will be a second trial for the divorce in six months. And if still the divorce is not given, then there follows a third trial in six more months, and this time the divorce must be given. Is the law."

"A whole year," I said.

"No, no," he said. "Frederika will give the *first* time, I am sure. Many times she has said she wishes to divorce."

But then why had she sworn to make trouble? And what kind of trouble?

Back in Riga, Indra and Imant and Ausma, who was a professional photographer, and I sat in a circle on the painted floor, dining on crayfish. The crayfish came served in a pot of salted water dressed with what looked like sea kelp. Food in the Soviet Union is wonderful—when you can get any. There's a Georgian dish, *shashlik,* a kind of highly spiced shish kebab. There is the omnipresent beefsteak, often wrapped in fried

eggs. Trout, sautéed zucchini, a string of open-faced sand-
wiches all day long, fruit and vegetables homegrown on the
cottage plot allotted to each city family . . . but not lettuce or
asparagus, at least none that I ever saw. And I was in one store
where the vegetables all looked half-rotted. There was nobody
else in the store, not even a clerk.

We sprawled on the floor, stuffed and languid, listening to
tapes. A breeze belled the curtains into the room and then
dropped back, sucking the thin cloth nightward. Imant asked
if I liked Joan Baez. I hadn't heard any Joan Baez since my
school days, and Indra caught the confusion on my face and
laughed. I had to ask Imant what she was laughing at. "For
years," he said, ruefully, "I make everyone listen to Joan Baez
sing this song which says, 'The pleasure of love lasts but a moment, the pain forever.' They know I am thinking of you."
But he had a tape I liked better; it was the music he'd written
for a stage production of *The Glass Menagerie*. I called it the
lonely music, the music that comes and goes. *Though its name
is Calliope, some call it Pain, pronounced like "rain."*

We were going to spend the night at Karl's place, and drove
by the hotel to collect my gear. That was when Vera told me
someone had called and hung up; she took me out into the
hallway to tell me this, so Imant wouldn't hear. "Imant's wife
is just curious," I said to Vera. "Besides, everyone who stays in
a Soviet hotel gets at least one weird call. It's the Soviet telephone system."

Imant was putting together the stuff I'd pulled out of my
suitcase. I'd brought toys for the children: Frisbees, yo-yos, water pistols, an Indian papoose doll, and chewing gum. Three
packs of chewing gum, but Imant said, "One will be for
me, yes?"

Vera saw us off, but the next day she had another call to report. And then another.

I checked in with Vera to find out what the group was doing, or to pick up clothes, and once the phone rang while I was
in the room but Vera took it. She held out the receiver when
the line clicked, and then it began to buzz in her hand like a
trapped fly. "It's his wife," she agreed. "Who else?"

Finally I told Imant. He was quiet. I listened to our own

tires turning beneath us, changing key as the road switched from macadam to cobblestone to dirt lane. "Yes, he said, "it must be Frederika. I will ask."

"Will she tell you?"

"I will ask my father to speak with her."

I had not met his father; he was still at the country cottage. Imant's mother was there too, or had been, tending *her* mother, who was dying.

I was as caught up in Imant's life as if I'd been sharing it with him for the past ten years. And actually, it felt as if we'd been married for ten years. There was none of that tension that accompanies infatuation. The peace I'd felt with Imant ten years ago had turned out to be real, wasn't romanticized; it was as immediately present as his profile, the thick shadows of eyebrow and beard, the tiredness at the corners of his eyes and the kindness in them when he turned around to look at me.

I'd always seemed to attract men who wanted to remake me, perhaps because I seemed uncertain of my right to be myself. Imant never did that; he trusted me with my inner life and looked only to share and increase the outer one. He couldn't get used to the idea of psychoanalysis. He had never heard of the way Freud is taken as gospel in some Western quarters, and when I told him about it—describing my ex-husband—he only shook his head wonderingly. "Is very strange," he said.

His willingness to leave myself to myself was, in my book, real gentleness, and I know nothing sexier than gentleness.

Imagining I was taking all this away from her, I had felt a sneaking sympathy for Frederika, but Imant was going to divorce her whether I encouraged him to or not. In the end, Frederika set my conscience at rest, convincing me that she was my enemy as surely as if we'd been at war: a cold war.

Imant's father was in Frederika's camp. He was furious about my involvement with Imant: "All Riga is talking," he said—to Imant, not to me, who still hadn't met him.

If Riga was talking about us, it was because Frederika had spread the news. I first heard it from the Intourist guide assigned to our group, Pavil. I was wearing three-inch heels and had to look down into his face, round as a globe. He had extraordinarily long, dark lashes; his cheeks were freckled and very red. "Frederika has been here," he said, plainly titillated, "to the hotel, to call you bad names."

Bad names? I almost laughed, but that would have been a mistake. Pavil was less charming than some Intourist guides I had met, but they are all tried and true Party members, obliged to report anything "interesting" about their groups. Not that Pavil believed in Communism, or in anything else—he was frank enough about that. But he earned a good living, saw the world, and encountered no difficulties with the authorities, since he was engaged in no work that might ever bring him into conflict with them. Life was simple for him precisely because there was no black or white for him: everything was the same convenient gray. He used to poke fun at the elderly people on our tour; he'd sit around and drink, the red patches on his cheeks on fire, and say how ludicrous people were when they got sentimental. But when he learned I knew Imant, he was too impressed to hide it. I had written a letter to the Department of Visas—the hotel Intourist office—which had to be delivered through him, requesting permission to go with Imant Kalnin to Muriyana, a sort of summer colony for writers and artists just barely outside the city limits, to visit the poet Imant Ziedonis. "But these are the two most famous men in Latvia!" Pavil said. "You did not tell me who is your friend." He seemed to be accusing me.

Imant came with us on one of the afternoon expeditions, and Pavil couldn't wait to announce his presence in the back of the bus, but later, when Imant had gone to check on his grandmother, Pavil said to me, "I know his wife. She is an actress, a minor actress. She will never give him a divorce, never. Why should she give up so much prestige?"

Her "bad names" had given me a certain notoriety. People stared at me. When I walked through the lobby or joined my group in the dining room, I could practically hear the heads swiveling. One intense septuagenarian stopped me in my tracks by planting herself in my path. She was wearing a lilac flower-print dress and smelled of lilac water. "I want you to know," she said, under my chin, "that those other old ladies are stupid. I can tell from your face that you wouldn't harm anyone. You have a kind face." Eventually the whole group absolved me. Now that left only the rest of Riga.

Since our attempts at discretion had already been waived for us, Imant and I decided to tell everyone our plans, and we purposely went wherever we would be seen together. Imant's father asked him what he was going to do. Imant said he was going to divorce Frederika. But Pavil said Frederika said Imant was going to go away with her. Imant did drive her and the children to a friend's place in the countryside, but when they got there, he turned to leave. "Where are you going?" she demanded. He said, "To Riga." She nodded. "The only thing left," he said, "is to settle who will file for divorce." She agreed. "You do it," she said.

My application to visit Muriyani was ignored. Pavil explained that when Intourist doesn't want the responsibility of refusing a request on paper, they simply pretend that it hasn't been made. But Imant and I had already understood that Intourist would be of no help, and we had submitted another application, this time to the Ministry of Culture. We were asking for an extension of my visa so that we could write the opera we had been discussing for months.

And "there will be no problem about it"! So we were told by a top official, at a long table in a bare room, with Lenin looking down at us from the wall. We needed only one other signature, a mere formality. All *would* be well. As we left, I scratched the side of my face, near where an earring dangled.

The reason I was scratching was that I was turning out to be allergic to Imant's beard. Every time we got close, I broke out in a rash. Imant thought this was very funny and laughed while I itched; I tried laughing with him, but I still itched. Short of shaving Imant, the only thing was to see a doctor. The *doctor* laughed.

The doctor knew some English and was delighted to see us. He was associated with the union, and his patients were all musicians and writers; he wrote some poetry himself in his spare time, he said, and wanted me to tell him about American poetry. Then he turned to Imant. "Is it true," he asked, "what we hear, that you are going to leave us for America?"

"Nē, nē," Imant was saying. He was smiling, and the doctor, an attractive, open-faced man, was smiling, and the day was so sunny we could see the dust motes filtering lazily through the closed room; yet an invisible warning flag had gone up at just this innocent juncture: I felt as if some crazy conductor was driving a train through my brain.

What, or who, had led the good doctor to believe that Imant was planning to leave the USSR?

The doctor walked out with us to the narrow, winding staircase and smiled us down the steps until we curved out of his sight. At the bottom, we collected a prescription cream which cleared up the rash almost immediately. It was just as well that it did, because nothing was funny anymore.

At three that afternoon Imant and I went to the Union of Composers to ask for his chief's signature, the signature needed to complete our application to the Ministry of Culture. A mere formality. I waited in the car.

He didn't get it.

The chief said the Central Committee said that if Imant valued his work and his family, he would quit seeing me. "Think of your work," the chief said. Imant was baffled and furious; he couldn't understand how his work could suffer. Weren't we, on the contrary, planning to write an opera, if only the chief would sign this paper? "I cannot sign," the chief said.

We had driven in silence and were now talking parked on the side of a suburban road. Imant went into a store, bought a pack of cigarettes, and came back and began to smoke, tight-lipped. (In the ten years since we'd first met, he had quit drinking and I had quit smoking.) "He wanted to know," Imant said, talking about the chief, "if you are so important that I cannot to give you up. Women are women, he said. But you are not women, and I cannot to give you up. This I told."

"What did he say to that?"

"He said, then it is a pity I did not divorce Frederika before you come." He threw the cigarette away. "A very great pity."

The scenery on the other side of our windshield was flat and—the adjective that stuck in my mind whenever I thought of the Soviet landscape—unfinished. Buildings are always going up and coming down; great unfunctional gaps stretch between one place and the next, waiting expectantly for something to happen in them. That's partly why Russia appeals to Americans: it is frontier country, it cries out for pioneers.

Imant said Frederika must be behind this. I asked how Frederika could be behind a telephone call from the Central Committee. He said it was possible, he knew she knew someone. Then we thought: Why shouldn't *we* call the Central Committee? But there were no telephone directories in Latvia, and when Imant walked to a pay booth and dialed his chief to get the number of the appropriate representative on the committee, the chief refused to give it to him. I hated that man. I thought he was evil. "No," Imant said, "he is not a bad man. He is no worse than anybody else here. Simply, he is scared." And that, of course, was when I began to cry.

III

When Imant's grandmother died, his mother returned to the apartment in town.

I had already met her once, a short, broad, quiet, sweet-faced pensioner in mourning. Speaking English, Imant called her his "mommy." I tried to explain, gently, that in America thirty-four-year-old men don't call their mothers "Mommy." I said "Mother" is often used. Imant thought that was terrible. "No, no," he said, amused, "is too formal!"

"Okay. Mom."

This was even more ridiculous. "Is not affectionate!"

"Ma?"

"Is too ugly—"

In Latvian, almost any noun can be rendered diminutive. Children talk, and are talked to, in diminutives, but adults use diminutives for themselves almost as often. *Māte* becomes *māmiņa,* for example: "dear little mother."

Imant's mother was definitely more *māmiņa* than mom. We couldn't talk to each other but she told Imant, "Kelly's smile says everything." It must have told her how I felt about her son.

"Imant's mother is *good,*" several people said to me, on various occasions, underlining the moral dimension of that word. This is still, border to border, the land of unthinkable suffering, in which the Christian hope of martyrdom is yoked with an almost Oriental passion for self-abnegation.

Imant had shown me the family albums; his mother showed me slides of his children. In the background were glimpses of the farmhouse Imant and I planned to live in, Vecpauleni. No one lived in it yet—Imant had bought it only a few weeks before, and it was "exotic," which, translated, meant it dated from the turn of the century and desperately needed work. The apartment in Riga would go to Frederika. Imant's mother pointed and made an apologetic face whenever Frederika appeared on the screen.

Frederika and Imant's wedding pictures were still in their stands in another room. She looked like a movie star, blonde, imperious, and Teutonic as all get out. (In fact, she's half-German.) I hadn't expected her to look like that. Finally, one night after I'd climbed into bed and was waiting for Imant, I said, "She's beautiful." He thought for some time, a peeled sock in his hand. "Not to me," he said, after a while.

Imant's father, the only one among his family and friends with whom Frederika was on good terms, was not with us when we viewed the slides. Latvians move about all the time, splitting up the week among flat, cottage, farmhouse, or friend's flat. It's a way of living in cramped quarters: if you have to share your four walls with umpteen other people, you vary the people by varying the walls.

After our first meeting I had sent Imant's mother a box of candy. This box of candy greatly impressed everyone who saw it, and yet, at the dollar shop where goods are available for foreign currency, it was incredibly cheap. I don't know how much it would have cost in a Russian store. (I bought a bottle of co-gnac in Leningrad for ten rubles, or roughly seven dollars at the official exchange rate—but ten rubles is one-tenth of many a worker's monthly salary.)

After what had happened at the Union of Composers, we went to Imant's mother's, and I waited in the main room while he reported to her. Then I heard Imant's muffled voice saying, "Thank you for the candies," and his mother's painfully enun-ciated voice repeating, "Thank you for the candies." Afraid of forgetting, she said it over again, coming down the hall, and when she opened the door, she smiled utterly broadly and said: "Thank-you-for-the-candies." But she wouldn't stay; she scurried back to the kitchen to fix bowls of potato soup for Imant and me. We waited at the round table by the window, the white tablecloth riding up under our elbows.

Imant said it was possible that "they" might have photo-graphs of us. He couldn't think of the word he wanted. I sug-gested *blackmail*. He nodded. "Yes, yes," he said, "that is the word. If they make trouble, you must tell our story. Go to the world. Say them, what the Russians are signing in Helsinki and what they are doing here."

I asked if that would place him in any danger.

"What can they to do me? They can refuse to buy my mu-sic. But this I think they will not do, because the people love me. I think the authorities do not wish to upset their relations with me."

We went on saying these optimistic words to each other, but we were like a station on a shortwave radio, and foreign notes kept creeping onto our band, jumbling the tune, and slipping away again. We ate our potato soup while the late afternoon sun shone triumphantly through the white lace curtains, yet even now we were talking partly for the benefit of hidden microphones.

On our way out again, we stopped to say good-bye to Imant's mother. She came out of her room, puffy-eyed with weeping. Her mother had died only that morning. "Granny" had lived to be a very old woman. Imant recalled how she took care of him during the war, when Latvia was under Nazi occupation, and afterward. I told his mother I was sorry. She clasped both her hands to one side of her head and rested her head on them as on a pillow. She didn't try to hide the fact she'd been crying. "Thank you for the candies," she said.

IV

In the morning, we drove to the now-unoccupied cottage near the airport. Karl was with us. The sun was bright but clouds damped it periodically; then it would suddenly blaze up again, raining fire on the garden. Karl was gathering fallen apples; Imant, trailing a hose from the water trough in back to the Fiat in front, was washing his car. I had no job to do. I didn't want to stay inside, although there were two or three large rooms, a screen porch, and a heating stove: this was where Granny had stayed until she was too ill to refuse to go into the hospital any longer. I borrowed Imant's jacket and waited in the backyard, where I found an ancient, outsized wooden rocker to sit in. The apple and pear trees were to my left, and on my right, shoulder-high lilies. The cottage plot was small, and it was sided, backed, and fronted by similar plots, but the garden was so luxuriant that it seemed as though we might be miles away from anywhere. A bee, stupid and drowsy from honeyglut, fumbled at my hair; the low drone of the bee harmonized with the high, climbing drone of an airplane, and still, silence seemed to hang heavy from the branches of the trees in the garden, like fruit. I couldn't imagine a better place to live, or die.

When Latvians suggested I'd have a hard time living in Latvia, they weren't talking about the KGB, or the problem of censorship; they meant that the standard of living was too low compared with America's. Pavil insisted no American could become accustomed to the style in which she would be supported in Latvia. What I saw as a step up—a home of my own—he saw as a step down—a house in the Soviet Union.

I thought I could teach part-time, or learn Latvian and translate Latvian poetry into English. My own poetry, written in English and, as the property of a U.S. citizen, not subject to the Soviet copyright office (VAAP), would be published outside the Soviet Union. They ran only the risk of my poems describing their people, houses, and streets, their weather and their trees.

It *is* true that a certain dreary atmosphere oppressive as a cloud hangs over the Soviet world on even the sunniest days. I developed a craving for color; I found myself going on at length to Imant about the dishes I wanted for our farmhouse. Coffee mugs became fantastically important, and I wanted them fire-engine red.

Where had this concern with crockery come from? My very own, private standard of living in America had never financed anything the State Department could hold a kitchen debate in. One room and a battered (but uncensored) typewriter would be a truer representation of my life-style, whereas Imant derived from his commissions an annual income considerably above the average, the Soviet Union being anything but a classless society. As would have been the case in the West, Imant's main money came not from serious work but from what was marketable. Imant earned about one-third of a Russian penny on each copy sold of his records, but he lived off his movie scores. "Is very simple," he said. "I write one, maybe two each year." Personally, I think the workers should revolt.

(Waiting in front of the hotel for Imant to pick me up, I was approached by a handsome blond boy. It was ten o'clock at night and Riga was as deserted as a ghost town, but I knew what he wanted: not my bod but my watch. Smiling engagingly, he pointed to the watch on his wrist, and then to mine. "Trade," he said, "swap . . . nice Russian watch for nice American watch." I held my arm up to the dim light seeping out from the lobby. "Nice Russian watch," I said, and left him standing there.)

I didn't give a hang about the standard of living, but the KGB, and the problem of censorship, were a different story. Imant spoke wistfully one night of the "Magdalen" he wanted to write: the beautiful song of the repentant sinner at Christ's vacated grave. "If I write this," he said, "it will never be heard."

We wanted and needed to live in Latvia. Imant's children were there; his work was there; and my work is, or is supposed to be, portable. But I didn't want to go unprepared for the worst. The fact could be that I would never be able to publish again. Before leaving the States, I had checked with my specialist friend, finding out what answer to make to the KGB when they knock on your door in the middle of the night and demand to know how it is that your manuscript has recently been printed in the West. . . . You clutch your robe to your throat; you blink ingenuously at the sudden white glare and say: "Impossible! My book has never left my desk. Look, here it is!" And managing to appear indignant and beseechful at the same time, you produce the original manuscript. You are able to do this because you made a carbon, afterward destroying the used carbon paper. You would have preferred Xeroxing, but all photocopiers are kept more or less under lock and key, and in fact you're lucky to have a typewriter, which you brought in with you from Europe. The men look disgusted and leave. Their white Volga spits gravel. You go back to sleep, if you can.

V

We had a place where none of these complications could impinge on us, a place of peace—Indra's place. In English it was located on "Nightingale Street," a narrow dirt lane bordered by high hedges. A crooked gate led to a crooked walk, and in a lot less than a crooked mile—in about ten steps, to be exact— we entered a crooked little house. Indra had only the downstairs, though the whole affair was so low that it was hard to envision where the architect had stashed the upstairs.

Actually, not even the downstairs was Indra's, only one room with a blue floor, and a triptych of tall windows opening onto a lush-leaved flower garden. The other downstairs rooms belonged to her retired parents, her sister and brother-in-law, and a small niece and nephew. Like everyone else, they shuttled among residences, including a house in Jurmala, countering smallness with variation.

Indra herself was mostly away, staging Anouilh's *Medea* (I wanted to go, but it was off limits to tourists). Imant and I had her key and room. Sometimes other members of the family were there, and once I shared with her father, in total silence, an elaborate meal, replete with cognac, served in his one room with Old World courtesy and New World informality, but sometimes the family would simply vanish, like sheiks stealing away with folded tents under cover of darkness, or so it seemed to me, since these arrangements were always concluded in Latvian.

On Saturday night, the family left and Indra returned, bringing a friend—the friend who had endured six years as a political prisoner in a camp in Siberia. Teodor was our age; his sufferings couldn't be attributed to Stalin—they had happened more or less yesterday. And what did this "criminal" do for a living? Did he throw Molotov cocktails at Party bigwigs, or subvert the State by beating up on little old ladies? Was he a hooligan? Well, he was a ceramicist, and everyone knows that nothing is more dangerous than a ceramicist.

Teodor was to leave the next day for a month in the Ukraine. But the next day, his trip was mysteriously canceled, no reason offered. Was I the reason? Teodor and I said nothing remotely political to each other. Teodor, like many Soviet citizens, was both eager to try out his English and reluctant to make mistakes. But a deeper caution than this held him. As if an invisible fence surrounded his words, he let them out only under guard.

About Siberia he would say nothing. And others would say only, in the implicatory phrase that gives *good* its moral weight, that he had "suffered much." This is a phrase you learn quickly to respect, as bespeaking experience unparalleled in your own country, even at its most brutalizing. *Anguish* perhaps is ontologically pure, being entirely subjective; the anguish of a child over a dead pet can equal a mother's over her dead child.

But to suffer is to be acted upon by outside forces, and outside forces may be more or less persuasive, they may exhibit greater or lesser degrees of viciousness, they are not equal. Teodor *suffered much,* and his friends honored that fact by recognizing it as a distinguishing mark, like ashes on his forehead.

Indra and Teodor hadn't eaten; she cooked supper, and we carried the plates into her father's room, the one she was using, next to her (our) own. In here, there was a fireplace, a huge open grate that ate up a square yard of floor space. Teodor brought in the logs, but then he told me I had to lay the fire. I didn't know how. He said I had to do it anyway. I asked him why. "Because," he said, "it is the custom. The fire must be lighted by someone in love." So I said Imant could do it. The fire cast an orange glow over the whole room, the faces. The other side of the chimney, the side we couldn't see, ran up the inside wall of Indra's room—a facing of bricks which the fire in her father's room would turn as hot as a grill. Someone has said that this is how homes in colonial America were heated. If so, the colonies were cozy indeed.

There was a wood stove in the bathroom also, and when hot water was needed, a fire had to be laid in the stove. I washed my hair in there once, a feat I managed with good cheer but not much grace. Imant offered to help but I rashly declined the offer, and when I came out, wet and slightly wild-eyed, his amusement showed, as if to say, I guess, That's what life in America does, makes you think hot-water pipes grow out of the ground like trees. "Is it true," he had once asked, kidding, "that in America tomatoes grow in slices?"

He must have thought America's tomatoes were progressive but not plentiful, because he also thought I was underfed. "Women should be fat," he stated, expecting no argument— and everyone I met agreed with him. I read that newsmen are told not to photograph the stouter specimens of Russian womanhood: their silhouettes are said to be not "consistent with Soviet reality." Maybe the Kremlin admires the new Soviet woman, but Soviet men still prefer the ones they know from childhood—they like their women to look, well, comfortable.

I couldn't eat any more, though, and when the orange glow

had faded and the fire was only a bed of embers, we said good night and returned to the other room, which was by now radiantly heated by hot bricks. The blue floor was as warm as a rug to the soles of my bare feet.

Imant and I found ourselves staying up, talking; we couldn't go to sleep without moving Indra's cat, Lalita, who had stolen the middle of the bed. And we had everything to talk about— ten years—and it wasn't often we could talk at all without the subject of politics intruding. I thought of Teodor in the next room, his refusal to acknowledge a political dimension to our lives as eloquent a protest against it as any he may ever have voiced. Even now, politics was present, as a kind of third, silent party, the secret agent whose code name is Time. One week was up.

One week was up. In a world where people aren't allowed to love each other because they were born in different places, time is the last thing you can trust. "Someday," I said, "we'll be together, and then we'll grow old together. We'll both be eighty years old. I'll still be writing poems for you. In a very shaky hand." Imant slapped his face in that way he had. "Ai-yai-yai," he said. "To be eighty is to live again longer than we have already lived. How can anyone live so long? No," he said, tickling himself, "is not possible." He put a tape on the machine and the words filled the room, soft as starlight: *The pleasure of love lasts but a moment, the pain forever.*

Sometimes I would find on my pillow in the morning a note: "I love you very much. Wait me, please." Imant had to fetch Frederika in from the country, drive his parents from one house to another, or take his eight-year-old shopping (she needed clothes for school, which was to start the following week). I passed the morning in an empty room; the cat sat on the sill, washing her paws. I read a biography of William Carlos Williams which I'd agreed to review, and wondered whether the Soviet government would let me send my reviews to Chicago after I was married and living in Latvia.

So I learned to ask in Latvian: *Kur ir Imants?* "Where is Imant?" He was never gone long, but even a five-minute delay reminded me of the anonymous calls, of the Central Committee's threat, of Frederika's threat. *Kur ir Imants?* Indra speculated—Imant translated—that some future day she would turn on the radio and lo, there would be Kelly's small voice, the voice of America, mournfully calling, *Kur ir Imants?* When Imant wasn't there, Indra sketched another forecast—on a notepad at the oilcloth-covered kitchen table. A wavy scrawl represented the Atlantic. Then she drew a boat, christened it *Kelly,* and set it sailing to America. Imant stood on the receding shore. I objected to this vehemently and turned the boat around, drawing arrows toward Latvia. I said Imant and I were going to be married. She pointed at the open kitchen window. "When children come"—cradling air and patting the heads of invisible infants—"love flies out the window." And she heaved her "heart" into the front yard. I denied it. I denied it strenuously. She squared her shoulders, thumped her chest, said "Frederika," and mowed me down with an imaginary machine gun. I collapsed—into giggles. Indra sighed, and clucked her tongue. Then I explained that Imant and I would live in the farmhouse at Vecpauleni, and she taught me the word for house: *māja.* Say: maah'yah. Any house is *māja;* but the special house you dream of, the one home that is your place in the sun, that, too, is *māja.*

Imant had shared a *māja* with Frederika, on Suvorova Street, and most of his things were still there, and after the funeral we went there to claim some of his tapes. I was going to wait in the car, but Imant wanted me to come up.

From the landing, the building looked like a slum: the staircase stank, mailbox lids were half off their hinges, paint was chipped, and many moving fingers had writ on this wall. This was nevertheless a desirable part of town, old and central, and the apartment we entered was much larger than anyone I knew in New York could have afforded: a living room, two bedrooms, all three quite large, a kitchen big enough to eat *and* sleep in, and one tiny, truncated room which was Imant's. Practically everything he owned was contained in this one room. I sat on the bed, a made-up mattress on the floor, while Imant looked through his shelves for the tapes. I saw, on the shelves, my novel, and on the wall there was a poster of the writers' conference in Port Townsend where I'd taught at the beginning of summer. This evidence of my own existence pleased me, but it also gave me the willies: I wondered what Frederika had made of it. Imant said she used to fling the door open—at night, say, when his friends were visiting him, stand there with her hands on her hips, and then slam the door shut again. Now that's what she's always doing in my mind: flinging the door open, standing with her hands on her hips. (I'd have done the same thing, in her shoes.) Then Imant showed me another scrapbook, mostly of his rock tours, but there was in it one stunning, grainy newspaper profile of Frederika. I said I wanted to leave, but he had other things to show me: a fine edition of the Renan *Life of Christ,* the Dhammapada. . . . I saw my brother's first book on his shelves, but not my mother's, which couldn't get through Customs. (The title of her evidently subversive book was *Would You Like to Live in England?* "Yes!" Imant had answered when I told him about her book. "London is city I dream most about.") We gathered up the tapes. One of the tapes he took, because I asked him to bring it, was his cello concerto, a piece he wrote as a student. Later, playing it for me in Indra's room, he would say, with amusement and resignation: "A young man, not knowing what is a tragedy, proceeds to write a tragedy." He smiled and said, "Oy!"

I didn't like this hanging around on the stage after the final curtain had been rung down. I jumped up and announced we were leaving, and as if we'd simultaneously shaken off some strange debilitating spell, Imant and I grabbed our things and fled down the stairs to the car. Good thing, too. Frederika was in town, and if we'd waited just a little while longer, she would have been standing there at the flung-open door, hands on hips, fuming.

Before we could marry and live in our *māja*—where, Imant proudly said, we would have our own cow, since each country family is entitled to one—he had to get his divorce. He had taken the first step, but now his lawyer told us that one more piece of paper was required before the divorce application would be complete. There were two copies of this piece of paper. One was at the apartment on *Suvorova iela,* and going back there would mean confronting Frederika; the other, the original, stayed on file in Liepaja, the port city where Imant had begun living with Frederika. I was not allowed to go to Liepaja. Liepaja is closed, chiefly because it's full of naval secrets. I wouldn't recognize a naval secret if it fell on me, but I was still not allowed to go to Liepaja with Imant. It was an overnight trip. We decided that he would go to Liepaja with Emil. I would spend the night in the hotel.

We went to pick up Emil.

Imant wears a ring that belonged to Emil's grandfather; he wears it as an emblem of his friendship with Emil. When Emil and I met, though we couldn't talk to each other, he made it clear that he knew about me. He had helped Imant to telephone America on at least one occasion when Imant was too drunk to put the call through himself, and now here we all were, in person. Introduced, I said hi; he kissed my hand.

Thin, tallish, in his midthirties, with graying hair, Emil had a kind of scholarly good looks. He was the model of the born student, the lifelong learner, ardent and hesitant, who figures somewhere near the center of every Russian writer's work. To support himself and his son, he would clear the top of the very small table under the window and hand-make pairs of amber drop earrings. When we visited, he cleared the table and set out cups and saucers and boiled eggs while we produced a paper bag of pastries. Over his shoulder I could see his wife's paintings—which she was not allowed to show. One painting I couldn't stop looking longingly at was a portrait in oil of Imant.

Emil and Imant both spoke proudly of Olga, and they always called her Emil's wife, although, I found out later, she was his ex-wife. But Emil had never ceased to love her, and she now realized she still loved him. As I understood it, the thing was this: they couldn't go back to living together, because she had married again, to a man who had, like Teodor, *suffered much,* and no one may inflict additional suffering on such a man.

Olga was there when we drove by to pick up Emil. So were Olga and Emil's little son, Emil's brother Bruno, Bruno's wife, Annele, and Bruno and Annele's three children, all of whom shared with Emil the first floor of an old wooden house planted on a piece of unweeded earth. You couldn't call it a lawn. We drove the car on it up to the door, and the kids peeked at me from around corners. The littlest one smiled bashfully, was shocked at himself for going so far, looked at the floor, and ran away, but I still caught a glimpse of his towhead around the open door. I finally figured out that what fascinated them was my hat; they thought I was an American cowboy.

The window over the table in Emil's room opened onto a dirt lane; wild flowers waved their blue and yellow heads, and fragrance filled the room: flowers and tea. Emil set the phonograph's needle at the start of the flute solo from Gluck's *Orfeo ed Euridice,* and a limpid sweetness, like sweet water, poured over us. I looked again at the portrait of Imant: there was a suggestion of icon about it, and the eyes, Imant's eyes, looked back at me. Olga wanted to make me a present of the portrait but didn't know how I could carry it out, to the West; I wanted it very much and said Imant could take it to the farmhouse; it would be a housewarming gift. In the painting, Imant was dark and handsome and rather saintly-looking; Olga had painted him during his "prime." She and Emil razzed him about his "prime"—his stint as a rock star. The Imant I knew was past his "prime," with his receding hairline and nicotine-stained fingers, and besides, she couldn't paint the Chaplinesque silhouette of his splayed feet when he walked away from me—or the look on his face when he walked toward me. And I was glad of this, because my Imant was mine.

In another room in this house there were dozens of paintings by Bruno's wife, Annele. Annele did all her work in a shed in the yard hardly large enough to hold light, much less air, much less an easel.

The men took pleasure in the women's work, and they made real sacrifices so that the women could do it. That didn't stop them all, men and women, from insisting that women and men should be treated differently. Indra herself said, "A woman's physiology is different," and Imant and Rudolf agreed absolutely that this meant a woman couldn't be expected to work like a man. But when I pointed out that Indra was a highly successful stage director, Imant said, "Yes, she is *pathologique.*"

"What about me?" I asked.

"You are very *pathologique.*"

"And Olga? And Annele?"

"*Pathologique,*" he said, grinning. A world full of pathological women delighted him no end: he was very pleased with this picture of the relations between the sexes.

VI

I had dinner with my group in the main dining room. I thought this grand room, with its draperies and paintings, was as decadently bourgeois as any I'd ever eaten in, but the old people said the hotel, like Riga itself, was pitifully run-down. They remembered the silver, the china, the crystal, and the service before the war. Wasn't it George Kennan who had called Riga "the Paris of the North?"

Perhaps the old people's memories were filtered through the soft focus of nostalgia. At any rate, Riga seemed to me to be still a wonderful city of three corners, where East, West, and North meet. No amount of earnest Soviet television extolling collective farms or factories disguises the romance of Latvian culture. Alfreds Bilmanis, once a professor of history in Riga, in his *History of Latvia* contrasted the national character to "the passive, mystical, fatalistic Slavs." He emphasized the Latvians' "temperamental affinity with the institutions and ideas of Western Europe to whose community . . . they have always belonged geographically, ethnographically, culturally, and historically."

I don't know if nations have temperaments, but they certainly have ways of structuring time and space, and Latvians are Western in their perception of every man as a unique act deserving a free stage, and their period of independence between the two world wars bears Bilmanis out. But during centuries of subjugation to foreign rule, they have also adopted the Eastern way of cultivating an inner freedom. Inner freedom won't, of course, provide you with a tourist visa to France or Sweden, and it won't ensure that your mail isn't censored or let you read, say, John Updike, whose *Rabbit Redux,* every time I tried to send it in to my friends, was confiscated by customs officers. When one friend there inquired at the main post office, he was told, "Updike is not allowed"—but the books would be returned to the sender, me, only if I wrote to the post office myself. Of course, the Soviet post office never voluntarily notifies the sender that certain books and records aren't delivered, and many such articles are simply, shall we say, rerouted, to the customs officers themselves and thence to the black market.

What inner freedom does do, besides rescuing sanity and conscience, is bind friends closer together. There is a Warsaw ghetto of the mind and heart, a defense, a last-ditch defense, against infiltration, behind which individuals knit themselves into a feeling community. Trust and friendship go hand in hand, like European women.

I like this sisterly way of walking: you take your girlfriend's arm and stroll, sharing confidences.

Hand in hand, I went with Vera, after dinner, to see a friend of hers, the daughter of a stage designer. The house was in a part of town I hadn't visited before. It was big, and out back, grapes grew on twining vines, throwing onto the ground bunches of purple shade. We ate some of the unwashed grapes wet with dew; they tasted for all the world like grapes from Virginia, and their shadows fell on nonpartisan grass. The *Aggada* claims that each blade of grass on earth is watched over by an angel in heaven who tends it and cares for it and commands: Grow. And so it does, even in the Communist sector. When Vera's friend walked back with us as far as the tram stop, we all linked arms.

I was feeling very *alive,* quick and exuberant, in touch with the moist air against my cheek, attuned to the crunch of gravel underfoot. Then Vera's friend, the stage designer's daughter, said, "Imant Kalnin is an artist." Not sure what was coming, I merely smiled. "A man who is an artist," she said, "needs to seek his inspiration in women. What will you do when he begins to feel the well is running dry?" As she pointed out, there *were* those two wives at the beginning—affairs had he lived in the West, marriages here.

Waiting for the tram, I slipped off my sandal to shake out a pebble. I needed to do something like that to my thoughts. Trust and friendship, yes, but you have to know who your friends *are.*

At the hotel, Vera and I climbed into our beds, turned out the lights, and talked idly. Our one large window gave onto the courtyard, and our one moon shone on concrete. A long, rectangular wooden diptych given to Vera by her relatives was propped on two chairs against the facing wall; in daylight it showed the skyline of Riga, but now it looked like a painting of darkness hung on darkness. Vera was asking me how I could consider living in this nervous, cryptic country. I tried to explain: in Imant's presence I felt free. To let go the secret vigilance you exercise over your deepest hopes and needs, to escape from all those warnings *contra* possibility . . . what greater freedom is there? But I didn't dare use words like *freedom,* because of the microphones. (Someone we knew had entertained a long-unseen cousin in her hotel room one afternoon; he put a finger over his lips, turned over the radio on her night table, and exposed the microphone inside. Another acquaintance visited relatives in their home: the man of the house prefaced their conversation by wrapping the telephone in a towel. "Poor little thing," he said, "it must be cold." And he winked.)

Our talk drifted. The sheets were beginning to give me back the warmth of my own body and I could stretch out my legs and think of sleep. It was midnight. I shut my eyes.

The telephone rang.

I picked it up. Vera had a great many relatives, but I hoped it might be Imant, calling from Liepaja. There was a pause, which lasted an eternity or a second, depending on your point of view. And then a woman's voice, accented but eerily flat and clear, and full of innuendo, said, "Kelly, she's dead."

The words dropped into my brain like coins into a telephone slot, one at a time. "What do you mean?" I cried. "What are you talking about?"

I went on asking my question over and over, automatically, as if somebody had wound me up and I had to keep on playing until I ran down, and my caller must have felt the need to elaborate, because she said, with great precision, still in that soft, macabre, and *presumptuous* voice, "Kelly, she's dead. Imant's wife is dead." Then she said: "Are you happy now?"

I was shaking. My tongue felt like a rock in my mouth. My wrists had turned to air, leaving my hands independent of my arms and useless. I just kept saying, "I don't know what you're talking about."

Vera had got out of her bed and was sitting on mine, and she grabbed my arms and shook me. I told her what the woman had said. "It's not true," Vera said, "it's a joke. And if it were true, so much the better." I was horrified, and yet, as soon as she said it wasn't true, I knew it wasn't true; I think I knew it all along. I hung up.

But the lady tapped reserves of guilt, and nothing Vera said could stop my palms from sweating or my knees from trembling. It was midnight in Riga—and who knew what might not happen here, in a country where the unbelievable had happened time and again, year after year, century after century?

But the possible, as the philosopher explained, is not always the same as the believable, and my caller gave the game away. Fifteen minutes later the telephone rang again; this time the caller hung up. The third time, I held on without saying hello, and so did my caller. I hung up. When she called again, I said the only words that came to mind: "You really are a very lovely person." After that the phone was silent.

Vera and I pushed a bench against the door and switched on

the bathroom light. In case anyone tried to break in. But we left the window open, since only a KGB man or a cat burglar could scale it, and we were, after all, now that I was calming down, pretty sure this was only Frederika. An actress! I no longer felt an iota of sympathy for her. I'd been a shafted wife myself and knew how it could hurt, but ratting to the Central Committee on your husband, or terrorizing people in the middle of the night, went beyond *all* boundaries.

And I thought: What kind of woman could say of herself that she was dead without spooking herself? The moon was lost to me now, gone from my window, and the stark, unmoving light from the bathroom bulb seemed the dead outer skin of that earlier light, cast off and glowing on the floor. And *did Frederika understand English?* But maybe she hung up simply sensing the changed tone in my voice. Maybe it wasn't Frederika. Maybe it was her informant in the hotel. Maybe it was the KGB. Maybe the story was even true.

I stayed awake until the sky began to pale and Vera's skyline of Riga began to come into view.

VII

Before I came, Imant had counted the days in his diary, which he kept in the glove compartment of the Fiat. He had shown it to me. It was all in Latvian except for one sentence each day— and one painful paragraph. The recurring sentence was, "150 days to go," "149 days to go," "148 days to go . . ." As for the paragraph, it was written the night he told Frederika that he wanted to marry me. "This is the most dark night of my life," he wrote. "Will it be worth it? We shall see."

Now he was recording the days of my visit as they passed. He regretted not having kept all of the diary in English, "for the practice."

I asked him if he remembered how he'd felt on the first day. He slapped his face. "Ai-yai-yai," he said. "Awful! I was so excited that I forgot to be happy." He paid the waitress. "Indra saw us kissing," he said, "do you remember?" He looked energetic, convinced. Happy.

VIII

One night we went to a restaurant with Rudolf. It was the Luna, the place where, ten years before, I'd been taken for a prostitute. This time I was wearing a vampish dress with red and yellow birds on purple leaves against a brown background. Our plan for afterward was a late-night underground concert of Imant's songs. But our consciousness of those ten years weighed on us. Rudolf, on my left, had that lonesome Modigliani look; his high forehead and pointed nose reflected the candlelight. Imant is swarthier, and that evening he looked deep-down dark. Queuing to get in, he had asked me how I usually felt. Did he mean my moods? "Yes," he said. So I explained: up and down, more or less. With so little time to cover so much territory, we gave each other these quizzes. So far, the only point of disagreement we'd discovered was a convenient one, having to do with grapefruit: I liked the pulp, and he liked the juice. We both liked the inside of the bed, but there he gave way to me.

"Me too," he said, meaning his moods. Rudolf chimed in, saying *ja* with exaggerated emphasis. He went on to indicate that Imant's mood swings were pretty spectacular. Normally mellow, easygoing and optimistic and believing the best of everyone, Imant fell into gloom with as little forewarning as if he'd plunged into some emotional trap door. I tried to guess what had brought him down now. "Are you still angry about that call?" I asked. He had said he was—"very, very angry"— though his anger was visible only to someone who looked closely enough to see the way he clenched his cigarette in his fist, or the tenseness in his other hand as he used it to drive Indra's key into the lock on the front door. But now he said he wasn't angry, only sad, but he looked angry and depressed. He was still convinced that Frederika was responsible for all the calls. And yet his father had told him that Frederika denied making the calls. "Do you believe her?" I had asked. We were sitting in the car, in the lane in front of Indra's house, when I asked him that, and for a moment I thought he was going to say yes. He stared straight ahead and then he smacked a hand against the steering wheel and said, "It must be Frederika, it must be," and then we got out and he slipped off the windshield wipers and locked them in the car and locked the aerial, because spare parts are hard to come by in the Soviet Union and people are always stealing them. "Of course it was Frederika," he called over the roof of the car, momentarily gay, and then he gave it up.

But Rudolf was right. By the end of dinner Imant was definitely more cheerful. We were talking about music qua food-of-love. I get cravings for certain musical sounds, and recently, I could practically taste piano music; I was starved for the keyboard's passionate intelligence. I told Imant I wanted him to write some piano music. He promised.

"Sonatas," I said, stipulating.

"Yes, yes."

"A *lot* of sonatas," I said.

"Of course," he agreed. "Thirty-two." And he raised one eyebrow and smiled with his tongue in his cheek.

I looked at my watch—Imant's watch. It was nine or ten, time to go to our underground concert.

Underground does not mean that the KGB did not know about it. As Imant explained to me, the KGB knows everything. It's not that KGB agents are supersleuths or even especially bright, but they are numerous, and there are many *more* people who report to them and *tell* them what's going on. They knew about the concert but had given their go-ahead, or rather had not *not* given their go-ahead. A certain amount of "underground" activity is tolerated as an inexpensive and harmless way of pacifying the people.

These songs of Imant's were set to texts no one else dared to utilize; they were about Latvia. They were ballads. Spreading his arms and then drawing his hands in to form a tiny O, Imant said that they would be sung by a very big woman with a very small voice.

We waited near the stage manager's door. Imant was surprised to find it locked. People, mostly young people, were milling around in the lobby. I don't know how they knew to come—there was no marquee. They were chatting and smoking and revolving in little clumps the way people always do before the lights dim.

All at once the people apparently all understood that it was time to leave. They dispersed in a wink; I blinked, and they were gone, the lobby as cold and blank as any on Broadway after the last curtain. Except that here the curtain was still iron.

Imant grabbed my hand and we raced out to the Fiat. Rudolf sat in back, silent. Imant rolled down the window and exchanged a few words with someone I didn't know, and his voice was low and urgent. Then we took Rudolf home, and then we went home to Indra's house. Imant sat on the blue floor and dialed one number after another but no one he wanted to reach was at home. So. We got into bed and turned out all the lights but one. Lalita the cat bounded through the open window and landed on the floor with a thud; her shadow on the wall was gigantic. Then we turned out the last light. I said, "Somebody doesn't like us." Imant lit another cigarette and smoked it in the dark; when he drew the smoke in, the red dot intensified, and I could hear the faint crackle of cigarette paper crumbling to ash. "It may be," he said. "I find out in the morning." He stroked my hair. "Go to sleep, Kelly," he said. And the next thing I knew it was broad daylight.

The very big woman with a very small voice was later summoned by an official; he reviewed her program, decided it was acceptable after all, and let her reschedule the concert for a couple of days later. The "underground" concert now had the stamp of approval.

This time the concert was to take place in the early evening. We were late and raced up the stairs. At the top we turned right, into a darkened, elongated room. It was already packed, and Imant and I were going to take seats in back but people kept calling his name and pulling him forward. Down front, a bunch of people, some of them professional singers themselves, sat cross-legged on the floor. This left a smallish area, defined by the audience, which served for a stage. On the not-very-far side of it, a dozen candles standing on trellises burned steadily, tips of flame neatly tapered like Christmas tree lights, as if somebody had pinched them into shape.

Two people in the front row gave up their seats and more or less pushed Imant and me into them. No one spoke—or at least no one was speaking—English. The room was hot, crowded, and clandestine.

I had on a blue pullover and didn't think to take it off in time, and the room kept growing warmer. If only everyone would stop looking at us. I could sense Imant's discomfort. For most of the hour Imant gazed at the head of the man below him as if he were a phrenologist instead of a composer. I wanted to hold his hand but didn't dare, knowing someone would see and talk.

The performer came down the aisle, a guitar slung from a strap around her neck. She wasn't really so big, but her voice was minuscule, the voice of a café singer. She waved to Imant and began. I could almost translate the words, using the faces around me as a gloss. They were absorbed, rapt, discovering themselves. This was more than a concert; it was a congress. And the big woman with a small voice wasn't only a singer; she was a speaker. And what the audience was hearing couldn't be picked up on a microphone or even by an official in his office. I wondered if the Kremlin really comprehended the depth of Baltic nationalism.

One of the singers on the floor stood up for a duet, a children's song about two clouds who meet, fuse, and blow up into a storm. But there's a happy ending: a rainbow.

Everybody's mood lightened. The candles dripped wax and the flames danced, their elegant forms becoming erratic.

Some kids started calling for a certain song. Imant looked as though he were about to slide under his chair. "Karl wrote," he explained sheepishly. All I could tell about the song was that it had a chorus of one word, *Imant.* The whole audience joined in; Imant looked miserable (and pleased). Then the concert broke up, but before we could get up from our seats, a gray-haired woman gave Imant a long-stemmed red rose. As she handed the rose to him, she seemed to be looking at him with great tenderness. It was more than a rose; it was also a flag.

The entire concert had been a flag, a Latvian flag waved under the noses of the Russian invaders. As Georg von Rauch puts it, "In terms of international law, the Baltic republics continue to exist as legally constituted states, which happen to be occupied at present by a foreign power." But maybe the Russians thought: Let them wave their flag, no one will see it. I saw it.

Outside, Imant passed the rose to me. I asked him what the song Karl wrote, said. "Is nothing," he insisted, blushing royally. I made him tell me. It had been written for his birthday last May and went on about how clever he was "and so on." His birthday. Time was running out. Time was a *double* agent. I tried not to think about this, and we were having such a *good* time that most of the time I succeeded. Nevertheless, the clock ticked, the calendar turned. But Imant quit writing in his diary at night. I didn't give him time.

IX

The second Thursday, the day before my last day in Riga, Imant and I swung by Emil's place. Emil looked tired; he'd been up all night, working at his little table under the window until the sun came up over the sill. He swept the earrings out of sight and set tea on the table. There was birthday cake as well—his son's. The boy came home at noon. With his somber suit and black book bag, knobby wrists and wide, unblinking eyes, Emil's son looked more like a little man than a birthday boy; he was nine.

The boy ran off to play with his cousins in the dirt lane, and Emil showed me his son's school books, Greek to me. The music book included a couple of children's songs by Imant. While Emil exhibited samples of his son's penmanship, I pantomimed my admiration. But it was clear that Emil had other things on his mind.

Imant explained to me that Olga had telephoned Emil from the sanatorium in Jurmala, in hysterics. She was supposed to stay there until the birth of the child she was carrying, about another month. I had seen her in Riga only because the doctors granted her an occasional leave. She hated the sanatorium and was lonely and wanted Emil to come out for an hour. In Soviet hospitals beds are crammed into corridors, and round-the-clock care is rare.

On the other hand, health care is essentially free, as it should be everywhere; the doctor I had seen in Riga was a good one; and Olga's sanatorium, from the outside at least, looked as modern as anyone could wish. The white building gleamed like a sand castle in the sun; the grass was as green as the sea.

That particular day, the weather changed.

We were all hurried. Imant and I, having gotten the divorce application in order and on file, wanted to go to the Marriage Bureau (ZAGS). We had tried every way we could think of to get my current visa extended, but Intourist, despite the promises in their travel brochures, would not allow it. We had to find out how I should go about reentering after I left—and I was scheduled to leave Riga the day after tomorrow. After that, there would be only final weekend in Leningrad. We also had to drop by Karl's so he could interview me.

The atmosphere was taut. A cloud rolled in out of nowhere. Emil called the boy over, and as we all piled into the car, rainy gusts bowed the grass at the end of the lane and showed the silvery underside. I put on my blue sweater. Every time we turned a corner, Imant's cigarettes slid off the dashboard. Emil was in a quiet mood, and the boy was too shy to talk. We crossed the Daugava. The highway unrolled like a red carpet, and for "ten minutes along the U.S.A." the bark of birch boles and tall pines glistened. I had sent Imant a postcard from Port Townsend. The front depicted a river and woods in Washington, and the printing on the back said, "Good fishing among birches and pines!" In Latvia we were constantly passing rivers, birches, and pines. "Good fishing among birches and pines!" Imant would say, smiling with his eyes.

Wind lashed at the walls and windows of the sanatorium. Imant and I waited with the boy while Emil went in to find Olga. Thunder and lightning danced in the distance. All at once the sky collapsed like a backdrop, and a full-blown summer storm came crashing down on us. Emil ran out from the white building, his jacket over his head, alone. Olga wasn't there; nobody knew where she was. We started driving slowly along the streets. Windshield wipers were useless against a downpour like that; it wasn't a torrent, it was an onslaught. Imant tried to navigate by the side window. Then, just as abruptly, the rain slowed, and Emil shouted, "Stop!" Imant pulled over to the curb, and Olga, in raincoat and scarf, got in. At first I thought her face was wet from the storm; then I saw she'd been crying.

She had no makeup on and the tears and the raindrops glittered like sequins on her clear skin; to dry them, Emil had to lean across their son and the barn-side stomach that was going to be her second husband's child. She blew her nose into his handkerchief. She kept saying—Imant said—that she didn't want to stay in the sanatorium any longer, she wanted to return to Riga with us. We drove to a side street near Olga's room, and she and Emil and their son went up to it for a while. They were going to ask the doctors if Olga could come back with us. Imant and I stayed in the car, listening to the rain on the roof. Leaves the size of lily pads spattered the sidewalk. An old woman was taking her afternoon stroll; a little matter like the lack of an umbrella wasn't going to stop her.

The doctors said no. When the unhappy family came back, Olga sat in the middle, her arms around her husband and her son, kissing both. She was weeping openly, and kept apologizing for it. Leaning forward, she said good-bye to me through Imant. I patted her hand. Then she kissed the top of the boy's head, and Emil took her back inside and left her. I had the feeling that they were saying good-bye for more than a few days;

it seemed less a leave-taking than a grieving. I shivered as if a cold shadow touched me, a foreshadow. When Imant released the stick shift, I reached for his hand.

The return trip was even quieter. The boy fell asleep in Emil's lap. Our tires on the wet road sang a gentle tune, like a lullaby. It was still raining, but not hard, and against that thin gray light the tree trunks glowed silver.

Imant dropped me at Karl's and drove father and son home. I stared out the window, remembering the vigil I had kept by the same window on the first evening. Karl said, "It's the first rain with Imant, isn't it?"

The idea was that Karl would interview me for the paper in which his translation of three of my songs had appeared. I jumped at the chance, thinking that if I could begin to have a professional life in Latvia, the Soviet authorities might hesitate to interfere with it. The Helsinki Accords were supposed to encourage professional connections too; well, Imant and I had had a professional relationship for as long as we'd had a private one, and if détente was for real, our professional relationship could only work to everyone's advantage, as a proof and affirmation of it. The Soviet authorities might even begin to see that if détente meant a "relaxation of tensions," it meant agreeing to disagree. With the force of each side's nuclear fist neutralized, both sides could forget about the Big Punch, relax, and spar like gentlemen, with words (and secret funds and agents). But one of the problems with détente, aside from the problem of implementation, is the inconvenient fact of communism's being historically defined, by Marx and Lenin, as precisely the elimination of other systems, by violent means.

The hitch was that Brezhnev, while pugnaciously announcing that the ideological war would continue, like his predecessors actually meant just the opposite: there would be *no* contention of ideas.

But! It was fine with me if the Kremlin, for the sake of détente, had come up with a way to redefine communism as one system among many. That they *had* arrived at a justification of détente that was consistent with the theory of communism was something the Western world apparently had to take on faith (with a grain of SALT).

I suggested to Karl that he could write in his article that I planned to immigrate to Latvia; now, that would be détente.

He pulled an extremely wry face and said that would not be advisable. I asked why not. "It would not be printed," he said.

What would Marx, sending his articles to the New York *Daily Tribune,* have said about this? In the United States there is a kind of censorship dictated by commercial considerations that functions so pervasively that much of the time people don't even know they're guilty of it, or victimized by it. It's nevertheless a far cry from being kindly informed in reasonable tones that something you want to say simply cannot be said. You may have something to say of life-and-death import, you may be ready to give up your own life for the chance to say it, but *where* are you going to say it?

Karl had opened our interview by placing several sheets of white paper on his desk. (He had no typewriter, though he wanted one very much.) The empty pages were still in front of us. He took a seat at the desk and straightened the corners of the stack of blank pages. I paced the room. There wasn't much room to pace, but I walked up and down the narrow lane of rug between desk and crib, thinking. Not being able to say that one thing had knocked everything else out of my mind. Why on earth couldn't I say that I hoped to live in Latvia? I wanted to ask, but of course I had been warned about the microphones, and I couldn't ask Karl anything that might embarrass him. He had turned around and was tugging at the golden goatee, his rubbery body stretched around the chair, his elbows resting on the top rung, the lines in his forehead as deep as if they'd been inked in. A nice, worried man. I came up with some words about the American literary tradition and the Russian literary tradition. I don't remember what I said, but Karl would remember it. Whether it's the traditional emphasis on the recitation of poetry or just the difficulty of obtaining a typewriter, everyone in the Soviet Union, or so it sometimes seems, can speak reams of words by heart. Imant could quote freely from my poems and often startled me, doing this. ("How sweet those mountains seemed / how cool and tangy, the Daugava!") You can go for a drive along the Daugava, Riga's river, and look at the sweetest of skylines, fine-edged and lacy. The tall spire of St. Peter's and its companion steeples only accentuate the long, low line of river. "Tangy Daugava!" Imant will say, or Emil or Rudolph. In the names of these Russian rivers—Daugava, Volga, Neva—I find poetry, a gentle susurration lapping at the shore of sound.

It was Karl who finally brought up a subject we could safely discuss: minorities. He asked about "movements" in American writing of the sixties; what he wanted to know most of all was whether minority writers had trouble being published in the States; he was especially interested in American Indians. But at some point he made a passing reference to the situation of Latvia as an ethnic minority. He said nothing about it, but the two terms had been set up; all I had to do was draw the parallel. Although the Soviet Union's officially stated policy is to encourage "cultural expression" among minorities, the real policy is the subtler one I talked about before, Russification, which might otherwise be known as slow death. Leonid Plyushch, in an interview *he* gave, said that "Ukrainian schools . . . are carbon copies of Soviet schools. Ukrainian schools are offered as national heroes such figures as Peter the Great, the scourge of the Ukraine, or even the traitor Kochubei. In this way, the Ukrainians are given a warped version of their own history. . . . Even more tragic than the lot of the Ukrainians is that of the Crimean Tatars, Greeks and Meakhals, for they have all been deported to Siberia or Central Asia and are struggling today to get back to their native land and obtain cultural autonomy." A trick the Latvians have is to speak Latvian in front of the Russians in Latvia, though they are required to learn Russian in school.

As for "movements" in American writing, if the sixties accomplished anything, it was to remind us that every people is entitled to its past. That was the decade's true revolution: a reclamation of lost history. Lord Acton said, "The civilization of a state is best measured by its respect for minorities." Is there a more valid rule of thumb?

X

The Marriage Bureau was on the second floor of an old building—a house, really—and all along the wide, spiraling staircase, the kind of staircase that looks as though women in ball gowns once floated dreamily down it resting one hand lightly on the banister, applicants whispered in pairs, waiting. There were tall guys with tall girls, tall guys with short girls, short guys with short girls, and short guys with tall girls. We were all suffering from self-consciousness and studiously avoided looking at other couples too closely. When the bureau opened and we were allowed to enter an anteroom lined with mirrors, there seemed to be twice as many of us, as if we were going to be married in quartets.

Imant and I kept close to the wall. I tried to melt into the wall, but no matter how inconspicuous I willed myself to be, there I was staring back at myself from the other side of the room.

Imant found an empty room with a chair in it and no mirror and asked me to stay there while he went to check things out. So I waited: in a large room with bare walls, at a long, bare table, while lovers hurried hand in hand back and forth across the open end of the unused room. Every so often someone would peer in, see me, and back away, startled: a Marriage Bureau is not a place to visit alone.

At last we were actually in an office. While Imant talked in Russian to the woman behind the desk, I tried not to look at their faces, I was so afraid of reading bad news in them. Instead, I looked at Lenin's. The omnipresent portrait of "the greatest hippie in the world" glared at me from the opposite wall. I couldn't think: my heart was beating so loud it was like trying to think with the radio blaring. Just one thought kept going round and round in my head like a record with the needle stuck in a groove: how absurd it was that a man who was long dead before I was born could conceivably keep me from marrying the man I loved! Then another woman interposed her face between Lenin and me. The bottom half of the mouth in it clacked open like a ventriloquist's dummy and words began to fall out of it at a furious rate.

But when we were on the street again, in the Fiat, Imant promised that the second woman's anger and agitation had had nothing to do with us; she had been in a minor traffic accident on her way to work and was still upset about it. Well, she did have one thing to do with us: she was a friend of Frederika's and was surprised to see Imant in the Marriage Bureau.

A friend of Frederika's.

"What did they say?" I asked, dreading the answer.

"I thought you would see in my face—"

I confessed I'd been looking at Lenin's face, not his.

"I was so excited," he said, "I could hardly keep still. I was afraid to make people think I am crazy."

Then the news was good?

"Yes, yes, Kelly! All *will* be okay!"

A car behind us honked, and Imant swerved to avoid the curb. Imant told me a Russian joke. Officer waves car to side of road. Young man has one hand on the steering wheel and the other on his girl. Officer to young man: Both hands! Use both hands! Young man to officer: Yes sir, but then who will drive the car? I wondered if the woman who'd been in an accident had been driving to work with her fiancé.

We parked in our spot at the Opera and had breakfast in the hotel café while Imant repeated what he'd learned. I needed my divorce papers and a piece of paper stating that the United States had no objection to my marrying a Soviet citizen. These papers were to be submitted to the Soviet authorities, by mail if I liked but preferably in person in Latvia. I could come in as Imant's guest on a month-long visa or as a tourist on a two-week visa which could be extended for two weeks at the request of the U.S. embassy in Moscow. Getting married would take about a month. Marriages between Soviet citizens and foreigners were ruled on by the KGB, but there was a routine bureaucratic procedure to follow and no need to expect any problems. (Under Stalin such marriages were outlawed.) When the time came, I was also to notify the Soviet embassy in Washington, D.C., of my marriage to Imant Kalnin, *dzimis* 1941. *gada* 26. *maijā,* Rīgā Latvijas PSR.

That morning we had no reason to doubt the information we received. It came, after all, straight from the Marriage Bureau, and didn't the Soviet Union do what its officials, speaking officially in their offices, said were its official rules? I made Imant go over every point again and again. It seemed as if all *would* be okay. It had finally turned out—hadn't it?—that our only enemy was Frederika, and she'd lose interest in her revenge before long. We might even—and now *I* could hardly keep still—be married in time to be together for Christmas.

It was 11 A.M. At the table next to us, four Russian women were drinking cognac on their coffee break. I was going up to my room to pack a suitcase for Imant to take to the farmhouse, with Olga's portrait of him: some books, some clothes, and some cosmetics I'd brought in, knowing Rum Plum eyeshadow wasn't a priority item in the Five-Year Plan. "I come back in thirty minutes, yes?" Imant asked.

"Jā," I answered, and went on up.

As soon as I turned the doorknob, Vera came to the door and pulled me in. "Is Imant with you?"

"He's coming later," I said.

"There was a call."

"Frederika?"

"A woman from Imant's office."

"Imant's office?"

"She said she was a friend of his. She was looking for him. He was supposed to be at work."

"Work?"

"She said that it was very important that she reach him. She asked where you and Imant were staying."

"So whoever it was knew about me."

"She thought I was you, at first," Vera said, sinking into a chair—after removing from it the books, records, candy, loaves

of bread, and jewelry her relatives had given her, not to mention one-half of the skyline of Riga. On her pillow, sleeping
bodilessly, was a giant wood stylized head sculpted by her
niece's fiancé. "I told her the truth, that I did not know where
you and Imant were staying."

"Did she have anything else to say?"

Somehow I was sure that she did. If governments deal in assassination, why not character assassination?

"She said that Frederika will give Imant the divorce and that
you can have him but that you aren't getting much. Oh, she
went on for a long time. She knew the whole story, and once
she started talking about it, she wouldn't shut up. I was curious
to hear what she had to say."

"You're positive it wasn't Frederika?" Remember: an actress.

"Oh yes, it was a friend from Imant's office."

"Imant doesn't go to an office," I said then. "He works
at home."

Now it was Vera's turn to look surprised. We were held in
that attitude, stock-still between statement and inference, when
Imant knocked on the door. I ran to let him in and hugged him
tight. "What is this?" he asked, smiling.

"I want you to see my wedding dress," I said, leading him
to the closet. "See?" I said, showing him the floor-length red-
and-white striped skirt and matching sash and the white blouse
I had bought in Minneapolis. "Do you like it?" It *was* a dress
for a wedding in Riga, revolutionary and romantic.

Imant said, "You have the most beautiful dress in the world."

"But it's a summer dress. Suppose they give us a date in
December?"

"We will get married indoors." He was still smiling.

I folded the dress into the suitcase bound for the farmhouse.
"You'll put it on a hanger?"

"Yes," he said. "It will be like a good omen, a sign that you
are coming back."

We left Vera and drove with the suitcase to Indra's house. We
were going to have supper at Ausma's apartment, and then at
six o'clock I was supposed to give a talk to the English class

Karl taught at the university. In the morning I would leave for Leningrad with my tour group; Imant would come by car.

This last day in Riga was a picture-taking day. The day was sunny, perfect. In the garden, Imant and Indra and I were clowning around with our hats, while Lalita the cat observed us from the wall. Lalita yawned, her pink tongue careless with confidence. In the bright light, orange nasturtiums at the tips of their stems gave off a steady, heady glow, so that the garden looked as if it had been planted in torches. Maybe it was just as well that there were no telephone directories in Latvia: our last night here still belonged to us. And the Marriage Bureau said we could get married, and Stalin was dead and despised, and the world had a future and so did I, in a far but dear corner of it.

At Ausma's apartment we ate creamed mushrooms, and then she got out her camera and shot film for an hour or so. Imant left in time to bring Karl back and pick me up before the class at six; that left Indra and Ausma and me in the flat, unable to talk with each other. I looked down from the window. We were on the fifth floor; across the street there was a school Imant had attended. He went to the regular school until he was twelve and then to a special school where he studied composition. His family wasn't particularly musical; simply, one day he heard some music on the radio and decided he would write his own. Success came easily—too easily, he said. (You turn away from outward things; first you sin, and then you go in.)

I still stood at the window, looking out at the school or down at the street. Any moment now, the yellow Fiat would wheel around a corner and into view. *The class begins at six.* Teasing, Indra said, "*Kur ir Imants?*"

Ausma brought out photographs she'd made of some of Indra's stage productions, and we spread them out over the floor, dozens of black-and-white glossies, while they tried to tell me what each one was about. It was mostly hopeless; we needed a language. I got up from the floor and wandered around the room, always circling back to the window. No sign of Imant. It was almost six. *The class begins at six.* I resumed my wandering. How many people lived in this enormous place? So far as I knew, there was only Ausma, with her tender eyes and worried posture, a thin little moustache like a circumflex over the O of her mouth, rattling around from room to room, daydreaming in the darkroom, hoarding one tin can of imported Nescafe coffee for the day when someone special would come to call. I half-expected to open a door and find Miss Havisham seated in her white gown and veil at the end of a moldering banquet table.

The room overflowed with photographer's props: a love seat, rubber plants, a gold-rimmed demitasse service, threadbare velvet hangings of green and maroon. On one wall there was a wonderful photograph Ausma had made of the window in that very room on a rainy day: it seemed to speak of desolation outside and warmth within, and I fell in love with it. On the spot, Ausma took it down from the wall and gave it to me, for the *māja*. Just then, Indra grabbed my arm and spun me toward the window, saying, "Imant!" It was six o'clock. I raced down the stairs, but he met me halfway and said there was no need to hurry.

"But we're late already," I said. His hair was wet; he had stopped to shower.

"The class is canceled." I waited for him to say why. "The director said, that it is not possible."

Once again I thought: It's not Frederika; it is the KGB. Why did they have to do all this to *us?* "Is not *us*, Kelly," Imant said, trying to reassure me. "The director told, how can he know what you will say? He cannot to take a chance. It is what is wrong with everyone here. No one will take a chance."

"You're sure that's it?"

"Yes, yes. Is stupid and terrible, but it is to be expected."

"Karl promised his students!"

"That is the way it is here." He stopped to let me absorb this.

"Ausma gave us a photograph for the farmhouse," I said.

He nodded approvingly, holding it at arm's length. "It is very nice, no?" he said.

83

"Yes," I said. "Maybe when I'm living here they will let me talk to Karl's class."

It was still picture-taking day, and I wanted Rudolf's. Imant and I drove over to see him on Karl Marx Street. He posed in front of his apartment, in an alley, his delicate face whiter than the laundry on the line behind him. It made me sad. Rudolf was always special to me, someone who had been there when I first came to this distant city. He was eighteen then. I never saw any sign of his family; maybe they lived in the country.

But that night he was in good spirits. He was coming with us back to Indra's—she was home now, and the four of us were going to have a party with a little *p*. Again we laid the table in the garden for tea, adding wineglasses for Rudolf and me. Night was falling, gently, like a black silk scarf billowing downward on a breeze. The stars were out, wheeling west, faint blue and pale yellow stars and a red star like the one on the uniform sleeve of a pretty Pioneer, aged about twelve, holding her father's hand as they bought tickets for the ballet. Somewhere someone was playing power politics. Somewhere someone was law-making and law-breaking, and the result would determine our lives. Well, *we* had a round table, a round white wrought-iron table in a dewy garden. Why not let *us* convene a summit conference? Could we do worse?

While Indra and Rudolf boiled the tea, I sat inside on the blue floor and went through my handbag, pulling out everything that could go to the farmhouse. At the bottom of the bag, I found an old watch; it was only a cheap timepiece, not jewelry. I was wearing the watch Imant had given me ten years before. I asked him if he wanted his watch back, but he said that would be bad luck: I must keep it, because it was mine. He crouched on the floor beside me and tapped the crystal of the watch on my wrist. "Ah yes," Imant said, "*he* has waited a long time too."

Indra's face appeared at the third panel of the tripartite window. "Come," she was clearly saying, motioning for us to come out, "tea's served."

"Would Indra like the other watch?"

"I am sure she likes very much."

"You'll have to explain that it's not fine or anything."

"But it is American," he said. "It will work."

(Brezhnev must have held the same opinion about Soviet watches, a few months later begging the watch off Kissinger's wrist.)

I gave it to her when we were all seated at the table, and she liked it better than the Saks scarf or the Zuni bracelet; it was a souvenir of the consumer society. I asked what I should bring when I returned, and after much prompting, they finally admitted they would like Janis Joplin albums, Saul Steinberg cartoons, a history of fashion in the Western world. Imant himself wanted three things: a Bible in the English language, a tiny American flag for his dashboard, and a pair of blue jeans. Then, to even things up, Indra disappeared into her room and returned with gifts for me: a corkscrew in the shape of the key of the city of Riga, and one half of a ruble. She kept the other half. We had fulfilled the first condition of a successful summit: exchange of tokens.

A single candle guttered in the middle of the table. I could see the reflection of the moon in my wineglass. I had one flash cube, and we snapped four pictures at the table. In the camera's stark flash, the bark of the tree behind the bench looked like stone. And then it was no longer picture-taking day. I was going to throw away the burned-out cube but Indra asked if she could have it. Imant explained that she would make jewelry with it. The nightgrass breathed damp air, and sleeping nasturtiums wept tiny drops of water. We leaned across the table, drawing closer. This is the second condition: conversation.

Now the saucer in the middle of the table was brimming with melted wax. The nub of candle swam in it, and then the flame went out, a sudden blind spot. I said good night to Indra; she'd see me off from the hotel in the morning. I said good night to Rudolf; Imant would drive him home now and pick him up again in the morning, for the long ride to Leningrad. We weren't about to let my two days in Leningrad go to waste, no matter what Intourist decreed. Imant would meet my plane at the airport. It was midnight, and I set the alarm for five.

When Imant got back from driving Rudolf home, I was waiting for him. Lalita slept on the blue floor.

XI

Imant took me to the hotel at six; it wasn't light yet, and he walked me up to my room. At the head of the hallway the key lady was fast asleep, snoring. We didn't wake her; we crept by, and then Imant beat it back to the street: Intourist wouldn't tell in advance where our tour group was booked, so Imant and I couldn't run any risk of missing connections at the airport in Leningrad. I crawled into bed and dozed for a couple of hours, waking to the last Latvian sunrise. Vera's relatives came to see her off; our room was so populated there was no place to sit. Even the skyline of Riga and the wooden head had been relegated to the floor. But by this time I felt as if her relatives were my friends. One was a grizzly-haired man with an ominous cough who'd been forced—they said, anyway—to fight with the Germans; now he lived in a forest, and seemed ill at ease in a hotel. Another was an "Imant" who said if I couldn't marry my Imant, I could have him. A third, a woman, was to hang herself the following year. The sun from the courtyard fell on their complicated faces through the great open window; it was getting late, and I wondered if Indra might not arrive in time, but she did, bringing, wrapped in a newspaper, a present from Imant, which she pressed into my hands downstairs, as we stood in front of the hotel. And I climbed onto the bus, and Pavil the Guide handed out box lunches (but naturally Intourist forgot to include a bottle opener for the bottles). And Indra, in long skirt and crazy pale pink top, stood on the street and blew kisses and then moved off again through the maze of Intourist buses. I sat close to my window, watching her back recede, thinking about Imant, on the road in his Fiat, *He's half-way there.* When the Helsinski signatories disbanded, they fixed a date for a follow-up conference. The last condition of a summit is: to arrange to meet again. (Preferably before the day is out.) I wasn't sad about leaving Riga, because I thought I'd be back soon. But there on the bus, alone for a moment before everyone settled down for the ride, I relived how, just as I was about to leave the hotel room with Indra, the telephone rang. All the chatter in the crowded room ceased, and everyone watched as I picked up the receiver. There was a click, and then the line went dead.

CHAPTER 3

An Underground Hotel in Leningrad

I was standing at the window of my room in the Sovietskaya, gazing into the courtyard below. All at once a *window* whizzed past my line of sight—a pane of glass exactly like the one I was looking through. It touched down with a tremendous ringing noise and splintered into silence. In the afterhush I glanced up and saw in their various rooms four or five hotel guests, all with baffled and blank expressions. Then the man whose window had fallen out smiled guiltily and shrugged, and the man with him slapped him on the back. The first man began explaining loudly that he hadn't done anything; he hadn't even been near the window. Across the courtyard, another man leaned out of his open window, calling condolences. A fourth man laughed and turned back into his room. Nobody ever came to sweep up the glass. That might have been laziness, or it might have been prudence: you wouldn't want to be under it when the next window came crashing down.

Imant was waiting for me. He had met me at the airport, with Emil, Ilze—who seemed to be Emil's girlfriend—and Rudolf, and then followed the bus to the hotel. Imant didn't know Leningrad well. We were all tired, and Imant's face was drawn. He had a friend in Leningrad and he'd been hoping we could stay there, but it developed that the friend was out of town.

Naïvely, I suggested to Imant that we could go to another hotel, surrendering the Sovietskaya to my tour group. That was when he explained the regulations to me: no visitors in your room after 9 P.M. I still didn't understand why we couldn't register as Mr. and Mrs. Ivan Ivanovich Ivanov. Imant's eyes lightened as he saw what the problem was. "Oh," he said, "you thought we could simply sign our names! Is not the way here. One must present one's passport." He meant the internal passport Soviet citizens are required to carry. Once Imant had asked me if it was true that in America anyone was free to travel anywhere.

"Of course," I said.

He didn't say anything for a long time. Then he said, so softly I could barely hear him: "*Free. . . .* Sweet, sweet word."

After further discussion we realized we had no choice: it was too cold to sleep in the car. (We left summer in Riga, and went to Leningrad to catch winter whipping around the corner.) We had to find a hotel: we'd fret about rules and regulations later.

It was still light when we started searching, but the light drained away quickly, as if somebody had pulled out a plug. (Or, seeing that this was a Russian sky, threw the plug away, since all Russians *know* plugs are unhygienic.) Reflected in the black canals, neon signs seemed to swim like brightly colored fish. The streets of Leningrad are broad and beautiful; I opened my window a crack, and air poured in like water. Ilze and I didn't care what it did to our hair.

Imant and I waited while the others went in to see about a room, but there was no room in this inn. We set off to try another hotel, but I felt subdued. And the next hotel had no vacancy either. Nor did the one after that. We had been driving around Leningrad for two or three hours, and in the end Imant took us back to the Sovietskaya. The trio went in to ask again for rooms, it was our last chance, and this time they struck gold, Russian gold. There were still no vacancies—but the clerk at the desk gave them the phone number of an *underground hotel*.

Now that we had a place to go to, the others stayed in the car while Imant and I went into the Sovietskaya so I could collect, from the room I was supposed to share with Vera, the overnight things I would want.

"Did Indra bring you something to the bus?" he asked, looking around the room. The package was on a shelf. "But you have not opened!" he said, taking it down.

"I waited for you."

"Open now," he said. "I want you to see—"

They were cups. Not the hefty red coffee mugs I had thought I was talking about; these were delicate teacups with matching saucers, two of each, hand-painted against a light brown background.

"Teodor made," he said. "They are very fine, no?"

"They are beautiful." And they were. "I don't want to take them with me. They belong in the farmhouse."

For our farmhouse we now had a painting, a photograph, and two teacups. On winter afternoons when the sun was sparkling on the snow, we would sit in our kitchen and sip tea from works of art.

Imant had said everything in our house would have to be "very fine." He was going to try to get a Dutch sideboard from someone he knew who had one for sale; the furniture in Soviet stores is all knockabout stuff, jerry-built, but you can get good things privately. Still, neither of us had owned fine furniture before, and I asked Imant why he was concerned about it now. He was laughing, though, as always, more with his eyes than out loud. "Someday this house will be famous," he said. "People will come from all over the world to see it, and so, it must be very fine house." That wasn't all. It also had to have alligators in the pond. "You're putting me on," I complained, but he said, "Yes, yes! Russian alligators," indicating a body length of about ten inches. He had already decided we'd have several cats, and a Borzoi puppy for me. And, of course, our allotted cow.

I tied the teacups up again in their newsprint and tucked them back on the shelf.

It was time to ask him about something that had been bothering me.

"You must have been in love when you got married before,"

I said. "How do I know there isn't going to be a Wife Number Five? I'm willing to live in the Soviet Union as your wife, but actually, I can't think of any place in the world I'd less like to be a divorcée in."

"You are only wife I want."

"Yes, but," I said, unable to stop, "is the way you feel about me"—I didn't know how to put this—"is it any different from the way you felt *before?*"

"You are asking me," he said, "what I cannot answer. I do not know how—" My face felt numb, as if the world had just blown up in it. He said again: "You ask me what I do not know how to answer."

I put together my gear for the night and gave it to Imant to carry. Walking back down the long hallway, weighed down by my flight kit and string bag, he said in a low but distinct voice: "I would give my life for you." I looked up, jolted. "I cannot live without you," he said, "I cannot." I smiled at the key lady at the end of the hall as if Imant weren't saying these things to me under his breath, but words which might be only romantic in other circumstances take on a startling significance when you know they could be overheard by the KGB.

"That's what I needed to know," I said.

We needed a gas station, and it had to be the kind of gas station for which Imant had coupons.

The beauty of Leningrad, simply speaking, stuns. The whole city is a measured spread of pastel set against a pewter sky carefully engraved with clouds; it's like a formal garden in which the ornately trimmed shrubs are made of stone. At night, the city's breath seemed cool and moistened, and the dark streets glistened. We spent another hour looking for the gas station, which we eventually came upon behind another building. I can't exaggerate the difficulty of these ordinary tasks.

And after we found the filling station, we still had to find the hotel. Now: like all underground activities, this "hotel" was certainly known to the authorities. The room shortage being what it is, private citizens, or comrades, rent out spare rooms for a few untaxed rubles. Some of these rentals are quite well organized: word is passed from guest to guest, or through official hotel employees who presumably receive a kickback, and if a "hotel" is booked up, it refers its overflow to another "hotel." Upstairs, it may be, or next door. Again, the room shortage being what it is, the authorities look the other way.

It took us another couple of hours to find our hotel; it was in a monolithic apartment complex in the suburbs. I thought we'd never find it. I asked Imant if the KGB were following us; he said it was possible. I had an idea. "Why don't we let them go in front," I said, "and then *we* could follow *them* to the hotel?" It was getting late, and every back alley and dead end we went down made it later. When we found the right complex, we couldn't figure out how to get into it. At last in utter disgust Imant jumped the curb, drove across three backyards and brought us to a halt in front of a building in a row of buildings. The only thing distinguishing it from the others was its number. We gave three cheers, discreetly.

Emil, Ilze, and Rudolf went on up. Imant clasped my wrist. "Kelly," he said, "do not speak to these people, okay? You will be my Latvian wife, okay? They may be frightened if they know you are American."

I nodded and followed Imant upstairs. Our friends were on the landing, talking (Russian) with the two old women who had answered their knock. They seemed agitated, and I immediately imagined some misunderstanding and dire consequence, but the only problem was that the room had only one bed. Neighbors upstairs had another room, one with two cots. At the time I didn't know what they were discussing; Imant introduced me to the ladies, I smiled, our friends raced upstairs, and I tried to cover up the name tag on my flight bag with my right hand while keeping my ringless left in my pocket and then remembered that in this country it should be the other way around, and kept saying "*Paldies,*" the Latvian word for "thank you," whenever anyone spoke to me. Our room was just inside the door to the flat, and as soon as we succeeded in getting inside and shutting our door, I sank onto the bed in relief. The room was small—and wonderful. A window looked out into the lives of other people in lighted rooms across the way. The wide bed had been pushed against a tapestried wall. The mirror was on top of a piece of furniture of indeterminable function. I got out my contact lens equipment—aseptor, cleaning solution, and so forth—and set it on the table and took out my lenses.

There was a knock on our door. Before we could stop her, the larger of the two ladies was in our room, urging cups of tea on us and talking a mile a minute. She was thrilled to be entertaining foreigners—Latvians—and she headed straight for the things I'd put on the table, picking them up and looking them over and seeing, of course, the American labels. Imant launched into an explanation; I could make out that he was telling her that he had to import these things for his wife. I couldn't say anything; I couldn't, for that matter, even see anything. When the woman left, I sighed my second sigh of relief. Then she came in again, with great hunks of bread in her hands. "*Paldies*," I said. She made motions that plainly meant, even to my myopic eyes, that Imant ought to fatten me up. "Da," Imant said. She seemed satisfied at this and left, and this time she didn't return. It saddened me to think she might not be so friendly if she knew I was American.

After she left, the apartment grew quiet; you could almost see the silence settling, like a cloth over a table. I stood at the window. In the building across the way, lights were going off. Soviet citizens go to sleep at night just as American citizens do: so much the better if they can sleep together, making love instead of war. I put on my long lavender gown with the low neckline. Wind was clawing at the trees, but in our small room we were safe. I could have holed up there a year, at least. Imant felt at home too; while I was looking out the window and musing, he drank both cups of tea and ate all the bread, and I gave him an apple from my string bag and he ate that too, and then he leaned against the tapestry on the wall and began to be happier.

Was everyone else asleep? I opened the door, stealthily. The rest of the apartment was dark, but to get to the bathroom, which was only a few feet from our room, I had to pass an open area from which a prodigious snoring issued. I crossed and recrossed on tiptoe, and then, having accomplished that much without waking anyone, Imant and I discovered that our bed creaked. Someone has told me that at one time the peasants used to overlay their hearths with broad platforms which became their beds at night, so that, in effect, they slept on their stoves. At least stoves don't creak.

We were making so much noise anyway that I asked Imant to teach me some Latvian. After all, I was passing as Latvian. And though the Latvian language, unlike Russian and English, isn't "rich" in vulgarities, it does have some words that were pertinent to the occasion. But Imant refused to teach them to me. When I asked why, he stammered and said that his *māmiņa* had brought him up to be "modest." On the other hand, she had not brought him up to be modest in a foreign language, and *he* wasn't at all averse to learning a little basic *English*.

Later, with the light out, as I was drifting into sleep, Imant began to speak Latvian. He was speaking his mother tongue, but as far as I was concerned it might as well have been tongues. My face was buried against his chest, and the mysterious words fell softly on my head, as if I were being anointed. I stirred, but he continued; it was almost a chant, alien and ritualistic, and I became alarmed. I thought he might be talking in a kind of half-sleep, that he might have forgotten I was only pretending to be Latvian, even that he had confused me with Frederika. I tried to interrupt, but he covered my face with his hands. His words were swift and sometimes so muted I could hardly catch the hard and palatalized *k*'s that lend the Latvian language its characteristic sound. In Imant's gentle and hypnotic voice the words seemed almost less sound than shadow, and gradually I grew used to them, like beginning to see in a dim room after coming in from a brightly lit hallway. Secure in his arms, I gave myself over to this grave music and closed my eyes. As naturally as day becomes night, the words became silence. The transformation was scarcely noticeable until it was complete, and silence filled the room. Then Imant spoke in a normal tone, in English: "All these things I have had in my heart to say you, but my English is too poor. So I have told them to you in Latvian."

*   *   *

Sunday morning, Emil rapped lightly on our door, took the car keys from Imant, left two boiled eggs on our table, and ducked out again. We were late getting down, and just as we thought we were ready to leave, I realized I'd better pack all my stuff and lug it along with me. I didn't think our landladies were light-fingered but they'd be bound to come in and take a look, and any of a dozen articles could have made them suspicious of my nationality. "Yes, yes," Imant said, smiling, "they are very curious. They are very typical, these old women, for they are simple but they are good." They brought us more tea, more bread, but I was kept busy biting my tongue. Imagine how hard it is not to let slip an "okay" or an "all right" or a "hi" or "thank you"! I was restricted to my *paldies,* which I used indiscriminately, looking helplessly at Imant whenever any longer speech was called for. I'm sure they thought he had married an idiot.

Emil, Ilze, and Rudolf were waiting in the back seat of the car. It was a brilliant day, not too cold. The first leaves of autumn lay on the ground but the trees were mostly still dark green, and the wide streets brought a bright blue sky clear down to eye level. Leningrad's palette is more variegated than Moscow's or Riga's, but its hues remain subtle; only the sky, the trees, the myriad canals will sometimes leap to the front of the stage like the *corps de ballet,* and dazzle. There's also, as elsewhere, the red of the banners overhanging the streets or draped across the cornices of factory plants and warehouses.

I've heard that many of these oratorical oriflammes were hung up to commemorate a given Party congress, and then after the congress no one had the nerve to take them down; and so they accumulate, congress to congress. They all say things like: COMMUNISM IS THE PARTY OF PEACE, or WE ARE MAKING THE WORLD SAFE FOR ALL PEOPLES. My favorite slogan was, TO LIVE, TO WORK, TO STUDY—LIKE LENIN! It struck my funny bone.

We parked, and walked to a café—to several cafés, in fact, before we found one that was "open." Along the way, Imant practiced *basic* English, at the top of his lungs. I tried to hush him up, but he argued, "Is okay! No one will understand," and the more I blushed, the louder his voice grew. He was testing his new vocabulary in sentences. "Is right way to use, yes?" he would ask, and Rudolf, coming up behind us, would say, "What does it mean?" Finally I capitulated: "Imant is learning the English that textbooks leave out," I said. Rudolf begged, politely but urgently, "Please, will you be so kind as to teach me too?"

So I rummaged around in the back of my brain for some expression or idiom that was slangy without being obscene, and so help me, what I came up with was this: "Wow, look at that pair of knockers!"

"Woo, look at that pair of knoak-erz," Rudolf repeated, his face contorted excruciatingly.

"Knockers," I said.

"Please, what are knoak-erz?" he asked.

I tried to explain. "Well, you know," I said, "a woman's chest. That is, her bust." There was complete incomprehension on both their faces, and in desperation I shouted, "Breasts!" I didn't know I was going to announce it so forcefully, and put my hand over my mouth, too late. Imant laughed. "I think you knew all along," I said, accusingly.

He wanted to know "if all American breasts are knockers."

"Only big ones," I said. "You're supposed to stand on a street corner, see, and then when a big-breasted woman walks by, you nudge your sidekick with your elbow, like this"—I nudged Rudolf with my elbow—"and you say, *Wow, look at that pair of knockers.* I promise you, this will make you extremely American."

"Knoak–erz," Rudolf said, with enormous seriousness.

"Knockers," Imant corrected him. "The *s* is between an *s* and a *z*. Woo, look at that—"

"Not woo," I said, correcting Imant. "Wow."

"Is impossible. How can there be such a sound as this: *ow?*" He made a face. "Americans," he declared, "are a peculiar people."

By this time we had reached the café; Emil and Ilze had caught up with us, and we were all standing around waiting for a free table. One of the patrons in the process of leaving was about five feet tall and five feet wide, with a grand smile displaying her gold tooth; as she walked toward us, she rolled from side to side like a sailor. A Russian grandmother, surely. She was reclaiming her coat from the attendant when I happened to catch Imant and Rudolf staring down at her ample bosom. Imant nudged Rudolf with his elbow. "Woo," Rudolf said, "look at that pair of knoak-erz!"

"Oh no," I said.

"Knockers," Imant said. "Yes?"

"Yes. . . . I mean, no!"

"But what is wrong?"

"Those are not knockers," I said (in a low voice, out of the side of my mouth, to Imant).

Imant looked perplexed. "But they are breasts?" And when I assured him they were indeed breasts, he was visibly relieved. "Big breasts," he said. "And so, knockers."

"Right," I agreed, once and for all. Besides, I didn't really want him to become overly American on this score.

The café didn't have the fish we ordered, so we opted for eggs, although we'd already had eggs once that morning. But the waitress tipped us off to the eggs' not being fresh. We wound up with the third—and last—item on the breakfast menu, beefsteak. I asked Imant if orange juice was ever available, and he set off in search of some. I don't remember what he came back with but it wasn't orange and he'd had to go to two other stores to find it. He didn't mind. Rudolf said to me, while Imant was away from the table, "Imant is cheerful today." Rudolf looked as earnest as ever. "Yes," I said, "thanks!"

We wanted to visit Petrodvorets, eighteen miles outside of Leningrad, an incredibly profligate spill of pleasure palaces and parks centered around the Grand Palace for which Peter himself is said to have done the first sketches, but we didn't know the way. I wasn't even sure it was within the permissible limits except by Intourist bus, but of course it is. I was jumpier than I needed to be. And yet, how do you know what's *appropriately* jumpy? We were heading out of the city, in clear weather, light breaking on the Neva in waves like water. A cop flagged Imant down, and he pulled over to the curb, got out his papers, and walked around to the back of the car to meet the cop. I had no way of knowing what this was all about. I tried to quiz Rudolf but he turned my questions aside. Emil shook his head, but whether he was shaking his head at me or over me, I couldn't tell. I did my best to look natural—also as if I weren't an American staying in an underground hotel—but I couldn't help casting furtive glances over my shoulder. When Imant returned to the car, he didn't say anything. After several minutes of studied nonchalance, I blurted out, "Why did he stop us?"

Imant seemed surprised by my question. "Why?"

"Did we do anything wrong? Did you break a Russian traffic law?"

"No," he said, as if that fact had been obvious to everybody, including the cop.

"Was he looking for someone?"

"For whom would he be looking?"

"I don't know," I said. "Smugglers maybe. Counterrevolutionaries. Enemies of the State."

"He was not looking for anyone."

"Do you mean," I said, slowly, "that he stopped you for no reason at all? Just to check your papers?"

"Yes, of course."

"Of course?"

We spotted a palatial-looking residence and hiked down one hill and up another to get to it. Stone lions guarded the gates. The palace was decayed and deserted, a windswept outpost, as if the czars had dug in at the last affluent fort. There weren't any czars here, however; only two or three contemplative picnickers eating their lunches singly in the "backyard," which looked more like the north forty. We paced the patio, looking down on the solitary lunching people. The formal layout of the former lawn was traceable under the overgrown grasses, and wind rippled the long grasses like green water.

I wanted to take pictures but my companions wouldn't let me; this wasn't our destination, and they wanted me to wait for the real thing. This was just your average spare palace, left lying around like a calling card from an earlier age. SORRY, SIR, says the card, BUT YOU WERE OUT WHEN I HAPPENED.

The real thing was a good deal farther up the road, and a herd of Intourist buses penned in the parking lot made it·unmissable. The whole affair is nearly as elaborate and decadent as the Tivoli Gardens, though higher-minded. From Peter's summer palace, steps pitch steeply down an escarpment to a string of parks on either side of a shimmering ribbon of tame water that unfurls into the Gulf of Finland. Viewed from the palace, the figured symmetry of hedgerows and footpaths is breathtaking, but at the bottom of the steps you join the throng of tourists meandering through planned walks past ingeniously contrived fountains and mechanical amusements. You blink before so much gilt—the very air seems like beaten gold. It's all enough to give a good Bolshevik nightmares, or at least dreams of capital gain. Children hop back and forth between a cupola and the sidewalk, giggling and shrieking as they aim to anticipate the next "waterfall" from the rim of the cupola. Toy ducks quack in a pool; you'd have to feed them toy crumbs. The event that took my fancy was a mechanical garden: there were big, painted, metal flowers that spouted like whales, and a tree with spraying branches. Coney Island, Disneyland . . . what won't people do, to entertain themselves and stave off death? We bought ice cream.

As we rounded a bend in the path, the Gulf of Finland came into view. Just before you reach the water's edge, there's a cottage now used as a museum; many of the visitors were headed there. Our friends joined the queue for the current exhibit, while Imant and I went shoreside to talk.

A mere eighteen miles away is Finland. It seemed I could reach out and touch it with my fingertips. We leaned against the railing. There was a bench, but it was totally occupied by two old Russian women, reading. "You could ask them to move over," I said, but Imant whispered back, "I do not dare." The pair held their books up to their noses. Imant ambled "casually" around to the back of the bench and peeked spylike over their broad shoulders. "They are *very* serious," he said, reporting back to me. "I think they must be retired Communists." We tried hard not to let them see us laughing.

"Did you ever think," I said, catching my breath, "of leaving?" Imant followed my gaze to the horizon.

Almost automatically, our voices dropped. "Everyone thinks I want, but this is where I belong. If I had been some years older when the war came, then, to be sure, I would have sailed to Sweden on one of the boats. There were such boats." Imant was five weeks old when the Nazis occupied Riga. Why had his father stayed? "I asked him," Imant said, "of course. He did not think, that it would be like this. Now, is my home, my people, and I belong here. A man must live in his country."

There was never any question of persuading Imant to leave; aside from considerations of law, morality (he thought defecting was wrong), and homesickness, for Imant to leave the Soviet Union would be even riskier for his work than moving to the Soviet Union was for mine; I knew this even better than he did. A young composer who writes on a large scale—symphonies and oratorios—can, in the Soviet Union, be performed and recorded; money is rarely available for that kind of thing—that large-scale kind of thing—in the United States, and although Imant would be able to write his "Magdalen" in the United States, he'd probably have to scrap most of his other compositions. Finding me a typewriter in Latvia, however tricky, still wouldn't be as difficult as finding him an orchestra in America.

"Sooner or later," I said, "after I'm living here, in your country, I'll have to write about it. If only incidentally."

"Yes, yes, is true, I understand."

"Will they make trouble?"

"There will be interference—of this I am sure. They do not know how *not* to interfere. But I think it may not be so bad. They will let you publish in America, I think. They will see that it is good for everyone that you live here and write."

"Will they let me send my manuscripts to America?" Again, it was a question that, according to the Helsinki Accords, shouldn't even have to be asked. My manuscripts would be my personal property, the property of a U.S. citizen, and I should be able to mail them to my agent, who would sell the first rights in North America.

"But why not? I think so," he said.

We looked out over the water—the jumble of rocks first, then the sun-spangled waves, then the jeweled horizon—toward Finland. Our hands, on the stone railing, touched. "Almost it seems," he said, "as if you can reach out and touch—"

I thought he was going to say Finland.

"—freedom."

The day's light had begun to go underground, like all radical activity. Our friends came out of the cottage, and we walked—a little faster, now—through the park, over one of the bridges to the other side of the blue ribbon, and back to the steps. I must say they seemed steep to me. I stopped to rest two-thirds of the way up. "I hope I get to marry you before we get old," I said. "You'll probably be bald by the time they let us get married."

"The men in my family do not go bald," he said, reassuring me. "Only a little."

"That means time is on our side," I said. But I was lying, and we both knew it. The crowd of tourists had thinned, and the weather was growing chill. Imant turned his collar up. We had a long ride back, and it was dusk by the time we got there.

It began to rain, a clear, steady, autumnal rain, the kind of rain that puts things in perspective. We were in the café at the Sovietskaya. One wall of the café was glass, so from where we sat we could watch the rain spattering against it, and across the driveway, the grassy circle changing colors from green to black. I had brought the teacups, Imant's present to me, down from my (official) room—Imant would take them to the farmhouse—and he unwrapped them for everyone to see. Even the waitress oohed and aahed. Just one table was oblivious. While Imant was putting the cups away, Rudolf leaned over to me and said, "KGB." I thought he was pulling my leg, as Imant did fairly often. The only people at that table were kids. "You're teasing me," I said.

"No," Rudolf said.

I looked at Imant. He was tying the string around the tea-cups. "Rudolf's joking, isn't he?" I asked.

"No," he said.

I looked again at the table of kids. "How can you tell?"

Rudolf answered, "One knows, that is all."

"They do not talk with one another," Imant said. "They try to hear what others are saying."

"But they're only kids—"

"Very often, a young person does something wrong—he takes something from a store, perhaps, or he tries to buy and sell on the black market. Then when he is caught, he is given a choice: to go to prison or work for the KGB."

We finished eating as fast as possible, got our gear together, and vamoosed. I don't know whether we were followed or whether, if we were, it was by the kids from the café.

It was early evening by the time we found a wine shop where we picked up the night's supply, and dark by the time we found a candy store. Emil and Ilze disappeared into the candy store for twenty minutes. The shop window glowed brightly through the rain, and my red umbrella finally got some use when Rudolf borrowed it to dash in after Emil and Ilze.

I had taught Imant another word: *privacy*. To Emil and Ilze and Rudolf, he had said, "I wish to have some privacy with Kelly tonight." (That was only for show, because he had to say it in Latvian before they could understand.) But Rudolf, in his halting English, said they hoped we would come to their room for a little while first. We would have a kind of party—a very quiet kind of party, in our underground hotel.

At our underground hotel, Emil, Ilze, and Rudolf decided to buy cigarettes across the way, so Imant and I went inside and waited for them by the window on the first landing. Light from the streetlamp, made misty by the evening rain—now slowed to a drizzle—shed a nebulous glow on the wet pavement. Three forward-pitching backs made a lunge for the store door, like football linemen. Emil and Rudolf were on the two ends; Ilze was in the center. I didn't know Ilze. She had sharp features, eyebrows carefully etched on a small face, and she spoke only Russian and Polish. I resented her for taking Olga's place, which was irrational of me. I surmised that Ilze herself felt like an interloper and tried simultaneously to defend and play down her position, but maybe I just imagined all this. Maybe not knowing Latvian limited her too. Today she had begun to unbend, be friendlier.

I thought of the other two, Rudolf and Emil: the one, Rudolf, with a young man's acute sensibility lending him outward elegance and a piercing inward sense of betrayal; the other, Emil, so much the man Rudolf would become, the inevitable older version, edges worn, the style grown scruffy with time and circumstance, the passion more accommodating, less ambitious, more forgiving, enthusiasm reserved for the attainable and not dissipated in dreams.

Dreams. Suddenly I wanted something to signify that my life here was real. I asked Imant if he knew what an engagement ring was. "Yes!" he said, excitedly. "I like this custom very much!" He said he would have a ring made for me. "I know a place," he said, "where they are making very fine jewelry." But he didn't think he would be permitted to send the ring out of Russia. "I will send letters," he said. "Each night I write to you and tell you what has happened in the day, and in morning I send." This way I could wake up each day knowing there'd be a letter from him.

We had somehow managed to shrug off the consciousness of time: it seemed as though we could wait forever by that window, speaking softly in a bare, echoing hallway, and never run out of time. I asked Imant if there was any chance we could be married in a church. He was greatly excited by this notion also and exclaimed, "Yes, yes! I have not been married in a church before." Considering the number of his civil marriages, I had to laugh. But Imant was serious.

He is Lutheran, though about Catholicism, he had said, "I like this confession very much." (He'd have had trouble with the Catholic ruling on divorce!) Before the war, the majority of Latvians were Lutherans, about one quarter were Roman Catholic, and nine percent were Greek Orthodox. There were

smaller but significant numbers of Russian Old Believers and
Jews. In answer to Imant's question, I had explained that I was
brought up more or less as a Presbyterian. He looked perplexed. "We have no Presbyterians here," he said. However,
when I mentioned Calvin, he'd immediately produced a book
on Luther and Calvin. The pictures of the two dour theolo-
gians were unmistakable in any language.

Now Imant said, "Sometimes it is allowed to marry in a
church if it is discreet." (Sometimes the churches are so discreet you can't even find them. We knew there was one church
in Leningrad where concerts are held on Sunday morning, but
we couldn't discover which one.)

And then I recalled a scene from ten years ago. Night, in the
old town of Riga: Imant opens an inconspicuous door, and I
find myself in a cathedral. There is incense. People are kneel-
ing, praying, rising. There aren't many of them, and some are
so old that it seems a miracle that they can get up from their
knees. There is one young girl, with a kerchief pulled so far in
front of her face that I can see her face only when she turns and
looks straight at me. Imant guides me out, his hand on my
elbow, and neither of us ever refers to any of this.

I had wondered at the time why Imant was showing me
this. To show, without stating it, that the Soviets discouraged
religion; to show that people worshiped despite that. But did
he also mean to convey a sense of his own spiritual longings,
to suggest that here, in a church, was where I might find a side
of him that not many people knew?

I began to think how much time had passed since we'd come
in from the car. "Where could they be?" I asked. And for the
first time we looked around us and realized we were in the
wrong building. Imant slapped his forehead and laughed.
"Well," he said, "they are all the same, these hallways, no?"

We sat on the cots in a room smaller than many closets. There
were no chairs, for the simple reason that there was no space
for any. Overhead, an unshaded bulb dangled at the end of a
string, glaring like an open eye. We had to keep our voices to
a whisper. It wasn't the merriest of atmospheres, but we were

merry. You're pretty much forced to be, on red wine and marzipan.

Imant asked everyone to estimate my ring size, and, by comparing the circumference of my ring finger with Ilze's, decided what size he'd order. If he couldn't send it to me, it would be waiting for me.

Meanwhile, Rudolf also arrived at a decision: he would learn to speak English well enough to conduct a real conversation in it when I returned. I grew sentimental about the English language, as a language that makes its own music, and then about Russian, which is also beautiful and rich in insight as well. Latvian isn't so beautiful, but it has other virtues, and the most beautiful of all is Estonian. By way of experiment I asked Rudolf to say something—the same something—in Russian, Polish, Latvian, and French. Emil threw in German, and Imant contributed Estonian. Then it was back to Rudolf for the English translation, but he was suddenly overcome by embarrassment. I had to look to Imant to persuade Rudolf to let me in on the little set speech. Rudolf had to struggle through the sentence, putting a period after each word. "We wish to thank you, dear lady, for your company and kindness in being with us." I knew if I started crying I wouldn't stop all night, so I smiled just as if none of us understood that we might never see one another again.

You could of course forge for yourself an iron heart to set in the place of this old mortal heart. This old mortal heart ticks like a time bomb, but the new heart lies in your chest like a dead weight. You try to walk and it drags you to the ground, you try to swim and are drowned. That heaviness keeps you in your place—your only place. This is a type of imprisonment. You would rather explode.

We set my travel alarm for six and woke to its clatter. Oddly, we weren't depressed; the thin light outside our window, the sense of secrecy and importance that attends any leave-taking done while most people are still sound asleep, buoyed our spirits. We packed efficiently—we were getting to be old hands at that—and when we were ready, Imant went to pay the land-ladies. The larger one came to see us out. She was in her robe, her hair looked as if she'd been fighting it during the night, and sleep still creased her cheeks, but she would have liked a chat. She stood with her hand on the doorknob, and she didn't want to let us go. I was afraid I'd muff the whole affair at the last minute, and as soon as we could slip out the door, I began to back down the stairs, saying, *"Paldies, paldies,"* but she wanted a final word with Imant. On the way to the car I asked him what it was. "She told"—he said—"my wife is pretty, I must take care of her." He grinned. I made a mental note that when I wrote my Michelin guide to underground hotels, this one rated four stars.

We waited in the car for Emil, Ilze, and Rudolf. The weather on this last day made it clear that we really were in a new sea-son now: a brisk and freshening wind, sky so blue it seemed as if the last traces of summer had been swept from it only that morning, and a fallen leaf stuck against our windshield like a deciduous parking ticket. The canals glint, glitter, wink, shine, blind, flash, and glow—how can anyone be sad, in Leningrad? But anxiety nips at the heart like a dog at a rear wheel, and by the time we reached the Sovietskaya, I felt emotionally out of breath.

Imant didn't see me onto the bus, because his scheme was to follow the bus to the airport. I couldn't see out back from my seat; I could only hope he was there. Then when we were out on the road that led to the airport, a little yellow Fiat overtook us, horn blaring, and all its passengers waved like crazy at ours.

But at the airport, I couldn't find them. We were driven in one way; they had to come another. We learned that we had a half hour yet, the news I was praying for—but what good was a half hour without Imant? Finally, we collided on the main floor.

"I am as excited as on the first day," he said, "but I know it will be okay. You will be back soon. I am sure of it."

"Before Christmas?"

"Is possible. . . . Yes, yes, I think so! I must make the house warm for winter."

We had gone off by ourselves and were sitting in the waiting room.

"You should keep your name when we marry," he said. "Here, is done very often when the wife has work of her own."

"Don't forget to take the things to the farmhouse—"

"They are calling your plane," Imant said, and suddenly everything became terribly bright and hectic and unreal. I said good-bye to Emil, Ilze, and Rudolf. The room all around us seemed to be in flux, but for that moment we were as isolated as an island. Ilze and I shook hands; Emil kissed my hand, and Rudolf was about to, but he looked so wildly forlorn that I pecked his cheek instead. Then there was nothing more we could say to each other, and we raced to the boarding station, the three of them following Imant and me. Imant, handing me over to the check-out officials, kissed me loudly and proclaimed for all to hear, "I love you." A short while later I was miles *above* ground.

CHAPTER 4

How to Wait

I

"As cold waters to a thirsty soul, so is good news from a far country." Or any news from Latvia.

While I had been in the Soviet Union, my parents had completed their move from Virginia to England. When I landed on their new doorstep, we all thought I was going to be there only for a short time, until I received a visa that would let me go back to the Soviet Union to marry Imant.

It was mid-September, and here in England it was still hot. The oak leaves sagged under a summer's accumulation of dust. I could see the oak from my window. I had a room with one window, one bed, one table, one chair, and one shelf; there weren't two of anything, and it seemed therefore just the sort of room to wait in, a waiting room.

Almost every day I mailed a letter to Imant. The rest of the time I worked on my poems. "Forgive me if I wander a little this evening," I wrote, quoting John Keats to Fanny Brawne, 1819, "for I have been all day employ'd in a very abstr[a]ct Poem and I am in deep love with you—two things which must excuse me."

When I wasn't writing, I watched my parents watching me. It was easy to guess what they were thinking: a month had gone by, and I had not gotten one letter from Imant. I began to make excuses for Imant, but the question remained: why no word? One day I had the house to myself, and I decided to make some telephone calls.

I couldn't call Latvia, unfortunately. There was no telephone in the farmhouse, and the Latvian friends who did have telephones didn't speak English. I set the London directories on the packing crate we had been using for a dining table.

The very first call was to Intourist in London; to my shock, they insisted that the information from the Marriage Bureau was inaccurate: getting back into the Soviet Union long enough to marry Imant, they said, was going to require special clearance. It was not possible to go to Riga for two weeks on an individual tourist visa. Five days was the maximum. There were no group tours for that long from London.

"Not possible." Suddenly the notion I'd had, that the Soviet censors might stop our letters, didn't seem so wild anymore. I rang the Chief Enquiries office of the General Post Office in London; he was sympathetic but said, "Sorry, luv! If the Russians are stopping the mail, there's nothing we can do. There's no point in even trying." What this told me was that the Russians *could* stop, perhaps *had* stopped, the mail.

The Latvian legation explained that a petition from them on my behalf would only worsen matters, since they represent Independent Latvia. The United States, Great Britain, Canada, Australia, France, West Germany, and Ireland refuse to recognize the incorporation of the three Baltic States into the Soviet Union, but of course, in the eyes of the Soviet Union, Independent Latvia no longer exists and its legations are consequently anomalies—though ones which the Soviet Union doesn't like to be reminded of.

A shipping company I called by accident—because they had the word *mail* in their title—wished me luck, but added that they didn't think I'd have any. "The Russians," said the shipping company, "do whatever they want."

I fixed myself a cup of coffee, collected myself, and dialed the Soviet consulate. One department kept connecting me to another, and then someone referred me to the Soviet embassy, where I completed a similar internal circuit. I was running—or calling—in circles. The imperturbably polite and uninterested voices without exception claimed that they had nothing to do with the post. Who did? They didn't know.

Last, I dialed the U.S. embassy, and there I met with outright hostility. "We have nothing to do with the mails," said the woman who answered. She didn't so much say it as snarl it. "Call the Soviet embassy." I said I had. "Well, there's nothing we can do. You'll just have to forget about it."

"If the Soviets have intercepted this correspondence," I said, as officially as I could while feeling utterly powerless, "it is a clear violation of the spirit of the Helsinki Pact." I paused. "Do you mean to tell me that the American embassy considers the Helsinki Pact irrelevant?"

"Just what is the Helsinki Pact?"

I couldn't believe my ears. This was an official representative of the U.S. government? The news had been dominated by the Helsinki Pact for weeks. "My god, didn't you read it?" I asked.

"I never heard of it."

I was speechless.

"Are you an expert in international law?" she asked.

I naturally said no, and wondered what that had to do with anything.

"Only experts," she said, with a voice like a hand laying down a trump card, "can understand these things." With a philosophy like that, she should have been working for the *Soviet* embassy.

It was her unique combination of stupidity and ungraciousness that finally overwhelmed me. I hoped it was unique. If it wasn't, I was going to be battling *two* governments.

Once, in a dream, I added a postscript to a letter I was mailing to a friend before leaving on a journey. I don't know where I was headed in my dream, but it clearly wasn't heaven. "If you hear from God," my P.S. said, "let me know."

It is an unhappy thing to lose touch. Anna Dostoevsky remembers a bad time when she and her husband were living abroad: "Fyodor Mikhailovich continued to work on his novel, but work was no comfort to him. To our already despondent state a new worry was added: letters addressed to us were getting lost, and so our contact with family and friends was hampered; and this contact was our only source of consolation. . . . Our misgivings about the loss of our letters were strengthened by an anonymous letter we received, in which we were informed that Fyodor Mikhailovich was under suspicion and that an order had been given for his mail to be opened."

One wonders, sometimes, how it is that so much effort expended on political revision can have resulted in things being merely rather more the way they were than they already were.

My misgivings were strengthened by a telephone call. Imant didn't have my number here because, while I was with him in Riga and Leningrad, my parents had been only just locating themselves in England. But one of the numbers I had given Imant was my sister's, a professional flutist who lives in London. On the evening of September thirtieth, he managed to get a call through to her, to say, first of all, that he had been writing to me every day. He also said—or Karl said, since Karl, with his fluent English, was there to help Imant make the call—that the first trial for the divorce had taken place the day before—and that Frederika had refused to give the divorce. So. It would be six months before the second trial would take place. Imant said that he had not received a single letter from me. Between us, that came to about forty "lost" letters. Apparently, things in Russia hadn't changed a whit since 1868.

II

Frederika could not have been alone responsible for this interference; she couldn't sneak into the post office and intercept our letters personally. Someone in an official capacity was conspiring with her against Imant and me—or else the Soviet Union all by itself had concluded our relationship was dangerous to the State. Make no mistake: the imperialistic might of the Soviet Union rests on four firm linchpins; namely, massive propaganda, a military allotment that makes chickenfeed out of the rest of the budget, a class system as rigid as feudalism, and the systematic abridgment of individual freedoms by the secret police. Andrei Sinyavsky says: The Russian writer of today must concern himself with imprisonment, exile, and "exactly how (interesting topic, you must admit) they shoot you in the back of the neck." Solzhenitsyn says: A woman was shoved screaming into a car—a white Volga?—and a hundred people pretended not to see or hear. My friend Karl, Imant's brother, says: "Very many young people have simply vanished."

Make no mistake . . . but I made a mistake. I thought that the Soviet Union waging its war against the individual on that monumentally collective plane wouldn't stoop to cutting off the correspondence between two nonpolitically aligned persons. Like a lot of people, I guess, I wanted what I wanted: a quiet life with Imant, a home, and my work. If I could live my one life the way I wanted. . . . After all, I couldn't do anything about the millions of lives forfeited in prisons and labor camps. Nevertheless, I couldn't forget those forfeited lives; I couldn't pretend not to know what I knew. Maybe the KGB knew this about me. It could be that the KGB is as expert at searching souls as rooms; maybe the KGB read my mind like a letter.

Here, when you come to it, is a mind-bending exercise, a conceptual backflip: what is *a mind?* Think about it. Descartes, of course, begged this particular question when he declared, "I think, therefore I am." Now it's been frequently suggested that the *cogito,* as it's called for short, presupposes the "I" which it purports to establish, but what I want to call attention to is the other word, *think.* And not in the way of a philosopher, whose interest in the subject must necessarily be vested, but as a poet, for whom the shortest distance between any two points is always a metaphor.

When I think about thinking, I imagine that my mind is a house. In the living room, my friends and family converse peaceably around a civilized fire. There's a room for every year of my past, and an inviting door marked FUTURE. I don't know what goes on in there, but I can glean hints through the glass pane. I can roam through the past at will—what I know of it—and sometimes it pleases me to explore the darkest rooms. The clutter in the attic is amazing: dreams, memories, imaginary numbers, imaginary people, advanced calculus (I studied it once), moral obligations, history, speech, and I-don't-know-what-all. *How* these ideas get into the mind is a question for the epistemologist; *that* they are there is a problem for all of us.

One way or another, this is a house I built myself: I added room to room and drew up the guest list, and sometimes I meet with an idea or person I won't give any house. At the same time, I can keep an open mind, like an open house, so as not to miss out on the meeting of minds. Passover celebrants include in their table setting a cup for Elijah and leave the door open in case he should come with news of peace on earth.

This is the way we move out of the solipsism of infancy into society: by bringing the stranger indoors, like Elijah at Passover. Plotinus put a "mirror" in his mind and said that the "ideas" reflected in it were those that could be termed "conscious." I put a "mirror" in my mind and see myself. Now I can point at other objects that look *like* me, and I figure they probably perceive me in a similar way. The mind that reflects on itself thus reflects a world as populous and varied as the "real" world, but it is not congruent with the "real" world, because it must always be the "real" world plus one—the mind reflecting on the world. This is solipsism defeated by introspection. I think, therefore you exist—and you do the same for me. To put it another way: scratch my back and I'll raise your consciousness.

And then one day you're standing, mentally, at an upstairs window, looking out, and, in the distance, you see, like unshaped puffs of thin cloud, the forgotten souls of forfeited lives drifting into nothingness, and you know that your first duty is to shelter them. "In my Father's house are many mansions." The least *you* can do is tack on a wing and say WELCOME to the millions who died and are dying for the sake of, so help us all, expediency.

This ingathering of souls is confirmation of the world's reality, but it is poetic confirmation, not philosophic proof. But it is the closest thing we will ever get to a proof that we are not alone—and it's all the confirmation we need. Clearly, the mind houses images, not things-in-themselves, and certainly not things: the brain surgeon who reached into his patient's skull and fished out a wife, three children, a Chevrolet, a mortgage, and a holiday in Bermuda would be a very surprised surgeon indeed. There is, however, no law that says we must rest here, philosophically, with Bishop Berkeley. We are free to make an imaginative leap and attribute similar mental processes to each other—and to others, those figures on the horizon.

In fact (as it were), the whole question of whether or not there is an objective reality is, if not exactly answered by Malthus, increasingly weighted on one side by more and more people seeming to enter into it. I couldn't possibly populate the world with four billion brainchildren. Some days I can hardly come up with one.

Why ask whether there is an objective reality? In the first place because, of course, if there isn't one, there's no point in being upset about its shortcomings. In the second place, once you imagine that other people exist, perceiving you in their "mirrors," you must also attribute pain and love to them, since pain and love—a desire to turn from and a desire to turn toward—are the two responses to perception.

(It may be that you are an inmate of an insane asylum; you think, wrongly, that you are Napoleon; for twenty years you have marched on Moscow, but the Russians won't fight, so you pace the space around your cot. Cold air seeps through the cracks around the window, the pigeon has flown, and you wonder if the time has come to beat a fast retreat to France. In this case, you are *out* of your mind.)

III

A letter came. Not from Imant. It was from his father. It wasn't even registered. Now. I was fairly sure that it wasn't only the letters from Imant that had been "lost": I wrote to Karl, Emil, Rudolf, and Indra, and never received answers from any of them. There was only one explanation for why Imant's father's letter got through: the censor found it agreeable. "Marry a man in your own country," it said. The thought even occurred to me that Imant's father may have been "advised" to write this letter.

When Boris Spassky and his fiancée, a French citizen employed in Moscow, applied for a wedding date, they were given one, all right; the wedding was scheduled for the day *after* his fiancée's visa would expire. When an Austrian girl working in the Soviet Union as a schoolteacher went home for a short visit, planning to return to marry a Soviet writer, officials at the border simply tore up her return visa. Both marriages took place eventually, with the help of international publicity in the first instance and, in the second, a hunger strike and a personal appeal from Chancellor Kreisky to Brezhnev. ("She will be a queen to help me win my games," Spassky said about his bride.)

I couldn't understand why the Soviet Union persisted in this barbarian attitude toward marriage between their citizens and foreigners (though the fear behind such an attitude is transparent, owing as much to a primitive psychology as to ideological resistance). I *did* understand why Imant's father objected to my marrying his son. The father was fond of Frederika, and even more fond of his own authority, and he didn't like to see things changed. When one morning the telephone rang—and it was Imant (my sister had given him my number)—and I nearly went out of my mind with relief—I was able to ask him if he knew about his father's letter. "Yes, yes," he said, "is nothing. He told, he was going to write you, but I have had a talk with him, and all is all right." His low voice with its heavy accent brought him close to me; I could wrap myself up in that voice and be warm forever. "Kelly," he added, "I call again in a week or two weeks, okay?"

"Okay, but does your mother think like your father?"

"No, no; Kelly, is nothing to worry about—"

"*Is* something, Imant. Why aren't our letters getting through?"

"I do not know. I wrote every day, as we said. And you?"

"The same." Then there was a silence which expressed as plain as words the anxiety we couldn't speak about over the telephone.

Imant's father's letter was written in Latvian; I picked out a translation, using a pocket dictionary and the text I had begun studying with a BBC translator. The Latvian House in London had referred me to this translator; my interest in his native country pleased him. Like most Latvians in the West, including his wife, he had left there during the war. He was still a boy when he saw Riga for the last time. Now he lives in Reading, and once a week I went to his house for a lesson (and homemade strawberry wine).

Latvian isn't, as everyone who speaks it will readily admit, a particularly beautiful language, but it has graces not common to English. It is inflected (but not as thoroughly as Estonian, thank God, which has *fourteen* case endings), and as in French, nouns are masculine or feminine. I had asked Imant the word for *writer*. "*Rakstnieks*," he said. "*Es esmu rakstnieks*," I said. "No," he said, "*tu esi rakstniece*." Thinking the distinction was like *author* and *authoress*, I said *I* was a *rakstnieks*. A month later, studying Latvian, I found out why this had struck him as so funny. In Latvian I couldn't be a *rakstnieks* any more than the table I am writing this on could be feminine. Everyone knows tables are masculine.

Latvian is one of the oldest, arguably the oldest, of the Indo-European languages and also, as I found out, one of the most difficult. In the Latvian language, the reflexive is extensive, tenses enjoy a freedom they're denied in English, and word building is quick and easy. It is a shy, rather romantic language, sensitive and polite. Whenever the word is used, *please* sits first in the sentence. Not "Pass the salt, please," but, "Please, pass the salt." And then there are all those diminutives. For kicks, and also to keep it straight in my mind, I translate the diminutive as "dear little . . .": *māmiņa* is "dear little mother" and *brālītis* is "dear little brother," *cepurīte* is "dear little hat" and *zvaigznīte* is "dear little star." And *labrītiņ* is, naturally, "dear little good morning." And aren't some mornings merely good, while some are downright dreary, but others are dear little good mornings?

The beginning reading selections in my text had about them an air of long-gone rustic simplicity, practically Arcadian. Yet something of that sentimental attachment to childhood and countryside is to be found even in the Latvia of my friends:

before the war, Latvia *was* a small, civilized society, with one of the highest literacy rates in the world, economically at least relatively well off, culturally and industrially more active than many larger countries, with a pastoral base. That nostalgia for a golden age which for most of us thins out into some vaguely shimmering mist at the far edge of historical and psychological consciousness is, for Latvians, right at hand, and so bright it hurts the eyes. Their golden age was 1918 to 1940.

Still, though Latvia is a Western nation, believing in the autonomy of the individual, the importance of work, and the malleability of destiny, close association must have lent it that Slavic intensity, a profound emotional life joined with a perfectly open awareness of it. In America this kind of self-observation is likely to be labeled neurotic; in the Soviet Union it's just interesting. The point of it is never analysis or control, but simply observation. It is a way of living doubly fully in a confined space.

I wrote an essay in Latvian: "One dear little morning, my dear little father with his dear little pick-ax chopped a hole in the ice, and my dear little brother caught a fish in his dear little bucket. I was playing in the dear little snow. Then the wind began to howl like a wolf. Night came early. In the sky, dear little stars twinkled like shiny new coins. The windows of the house were covered with ice-flowers. Lamplight glowed through the windows, making wonderful designs, like roses of silver. I went inside. In the house, a clock was ticking. My dear little mother was cooking supper. How hungry we all were! At last our meal was ready, and we took our seats at the big table. My dear little father said the dear little blessing, and then— And then we ate the dear little fish."

(A touch of dear little realism.)

Before Imant was supposed to call again, one of my letters to him got through: I had registered it. He answered by registered mail. We thought we had found a way around the censors. Once more we were fooled; apparently, the real situation was just that intercepting *registered* mail required the signature of some other bureaucrat, or a decision by a higher-up. Meanwhile I received six precious letters from Imant. One of them even contained some photographs Ausma had made on my last day in Riga. Once again we began to believe in the future— with a difference: "I am very scared about our future," Imant wrote, "because of being afraid of what they can do for not to let us live together."

I had come to England thinking I would be going back to Latvia almost immediately; now there were six months to wait. I had a little money left from the paperback sale of my first novel and it didn't make sense to use it up returning to the States, where, without a home base to be interviewed from, I'd have to forgo the chance of a teaching job and head for New York. So I gave my folks a token amount for room and board, laid in modest supplies of books and booze, and started work.

Starting work is a terrific feeling. I say to myself: Now it is time to start a new book, and I become positively elated, thinking that two years or five years or seven years from now—or fifteen—I will be able to look at that book on the shelf and know that all that time is not lost to the world, it is not time out of mind. That book convinces me that the past was real; it must have been real, I say to myself, because here is the evidence of it. For a reader, a book must be alive; but for a writer, it is a kind of fossil, the imprint of his mind, a clue to the mental life he lived in an earlier age.

This is why, for all that I was worried sick, I wasn't unhappy. I was too busy. And if the KGB suspected by now that I was easily scared, they must also have known by then that I am not easily scared *off*.

I sat at my table, a door laid flat across the room, under the window. I was becoming attached to the view from this newest window, the one in the waiting room. Imant, waiting out the winter alone in the farmhouse, wrote: "I never wanted spring to come so much as now. It seems for me that it will be like coming Paradise on the Earth." As the days fled down the long corridor that leads to Nowhere, wind and gravity stole the leaves from the oak outside my window. And what an underhand job it was: one morning the tree was festooned with leaves; the next, it was stripped, like a pinup. By mid-

November the tree was utterly exposed, but the branches took on a kind of dignity in the way they asserted their complex patterns against the sky. I saw in my tree a metaphor for stubbornness and resilience.

On November 18, I went with my teacher and his family to London to a celebration of Latvia's Independence Day. So far as its refugees are concerned, Latvia remains an independent country. No one can deny the illegality of the Soviet takeover of Latvia, whether he thinks it was for better or worse, and I don't know who could seriously think it was for better.

Latvia declared her independence on November 18, 1918, and in time, with the aid especially of Estonia, she routed the Red Army from inside her borders. In the 1920 Treaty of Riga, the Soviet Union "unreservedly recognizes the independence, self-subsistency and sovereignty of the Latvian State and voluntarily and for eternal times renounces all sovereign rights over the Latvian people and territory." The Soviet Union had arrived at similar treaties with Estonia and Lithuania. Twenty years later, "eternal times" notwithstanding, Stalin sent in his troops—he threatened to bombard the Baltic States if they refused entry—and within days overthrew the existing governments. There are documents dated 1939 showing that the takeover was planned well in advance, with guidelines for mass deportation of "anti-Soviet elements." Bilmanis says there were 800,000 Red troops in the Baltic States. The choice between invasion by Germany and invasion by Russia was no choice, though "in northern Vidzeme, the population had spontaneously withstood the Russian troops for three days."

The historian Andrew Ezergailis, however, notes that "if any sector of the Russian empire's population can be designated as a vanguard of Bolshevism, it seems the Latvians would qualify. . . . [T]he Latvians . . . were the main force of support for Lenin, especially in the first year of Soviet power." This earlier commitment, though not universal, must have considerably complicated Latvia's attitude of resistance toward the Soviet Union.

The Soviet Union then literally rubber-stamped its coup by

staging elections. A list of Communist candidates representing "the Union of the Toiling People" was offered to voters—and the voters had to vote, if they wanted their passports stamped. Without a stamp, they couldn't work in the Workers' Paradise, much less toil with the Toiling People. To help them get their stamps, voters received military escorts to the polling stations. To help them vote in their own best interests, the balloting was open. And miraculously, "election results for all three states appeared in the foreign press twenty-four hours before the count had been completed."

The U.S. Department of State noted, officially, that the independence of the Baltic republics was being "deliberately annihilated" by "devious processes," but the mass deportations of Latvians to Siberia and central Russia continued. In these twelve months of occupation by the Russians and nine months of rule by the Soviet powers, over two percent of the Latvian population, Bilmanis writes, were either massacred or deported.

The Russians receded before the Nazi advance, and when the Nazis receded, the Russians advanced. It was like the Castle of Light in the Latvian legend: the legend says that the Castle of Light, Latvia's symbol of independence, sank back into the Daugava when the Black Knight stole the key from the Bear-Slayer. Now it lies in silt on the floor of the river, laved and dimmed. The Bear-Slayer still fights with the Black Knight, and one day he will rise from the river, victorious and dripping, and restore the castle to the shore. . . . The Baltic States drowned under these successive waves of invading armies. Solzhenitsyn recounts his conversations in prison with Susi, the lawyer from Estonia, "that modest, work-loving, small nation. . . . I listened willingly to their fatal history: the tiny Estonian anvil had, from way, way back, been caught between two hammers, the Teutons and the Slavs. Blows showered on it from East and West in turn; there was no end to it, and there still isn't." You don't need to rewrite a word of that for it to apply accurately to Latvia. As for the Estonians themselves, Solzhenitsyn says that "neither Churchill nor Roosevelt cared about them in the least; but 'Uncle Joe' did. . . . Fifteen of them were imprisoned in various cells of the Moscow Lubyanka, one in each, and were charged under Article 58-2 with the criminal desire for national self-determination." But the West did readily accept Baltic refugees, refusing to repatriate them to countries that didn't legally exist, and now Latvians outside Latvia remember the old freedoms, hand on the old traditions, and keep faith with Independence.

Latvian history was not something I had much discussed with Imant, but I wanted to learn as much about his country as I could during this waiting period, and the deeper I went into its past, the more plainly outrageous its present condition appeared: seized as a front-line hostage against Germany, stripped of its freedoms, made to serve the Soviet lust for access to the sea. And to tell the whole truth, perhaps there was an even deeper impulse involved in my response, an American's sympathy for, even a southerner's identification with, the underdog.

There is a wicked and pervading arrogance loose on the earth, like a rabid beast, an overdog. Does it run, does it slouch, does its name have a number? This beast preaches contempt, for that's what arrogance says: that nothing is real but itself, and the bone and blood of another's being are as insubstantial as breath. Here is the solipsism of the true paranoid. In a one-man (or one-party or one-nation) world, history can be revamped to suit whatever present conditions hold sway. If you don't like to think you stamped out a nation, for example, simply turn things around and stamp it in. If you don't like to think you abrogate individual freedoms, say that you safeguard social freedoms. Call dictatorship—even by the proletariat—democracy. Who's to argue with you, if no one else exists *really?* (And if anyone did, you could still claim you knew what was best for him.) This is not just a political stratagem; it's the technique by which most of us live our lives most of the time. It's the way we revise reality to justify our deeds, or pocket the key to the Castle of Light.

Alas, if anyone at the Independence Day celebration mentioned the Castle of Light, I missed it; much of the evening was in Latvian. There were several speeches, a piano recital, and, naturally, Latvian songs. The younger people came in national costumes; each region has its own. The girls wore long, full skirts, full-sleeved blouses, and embroidered vests. The Latvian colors, red-white-red, were everywhere in evidence. Afterward, the kids in their costumes received gifts of books according to their accomplishments in Latvian classes, and everyone milled around the large auditorium, munching on little cakes. I remember wondering if the KGB would keep an eye, or a spy, on these very simple proceedings. We weren't far from the Soviet embassy. It strikes me now that that morning, November 18, was the day I got my last registered letter from Imant. I couldn't know at the time that it was to be the last. "If you could see how beautiful is here," he wrote. "I am alone with sky, forests and air. I feel only nature with me. It gives much peace but loneliness is here too." Coming out of the auditorium, around midnight, with the cold air biting my nose and ears, I took a long look up at the sky. What is the Latvian word for *eclipse?* Slowly, under the inexorable onslaught of darkness, the yellow disk of the moon, like a castle of light, sank out of sight.

IV

Whatever special steps had to be taken to intercept registered letters had now been taken.

Not wishing to "upset" the censors, I didn't dare to spell out in my letters to Imant the fact that I wasn't receiving his. I did what I could: I now wrote the first of many letters—I didn't yet suspect how many—asking for help.

I couldn't seek official political help, because I wasn't married to Imant; I had no legal "claim" on him—Frederika still held that.

As for publicity, I couldn't seek that either, and for the same reason: Imant was still married to someone else. And the Soviets were obviously hoping that Imant and I would lose touch with each other or give up on each other before the divorce became final. Until the divorce, any publicity might boomerang. That it was the enmity between our countries that had kept Imant and me apart in the first place, that Imant and Frederika had not for a long time shared anything like a real home, that Frederika had had the children out of wedlock and had then been in favor of a divorce before she knew about me—how could these things be explained in a brief news item?

"What can you do?" Pavil the Guide had asked, supercil-iously. "You cannot have publicity, because he is still married." Theoretically, this should have been none of his business, but as an Intourist guide he was a trusty, and when he advised me of the pitfalls of publicity—with such heat that his red cheeks ballooned and his dark eyelashes fluttered—I knew I was being warned. In England I made inquiries, nevertheless, and might have gone ahead with it except that I was told any publicity would give the Soviets an excuse for keeping me out of the So-viet Union. They already had an excuse for keeping Imant in—his children. But if we made no publicity and followed all the regulations, the Soviet Union would, I still thought, have to allow me to go to Latvia to marry Imant. After all, the Helsinki Accords said as much.

I wrote letters to Imant's friends, using an assumed name for the return address; sometimes the return address was bor-rowed from a friend in the States. So far as I know, none of these letters ever went anywhere other than straight to the cen-sor. This meant the Soviet authorities were keeping tabs on everyone I knew there. I continued to register the letters I sent to Imant. And after I found out about the Advice of Receipt, I began to attach this form to every letter I sent.

This form is supposed to be signed by the letter's recipient and returned to the sender. It is, in effect, a tracer. Of the ones I sent during this period, three were returned; the others disap-peared into the vast Soviet void.

According to Universal Postal Union conventions, each un-returned Advice of Receipt form is to be compensated for, in this case by the General Post Office to the tune, at the time, of £5.50 each, or about ten dollars. The GPO is then reimbursed by the country which has "lost" the mail. Nobody had in-formed me of this interesting fact, and I still didn't know how much time had to pass before an Advice of Receipt form quali-fied as officially unreturned. Even more interesting was a newspaper's excerpt from a letter by the GPO justifying its decision to discontinue compensation payments. The British post office admitted that the Russians "have now stated quite categorically that they will not accept liability . . . for registered letters confiscated or destroyed because of their contents. . . . The British Post Office is not prepared to pay compensation . . . since no fault attaches to it." In other words, the British government was willing to ignore international agreements concerning exchange of letters between different countries, precisely because the Soviet authorities were ignoring the same agreements. The British post office even went so far as to assert their belief that the Soviet authorities were acting within their own laws. The Soviet authorities were *not* acting within their own laws. These laws include the Soviet Constitution of 1936 and the Russian criminal code. The International Covenant on Civil and Political Rights and the Universal Declaration of Human Rights, both adopted by the General Assembly of the United Nations, also "guarantee" secrecy of correspondence. There is also, if one dares to bring it up yet again, the Final Act of the Helsinki Accords, which is morally if not legally binding. How on earth do the Soviet authorities justify censorship of *love letters?*

The British post office was, however inadvertently, cooperating with the Soviet Union in stopping my correspondence with Imant, and possibly, as a result, our marriage. It was months before I stumbled on Zhores Medvedev's ironic essay, "Secrecy of Correspondence Is Guaranteed by Law," in which he uncovers the way the Soviet post office really works. At the end of the essay, checking by telephone into the nonarrival of a scientific journal he subscribed to, he gave his "name and surname. The voice at the other end changed at once. With a faint note of respect, he categorically denied any possibility of anything being lost in my mail. 'Your name, Comrade Medvedev, is on our *check-list.*'" Medvedev also noted that "[t]he average time taken by air-letters from the USA has increased from 7.2 to 11 days. Evidently this is what one pays for the high honour of having one's name *on the check-list.*" My letters to Imant, if they got to him at all, were taking anywhere from nine to thirty days—from England.

Weeks went by. I think I held my breath, waiting. But it didn't matter that I couldn't breathe; my life wasn't in my hands anyway—it was in the hands of censors, bureaucrats, diplomats. I located some out-of-print books (not by Updike) on Russian composers and mailed them to Imant, just as if the Chief Board for Protecting State Secrets from Publication (Glavlit) wasn't given to confiscating any books that distress them, or that they can sell on the black market. In 1975 a deputy director of Glavlit was arrested when "a raid on his offices disclosed a total of 170 sacks of confiscated literature, all registered as already destroyed." For some years the deputy had enjoyed two vacations a year, two apartments, and two wives.

I kept thinking about the engagement ring Imant couldn't send me. I wanted it very much; it would have been a sign, and a promise. But whenever I thought about the ring, I caught a glimpse of another memory just out of sight of my mind's eye. One day it flashed into full view: a scene from a movie. A concentration camp. Women are lined against a barbed-wire fence. Their arms are upraised, their palms outstretched and pressed into the topmost wire: if a close-up showed a hand pulled back from the wire, you'd see a fresh crease across the center of the palm, a death line intersecting the life line. Only the arms and hands of the women are visible. The guards walk the length of the fence—on the other side—yanking rings from fingers. I don't have any idea if that's the way the Nazis actually did it or if it's only how a film director imagined it. And that is the point. I *don't* know.

It's useful, if oppressive, to remember these things, and you don't have to go to movies to find them out. They find you out. They settle in like squatters. You have to give them house.

A woman and her mother lived in comparative splendor in Latvia before the war, but during the mass deportations of 1940 the woman was forcibly transferred to Siberia. There she worked in the mines for years. After the war she managed to escape, making her way back to Riga partly by train but mostly on foot. The veins of her legs popped and burst, and by the time she reached her home, her feet and calves were so bloody she seemed to be wearing red stockings.

Her home had been divided into a number of apartments, and her mother now lived in one room in what had formerly been her whole house. The mother wasn't in good health either, after the hardships of the war, but she was overjoyed to see her daughter and for some months they lived in their room as secretly and quietly as if they had been shadows, but even that was too much of an existence, and someone caught on to the daughter's presence in the mother's room and reported her, and she was promptly shipped back to another labor camp in Siberia. There she worked in the mines again, this time for years on end; she didn't get a second chance to escape, but she simply outlasted her usefulness as a miner, and the camp officials retired her, and even gave her a "gold watch," only in this case it was—a decanter. Yes! And wasn't that decent of them? And what on earth was she going to do with a decanter? She might have taken it home to her mother in Riga—this time she could travel by train—but I guess the old woman was dead by now.

The world abounds in such horror stories, and an unreasonable proportion of them issue from the Soviet Union. There are so many of them that all you have to do to discover them is listen. These stories gather in your backyard, like beggars, and ask only to be invited into the kitchen and heard.

V

And there was still no word from Imant. I thought of that dream I'd had in which I asked my friend to let me know if he received any word from God. If the friend in my dream heard from God, would he be *able* to drop me a line? And could God write to my friend without being censored? Maybe it's like this. There's Good News and there's bad news, but first, the bad news: the Good News has been shredded.

That was a joke, but is it a joke? Soviet officials, on the lookout for anti-State literature, confiscate Bibles as well as love letters. What are they censoring, in both cases, if not the Logos, the Word as well as words? After all, a synonym for *messenger* is *apostle*. I'm no apostle, but I am a writer, and this logophobia intrigues me. Does this fear of the Word made flesh extend to the word made flesh? Is it possible that the men in the Kremlin have never known, really, what it means to communicate through touch, in the body's symbolic language, and have all their hearts always been dumb, as inarticulate as Newspeak?

In that case, nothing can be more urgent—for them and us—than to try to say what love means.

CHAPTER 5

Love

An article in *Pravda* stated that "the West is very willing to speculate about marriages between Soviet citizens and foreigners, and about exit from the USSR, painting a lurid picture of the obstacles that the Soviet authorities allegedly raise. But, this, too, is nothing more than a pernicious lie." Allegedly! How I wished they were only allegedly intercepting the letters Imant and I wrote to each other. How I wished the Central Committee had only allegedly threatened Imant: if you value your work, forget Kelly Cherry. And we weren't even trying to get Imant *out;* I was willing to go *in.*

In *The Conference of the Birds,* a twelfth-century Sufi poem, there are these words of good advice: "If it is necessary to seek knowledge in China, then go." *The Conference of the Birds* is a mystical poem, and the knowledge it speaks of is knowledge of love. I'm no mystic, but knowledge of love lures me— though I couldn't help giving thanks that Imant lived in Riga and not Peking.

Riga is closer, but far enough. Ever proud of its European traditions and affinities, under Soviet domination it is being inexorably removed, however subtly, from its own history. And this is what they put in place of the independent democracy that flourished between the wars: microphones in hotel rooms and private flats, KGB agents in white Volgas and political bosses in black limousines, a world in which a university dean is afraid to invite a lecturer without bureaucratic approval, even a world in which so-and-so—a friend of yours, it may be*—simply, well, disappears in glaring daylight. I don't exaggerate; I purposely subdue my voice, flatten it out into the barest possible prose, because what I recite here is not poetry. It is a pernicious truth. *Pravda,* which means "truth," lied.

Why, then, was I willing to live there, and why did I even have my heart set on it? First of all, I loved the country—and I mean the country, the land itself, rock, soil, and root. Who knows the reason for these connections, these unexpected linkages between personality and place?† Maybe it all hinges on something as elementary as what books you happened to read when you were fourteen. Or maybe something guides your hand to a certain book. At fourteen, I read *War and Peace.* I stumbled on the title in a movie magazine article about Marilyn Monroe (I got more out of *Photoplay* and *Silver Screen* than out of my high school—the worst high school in Virginia back when Virginia was second from the bottom in education). Then for long years, the beat of my heart said: Russia, and the echo returned: home. I can't explain this, any more than I can explain it away; but I can render it comprehensible by asking you to listen to *your* heart. Some place pulses there, as sure as air. Simeon the Stylite made his home on a pillar. I know a white man who feels truly at home only in the Congo, and another who sold all he had and went to live in Venezuela. My family moved to England. I even knew a man from Yorkshire who found it was necessary to seek knowledge in China.

All the same, considering the regime, I was willing to *live* there only because that was Imant's home too. His work and

---

*Or Alexander Dolgun.

†George Feifer writes in *Harper's:* "Two Russias alternate in the experience of long-term American residents: the oafish Kremlin of oppression and lies; and the sloppy, beguiling sitting room, or cramped, battered kitchen, where one is more alive and emotionally free than in the rational West. In these shabby rooms one feels surprising relief at having come home to one's emotional motherland—an odd thought, isn't it, in a country with such an alien political and economic system!"

children were there, and his people—that is to say, Latvians—
needed him. Imant wouldn't defect, and I wouldn't encourage
him to, even if it was possible, which it probably wasn't. Besides, détente, latterly called, of all things, "peace through
strength," ought to mean that I could coexist with Imant in
Latvia without relinquishing my "ideological orientation,"
quite as the Soviet Union announced it wouldn't desist in
theirs. But to be on the safe side, I had done my research, turning up several organizations my parents might appeal to if
someday they should hear (but how?) that one of their daugh-
ters had been packed off to the Siberian salt mines, or was
"under observation" in a mental institution. Such things had
happened to Americans, and though they were highly unlikely
to happen to me, they were within the realm of possibility.
Nobody, not even Brezhnev, could be sure that there wouldn't
be another Stalin in the Kremlin tomorrow. Imant had said,
lugging my flight bag down the long hall of the Sovietskaya in
Leningrad, "I would give my life for you." And again, my
heart gave back the words it heard, as if repeating a solemn
vow, or a pledge of allegiance.

The one you love is the one you will die for: your child, your
dearest friend, your God. You don't rush to it, but if it comes,
you embrace martyrdom, because martyrdom is the deciding
vote, the one you cast between you and the Other, declaring:
Choose the one I love. Let that one live.

In an ideal world, of course—Paradise, Utopia, or the Affluent Society—we escape such elections. Or we carry them
out, but in the privacy of our homes, in our bedrooms after
the kids are asleep, or in deep-carpeted conversations with our
spiritual accountants, when risk of public exposure is slight.
Ignorance clothes us, protects us from prying eyes—and our
own examinations. Maybe we march. But television brings
live coverage of the newly slaughtered, and, as I have said,
there's a snake in the grass in Eden, and in Arcadia, death.

We know these things, and I don't aim to trade in guilt or
fear. What I want to talk about here is not the world at large—
that comes later—but how *two* people love each other.

And not saints, either, but two *people*. I, at least, have to start with my body. Descartes' self may have been immediately evident in his *cogito,* but mine is a logical, or illogical, construct that can never be completely mirrored in consciousness, since it *contains* consciousness. So I start with what seems simple. It may not *be* simple, but it *seems* simple, and God knows it frequently behaves in simpleminded ways, and not at all subtly.

There are a lot of things about which I do not know what I think, but when Imant looked at me, I knew exactly how I felt. The ideas that came to me then were clear and distinct and not even remotely cerebral. He had a trick of expressing sexual desire at unexpected moments: over lunch, or while ostensibly contemplating a friend's paintings, even while turning the pages of a biography of Verdi. I must find out what kind of life Verdi led. Checking out the menu in a restaurant in Jurmala, Imant would say, suddenly looking up, "I want you." (I gave him carte blanche.) His language on these occasions was forthright but not, as I've explained, obscene, and though I was drilling him in the English vernacular, he kept forgetting the words. "What is called what we are doing last night?" he would ask, under his breath, deadpan in the middle of a public conversation. But however much we liked going to bed together, the more salient point is that ten years elapsed before we were able to. In this, anyway, the Iron Curtain, cruelly complicating our lives in every other respect, may have done us a favor.

I remembered what it was like, being divorced in New York City, shelling out two hard-earned bucks to attend a "singles' mixer" where a self-styled therapist (no certification) assumed command while the rest of us sat in a row of chairs that ran around the room's four walls like, literally, a chair rail, hugging our paper cups of weak punch. Or being asked to "make the scene" at Sardi's, say, in tennis shoes. Or waiting after hours in the executive room watching the big boys blow pot (that was what they called it then) and play pinochle. I was bored. Across an ocean, Imant felt it too, the sheer, paralyzing weight of life lived moment to moment, no matter how exquisitely. The very experience some mystics celebrate—of the present as a thing-in-itself—defeats moralists, and makes us feel disconnected from the possibilities of right judgment and right action, both of which are processes and like hands reach forward and back, into time.

Suppose you *held* in your hands, cupped, that mystical entity, a moment; suppose it had no consequences or precedents, and suppose further that your hands' bowl is not even a context but merely a convenient metaphorical construct. Here, now, is the living moment. Fine, but *what* is it? Is it the sun on the pinecone on the pine, light splashed on ground like water from a clay jar? Is it the flutter of your heart, like a dove beating its wings against a cote? Or perhaps it's the memory of a loved face in a loved place, or an open window, a rain-rinsed night, and the air in your hair? But it is none of these, because it's gone. It was ever only there, then.

You can look everywhere for it, behind furniture, in corners; you can chase it down all the rooms of your mind, and you will never glimpse more than a reflection on a wall, in a mirror, because all that we know of time we see through a glass, darkly. Or say that we see through water, wrongly. It's as if time is a reed in a river: water bends the reed's *apparent* shape, and when you grasp what appears to be real reed, what you come up with is a fistful of river.

I make a distinction here, between appearance and reality, and however skeptical I am of our ability to tell one from the other, the very fact that I make this distinction, without saying that one is somehow more ontologically "valid" than the other, places me squarely on the side of moralists. Mysticism swallows distinctions. Morality says: There are good and evil, right and wrong, truth and falsehood, fact and fiction, and these words denote significant differences even under the aspect of eternity. I find their *significance* in assuming there is someone else in the world. I am not alone. We are not alone. This is the door at the end of the long hall.

Open the door. If Elijah doesn't enter, someone else will. For me, it was Imant. In 1965 I looked up from my unaccustomed place on a couch in a lounge of the Metropol Hotel in Moscow, and saw Imant Kalnin. He was thin and dark, dressed in black, but his eyes were gray—the Latvian gray that may indicate some ancestral hanky-panky with the Finns a couple of thousand years ago. WELCOME, I said (but not out loud, because I was rather young and very shy). Seeing him again for the first time in ten years, in Riga, when it finally looked as though we would be able to marry, I asked him why he'd fallen in love with me in the Metropol. "Because you're Kelly Cherry," he said. How on earth could he know in that moment who Kelly Cherry was? The answer of course is that he couldn't, and ten years later we remarked what a relief it was to discover that, inasmuch as we were going to be married, we also liked each other.

But something did happen in that moment in the Metropol, though it wasn't (not quite) infatuation; some information was conveyed, though it wasn't about our selves. It was a greeting, an exchange, and an irrevocable shared decision to *make* that one moment morally meaningful by connecting it to every other moment of our lives, forward and back. If we were "in love," it was not so much with each other or even, as the expression has it, with love, as with the idea of making sense out of our meeting. (This desire to reform accident into significance is of course the aesthetical impulse.) From that day on, Imant lived in my mind, and I occupied his. We loved each other, and what this meant was, we believed in each other.

Do you believe in God? people ask, and what they mean— what even philosophers, when they let their hair down, mean— is, Do you reckon that God is *as real as you are?* I knew Imant to be as real as myself. To someone you love, you grant ontological autonomy. The still greater, harder thing is to grant it to someone you don't love. So babies in Bangladesh die of starvation, and holders of minority (or merely militarily unimplemented) views are incarcerated in Soviet asylums, and— But I said I would talk here only about "two." Okay. First, you admit another, and in that way step out of the solipsistic universe, even though you travel no farther than your mind's precepts and concepts. If you cannot get out of your house, you keep your house from becoming a prison* by building on to it; you enlarge; you make room.

Bear with me for a second if I go over old ground—it is fruitful ground. Seeing Imant—and being seen by him—ten years after our first meeting, I thought he might be disappointed in me. In fact, I couldn't stop myself from asking if he was. This was after he'd given lifts to Karl and Indra and come back to the flat, for our first few hours alone. It was dark by then, and the children playing in the dirt lot that served as a yard for this section of the building complex were long indoors, fed and abed. A window stood open, and the night air, filtered through wire mesh like flour through a sieve, seemed infinitely fine, like an invisible spirit divisible at every point and yet formally coherent. I was mindful that microphones had once been found in this flat, but Imant had brought a record back with him, and if the KGB's bugs picked up anything that night, it was just *A Little Night Music*.

I leaned against the door jamb while he put the record on. I was still wearing the sheet I'd used as a blanket—I took a nap while Imant was gone—and when I asked him if he was disappointed in me, now that I was, after so many years and letters, there, even to the extent of being draped in bedclothes, he said *disappointment* was a useless word. "Such a word is not for us," he said. To be disappointed in someone is to have expected him to be someone other than he is. You may not know who someone is, and you may expect to be surprised, but that's different from expecting him to be particularly this or that. In a sense, the extent to which we're disappointed in someone or something is a measure of our own faithlessness.

We were lucky, I think, in that censorship and the Iron Curtain imposed restraint on us. We had no opportunity to experience the sexual vertigo that so often skews relationships. We had to be respectable for the censor's sake. Restraint which seemed even in a sybaritic age reasonable—because without it,

---

*The spiritual claustrophobia of solipsism, that Sukhanovka among philosophical prisons . . . "legendary, diabolical Sukhanovka," says Solzhenitsyn.

our letters wouldn't have gotten through—delighted us both, and to the respect for each other that we began with, circumstance added a mutual *courteousness*. "Your letters discipline my time," he wrote. Some days after our reunion and my question, as we were waiting on the stoop for Emil to answer our knock, Imant said, "I feel myself changing already." He felt himself being freed *for* good. I was liberated by him in the same sense. "In truth," wrote Anna Dostoevsky, in the Afterword to her *Reminiscences,* "my husband and I were persons of 'quite different construction, different bent, completely dissimilar views.' But we always remained ourselves, in no way echoing nor currying favor with one another, neither of us trying to meddle with the other's soul, neither I with his psyche nor he with mine. And in this way my good husband and I, both of us, felt ourselves free in spirit." This is the free life you can't find until you are willing to give your other life for it.

The lover suffers; literally, he lets himself be acted upon by another being. This is how convinced he is of his beloved's existence, that he is *willing* to be acted upon by the beloved, even, if it were necessary, to be murdered by the beloved. (Like Christ by the world. Love is risk, as Good Friday, for example, reminds us once every year.) Please don't get me wrong; like almost everyone else, I recommend among mortals a healthy reciprocity in love, but we all taste unrequited love once or many times, and my business here is with the extrapolated extreme: the swill of vinegar on hyssop that Christ on the cross gags on. If, locked in our intelligences, we seek to impress the world with our reflection, to establish our existence (or our nation's) by stamping it so firmly on something *else* that we receive in return the impression (but is it seen through water, through glass?) that we are real enough to have wrought an effect, to have raped a woman or Czechoslovakia, then surely the opposite is also possible, and the voice that says "I am that I am" is the one with no need of a body. It just may be that an omnipotent God would show his love for the world by declining, graciously, to act in it. Or he could choose, as Christ in the wilderness did, to act in but not on it. I said I was skeptical;

I doubt miracles too. Like Thomas, I need to touch; I need to *know*.

The knowledge you achieve through touch isn't perfect knowledge, but it's knowledge of how something—or someone—feels. Thomas reached into Christ's side and *deduced* the resurrection, but he *knew* the man had holes in his flesh. For ten years, Imant and I, on opposing continents, substituted text for texture. This was the flesh made word. Every letter, poem, song, and symphony was a kiss and caress. Lucky you, if you sleep in one bed with your lover, but if you are far from the one you love, you will learn to touch without touching. You'll stand at a window in Virginia, New York, North Carolina, or Minnesota, and you'll think: This air that I breathe was blown here by a democratic spirit, sown everywhere. Mao Tse-tung at eighty-two inhaled this air; Brezhnev, ailing, still breathed it; Nixon, failing, breathed the same air as plants and ants and I. I could imagine that Imant's lungs churning air in Latvia caught my breath on the breeze and blew it back to me, that my life sustained his. I could imagine I was leaves on a tree, flung forward and back, all my green throats bared by a current of air begun in Latvia. Air isn't a free gift; it's a rare loan. All the air I received I gave gladly back to Imant. Go, I said: Keep him well . . . and intake of air became outgo of touch, and love was everywhere. "All my life is you and only you," he wrote, sending me my life by return airmail. And that was one way we endured our long years apart—until, that is, the KGB intercepted our correspondence.

Juliet had her own, famous question. My question, as Indra had known, was *Kur ir Imants?*, and the letters that answered it were not allowed to leave Russia; I wondered whether somebody shredded them, or if they were kept on file. *Kur ir Imants?* I didn't even have a balcony to declaim my question from and could say it only in my heart. Saying it to myself, silently, in the middle of the night in my waiting room, I remembered better nights, when I had, for however short a time, Imant to sleep with. I had known right well where he was then—at my side, touching my face, my hair. *Where is*

Imant? The anonymous telephone calls, the lost letters, the Central Committee's threat—these, I found out later, were merely par for the course, but I didn't think anybody's agents had yet developed a device for listening to the secret beat of a woman's heart or even the coded message transmitted by the pulse of her wrist. But I may have been wrong.

I don't mean to say that a woman can love only one man in her life. On the contrary, she spends her life learning to love her fellow man in India, Africa, Southeast Asia, even New York City, and if she won't spend her life for that knowledge, it isn't love she expresses but only self-indulgent sentimentality. But it's not every day—it's maybe once in a lifetime—that love is returned, and that's a day for rejoicing. God celebrated his covenant by causing a rainbow to appear in the sky. When Imant and I made our own pact in Moscow in 1965, there was snow in the clouds, ice on the pavement, and dark fell early, but we raised a drink—or two or three—to toast the occasion. Cheers! We said, in effect: We'll acknowledge each other's existence, for better or worse. Of course, each of us gained in that transaction; we both believed we'd wrought an effect upon another and so our faith in ourselves increased, but I haven't been saying our motives are ever without self-interest. Like another Thomas—à Kempis—I've been urging an *imitation,* rather as if, or exactly as if, we ourselves are works of art that hold the mirror up to reality.

If we believe that God exists—that is, if we believe reality is love—we unmystically base our belief on the conviction that love is real. This is not good logic—it is terrible logic—but it is very excellent reasoning. We are not talking about Venn diagrams or Turing machines but about the way people think. Beliefs and convictions may be called various things in various systems, propositions, axioms, or principles, but they are also, and importantly, metaphors. A metaphor is a kind of verbal or visual somersault. It gets you from here to there, but not always in the expected manner. But what have we to do, even metaphorically, with a reality that retreats *ad infinitum,* like the French from Moscow, through an eternal winter? I think we have everything to do with just such a reality, one which, *un-*

like Napoleon or the inmate who thinks he's Napoleon, manifests love by relinquishing power, but I want to discuss only two things here.

Mirrors only reflect. Set a bowl of fruit in front of a mirror, and the mirror, though it may be the finest mirror in the world, will not give back the image of a vase of flowers. We "mirrors" are not all "one"; we are one, and the other, and many, and we reflect "reality" in many ways. (Or say that we reflect different realities, and avoid assuming unity where there may be none.) But we are remarkable "mirrors" that feel pain and love in *response* to what we reflect; and since I reflect you— I have an image of you and can reflect on you (and myself)—I conclude that all the "mirrors" that I reflect are probably alike in this respect: that they feel pain and love.

I sit at my desk, rain stippling my window, and try to think about these things. It is as if pain and love were the fruit and flowers, and every mirror that I can see has before it both a bowl of fruit and a vase of flowers. Now suppose that there is neither fruit nor flowers: the mirrors are blank; they are dead mirrors, reflecting nothing. You wouldn't even be able to tell if they reflected each other; that is, you wouldn't know that they *existed*—were mirrors. It could be that, like mirrors which are what they reflect, we are, as has been written, images whose very existence is defined by the flicker of light batted down through history from one beveled pane to another. If this is so, we are not one, but that we are anything at all means that we are *alike*. Not same, but similar. Our different realities have something in common—do we dare to say "reality"? You could think of God as the First Metaphor, linking all othernesses.

The second point to be mentioned here is that the imitation or reflection of a God who relinquishes power involves relinquishing power. At least for the unflawed "mirror," it does. For the human state, it may involve only the right use of power. For the human *couple,* I am sure that to grow in love and wisdom, and to get along with each other, is to refuse to use the power over the other that each grants to the other.

There was an irony here for Imant and me. We found peace

and freedom as a result of international conflict. Our countries sowed the ground with bullets like dragon's teeth, and up sprang—not soldiers. Lovers.

There's an old saying that goes, He is mighty who makes a friend of an enemy. That was the one foundation détente might reasonably have been built on; we might have had guests to dinner, brandy and benedictine, some serious talk. Instead, we said that *serious* talk was out of the question: the "war of ideas" would go on being waged, wherever. As if you could just charge in behind a shield of propaganda, without ever actually becoming *engaged* in combat! The risks of serious talk are greater than that—you could end up having to change your mind. Brezhnev could have ended up believing in democracy. The world could change. No wonder we pretend that tensions can be relaxed without revising ideologies. No wonder we try to support this absurd self-contradiction, that the war of ideas is vital but it shouldn't be carried out head on, in case there are casualties. But this is the front; it's where we live, it's where the main fighting gets done, and it's where we die.

Socrates, about to drink hemlock, said that "those who rightly love wisdom are practicing dying, and death to them is the least terrible thing in the world. . . . They are everywhere at enmity with the body, and desire the soul to be alone." If I had to drain a cup of ground poison, I might, like Socrates, a hero of mine, give in to the temptation to ham it up a little—if I didn't fall apart completely. But I don't think philosophy needs to be predicated on enmity, even between body and soul. If logic can't unite body and soul, metaphor brings them together like any shrewd matchmaker with an eye on a commission. You know best what you go into deepest, as the Bible writers, recording all those begettings, have told us. To know is to feel—without reducing one to the other, as the Gnostics would, or as Marx, another mystic, reducing all spirit to matter, did. But whether any of this is right or wrong, it strikes me as "proper and worthy of the risk of believing; for the risk is noble." So Socrates said, about his farewell description of Earth and its surrounding regions, the hollow we live in and the rivers, chasm, and pure dwellings to which the dead are variously dispatched according to their merits and demerits.

I shut my eyes and tried to think of life after death, a place where even a modern philosopher might go. It wasn't the place Socrates had described, nor was it China. It wasn't even Russia, or Riga. I was outside Calcutta, and I had come in search of the Bengal tiger. I flew to Uttar Bagdogra, took the miniature train to Darjeeling, and came to Tiger Hill. The mist still hung in the air like an unspoken word. From the hill, I watched the sun rise over Mount Everest. First, it seemed as if snow was tipped with fire, and then the whole world exploded into flame, like a fire bomb, but I still hadn't found what I came for, and I pushed on, climbing. Now the mist seemed to fall away below me, as if I were walking not on water but on condensed water. Trees joining their tops overhead blotted out the light—until I came abruptly on a clearing, where the sun shone through like the Noon of noons. It stood in the center of the sky at twelve o'clock and seemed as though it wouldn't budge for all eternity, but it did, and I took my time, looking around. There were tigers everywhere, short-haired, striped, and, naturally, burning bright, even though it was high noon. They were blazing. They yawned, and stretched their huge bodies; a tigress whapped her whelp with her paw, and all the younglings played in sight of their parents, or sharpened their claws on bark, or napped. I was very tired myself, after the long hike, and looking around, I saw that each tiger had a collar around its neck, and each collar had a name. Some of the names were: Nuclear Nonproliferation, Civil Liberty, Suffer-the-Children, Self-Rule, Vox Populi, Sanity, and Pluralism. My pet was the amber-eyed tiger half-dozing, half-watching by the glade's blue pool, because he had a whole string of names, but they all summoned the same tiger forth: and the three names were Separateness, Neighborliness, and Love's Cause and Effect. Then I felt sleepy and peaceful, and lay down on the ground with the sun on my back like a man's warm hand.

CHAPTER 6

Nightwork

And so I read and wrote, and tried to say what love means. I tried to make waiting an activity. I studied Latvian. But often enough I just stared out the window at the tree, as if the future might at any moment fly in and roost on a branch. The dark question was, What kind of a future would it be, anyway? Would they let Imant be in it? The last week of the year, every magazine I picked up contained a horoscope for the New Year. Mine said: Right off the bat, things will go wrong. It wasn't kidding, because things went wrong on the second of January.

On the second of January, I rescued a scattered heap of mail from the hall floor. By this time, I knew there would be no letter from Latvia: the Soviet censors clearly weren't going to allow me that simple thing. But there was a letter from someone in America who had connections in Latvia. Maybe there was news about Imant? There was. The news was this: the writer knew, from someone who had talked with someone who knew Imant, that Imant had "given up and gone back to his wife. . . . Imant thinks, that you would not be able to adjust to life in Latvia and that it is not fair to ask you to come. And he does not wish to leave his country."

I scanned the letter, and, without registering any emotion, threw it down on the dining room table for my parents to read. "Imant has gone back to Frederika," I said. "It's all over."

I went upstairs to my room, the waiting room. What I was waiting for was for the screwy noise in my head to cease. I felt as if my brain was a gong, and J. Arthur Rank was going to go on clanging it forever.

Daylight is a state of mind. My mind had set up house in a gloomier region, a very real and specific location, precisely the place where the nights are so long that no matter how often you look at the clock it is still always only the black hour before dawn. But you tell me: What is the way from darkness to light?

If I lay down on my bed, the angle of my vision altered so that the oak tree filled my whole window like a painting in a frame. I did that now. The wild scrawl of the tree's bare branches seemed a manic handwriting on the wall.

Was the future I was reading there so bleak? Was I not merely greedy? I knew my dissatisfaction with life stemmed partly, or wholly, from wanting too much—or just from wanting—but I always wanted it all, a home and work. Some people, of course, are simply inexplicably lucky, and they *get* it all, but I figure they're statistically insignificant.

At various times, I gave up hoping for one or the other, the home or work. For five years, I tried to quit writing. This started with David. It wasn't easy. You will not write, I would say to myself every morning on awakening; you will *not* write . . . but in the end I did. You will *not* love, I said to myself, but my heart tricked me, and I did.

The point of these exercises, failures though they were, was to train myself for "reality"—what David said was reality. The reality in question was notoriously elusive, and kept sliding away under renewed hope.

But. My dissatisfaction is, I think, of more than merely local interest precisely because it didn't abate. I could dutifully chastise myself for it from now till Kingdom come, could do all the recommended things—consider those who are worse off, keep busy, don't think about yourself—and all day long the clock turns round like a wheel, moving, moving, but comes the night, and time stops. Instead of flying, or at least passing, time gets bogged down somewhere between panic and despair, and you spend the rest of the night in a sweat, wondering how on earth you are ever going to get out of this particular tight spot.

I could, as they say, count my blessings and tally them up alongside others' misfortunes, but this has always struck me as a suspiciously gruesome approach to feeling good.

One thing I could not do was deny that I knew some others, at least a few, who bore with amazing grace whatever vicissitudes they met, like Job causelessly covered "with sore boils from the sole of his foot unto his crown . . . and still he holdeth fast his integrity." Could I hang onto my integrity in a situation like that? I would have to work at it.

From the start, even before cause existed, I was closer to the middle-period Job of chapter seventeen: "My days are past, my purposes are broken off, even the thoughts of my heart. They change the night into day: the light is short because of darkness. If I wait, the grave is mine house: I have made my bed in the darkness. I have said to corruption, Thou art my father: to the worm, Thou art my mother, and my sister. And where is now my hope?"

It is interesting that the ancients—Greeks, Hebrews, and Chinese—yoked happiness to integrity. The happy man is confident of his wholeness, of being one, an integer, well defined in relation to one other. The paradox of solipsism is that you cannot be sure of your own existence unless you can believe in someone else's: without the possibility of "two," one is meaningless, and all our mirrors sigh, going dark, night reflecting night reflecting night reflecting night.

The unhappy man is oppressively burdened with what Arthur Koestler somewhere calls "the apocalyptic temperament": all or nothing. And *he* is all or nothing.

I remember Imant's saying to me—we were waiting for the light to change, and the tram in front of us was disgorging weary passengers homeward bound—"When I am not writing music, I do not exist. I am zero."

I used to experience moments of terror when my face would

begin to dissolve into thin air, like sugar in a cup of coffee; I'd reach up to touch it, and my chin would have distended, like a balloon, or my forehead would have moved back from the rest of my face. Or I stayed, but the world went: it folded up its third dimension and retreated, so that to walk from school to the subway took approximately an eternity. The backs of things disappeared, and I was afraid to look around corners for fear of finding—what? Myself, maybe, as if I lived on the other side of light. As if I lived in an antiworld.

In such extremity, psychoanalysis would be redundant— facing the same self over again. But love is potent. Love says, You are yourself, and I am myself, and the really great thing is, there are two of us, so let's have a drink and a smile and chat for a while. The lover, perhaps not a romantic lover, *seconds* the motion that the beloved exists. The lover becomes whole in being made incomplete. In the same sense, someone might argue that God exists, but infinitesimally. The lover is a ruler who abdicates from solipsism; he gives up the power to act as if he is alone in the world and acts as if he is not alone, demo- cratically. Inch by inch he signs away his kingdom, and in the end he is a beggar at the gates of his own palace.

My ten-by-six-plus room had been a waiting room. As there was nothing more to wait for, it was time, I concluded, to leave.

It was a Friday, and I couldn't go anywhere until I went first to the bank on Monday. Meanwhile, the sun was setting; it went down on the other side of the house, pulling night up over my window like a sleeve. The mock nineteenth-century streetlamp switched on: first, there was a tentative, other- worldly glow, a delicate ghostly white; then it blossomed into pale blue; and then it swelled into a full-blown yellow beacon. It shone straight in my window every night, so that some nights I could look up and see two moons, as if I were battling insomnia on Mars.

I got up from the bed and began to pack. I had thought out what I would do: fly to New York, find a hotel, look for a job, find an apartment. It wasn't as if I hadn't done all these things before. But the more I thought about it, the more convinced I became of the superfluousness of all these movements, and so I revised my plans: I would fly to New York, find a hotel, and slash my wrists.

In the longest nights one imagines that the only way to sleep *is* to die—or that this life is a nightmare, this restless awful dreaming, and the only way to *wake* is through suicide . . . the inclination toward which even Indra spotted, reading my palm in Riga. She made a big, silent O with her mouth, and then she grabbed Imant's palm, and, examining it, began to chatter excitedly. "She says," Imant reported, smiling, "that we both are capable of suicide." Feeling, then, anything but suicidal, we looked at each other with fond complicity, knowing this was an utterly irrelevant piece of information about ourselves.

I wrote Imant a letter, sealed and addressed the envelope, and placed the letter on the dining room table for mailing. "*Ardievu!*" it said. "Good-bye."

A fierce wind had blown up without my realizing it, and now it was raking the little house mercilessly. The next day we discovered the wind had flattened our fence. We also learned that along the coast it had been a full-scale gale. People had been killed. I was surprised; I didn't think there was ever any "weather" in England, only rain. Rain, and the "odd spot of sun." The weather reports on English television always predict "fair with scattered showers," except when they say "wet with sunny intervals." But people die of the weather in all parts of the world. Saturday dawned bright and cold. I woke slowly, fitting myself into the right time and place, remembered the previous day, and finally started to cry.

I cried for three days.

Unity is the number for mystics; writers and politicians cast the world in dualities, demanding drama in order to mobilize emotion; but the philosophers' pet digit is three, the number that takes account of relation.

There must be something philosophical about coming to terms with being jilted; it's a threefold process. The first day is for dying; the second day is the descent into hell; and on the third day you rise out of the deep slough of your soul and keep on rising, like leavened bread, like Christ. Imant dreamed of writing an aria for Mary Magdalen, which, though the Soviet authorities would never allow his audience to hear it, would heap hosannas on the great stone that is rolled back from the empty sepulcher.

I wondered what might have happened to Christ when he went down there. If you were going to think in these terms at all, you couldn't balk at his being legitimately, as it were, dead. Worms surely gnawed at the unseeing eyes; his fingernails grew senselessly; his odor ripened. And if he had a spirit, and it walked, what then? Was he completely cut off from the Father, and if so, could that amputation seem hellishly unendurable unless he forgot, for the space of a day, that he was to be resurrected, and truly believed himself "dead" for all time? And when he walked through hell, did he shine in the dark fire like a live coal?

You are dead . . . dead. Your lungs are clogged with mud, water seeps through your bones like marrow. You fancy you have given birth parthenogenetically from your forehead to a sycamore—or daisy—whose roots clasp your skull. Your left foot is a sumac bush, and your right arm is quartz. But at the same time you are dead, your spirit quickens and wakes; it walks abroad, or down; it races forth, not yet understanding that there is no longer any hurry: dead, you have all the time in the world. This thought slows you, it stops you in your tracks. You might as well take it easy, loaf a little; Lord knows, you never could when you were alive. Maybe you idle an hour away by the roadside, watch the play of sun on macadam and mica as you were never free to when you were still in your body—though come to think of it, you could use that body now, to feel the sun's heat on your back, breathe the day's fresh air. If you had a body, you could stretch your back. If you had a body, you could shake the hand of the man approaching from the east. He walks squinting, eyes shaded against the sun. You wave like mad, but he ignores you. Could it be that the sun's glare has temporarily blinded him? You shout, you stamp your foot—or you try to, but who ever heard of a peripatetic sumac bush? Now you don't so much want to shake the man's hand as tear it off, but he ignores even your anger, passing you by so closely his sleeve would brush against yours . . . if you had a sleeve, or an arm to put in it. What wouldn't you give for your body now? Oh, yes, you'd take it back, every rank and worm-infested, every stinking part of it. And you thought you had all the time in the world. The sun has rolled down the sky like an apple down a hill, and you have nothing in the world. Hurry, then, back to your body. But where did you leave it, and why won't the earth give it back? You can pound at that door forever, and it won't open. Or if it does, it opens from inside, at someone else's bidding and not your own. You cannot resurrect yourself.

And yet, somehow, you must. You feel yourself homeless, without the power to touch or be touched, and you have to find a way to live in the world. It amazes me that in all of the literature I have read about suicide, no one names the two most distinctive things about it. First, the person about to commit suicide always thinks he is choosing the logically necessary course. He thinks he serves no purpose alive, whereas his death will liberate others from the burden of knowing him. In spite of what psychiatrists may say about the "real" motive behind suicide, most people who are drawn to suicide are at least under the impression that they don't want to inflict damage on other people; but they feel that they have no proper place in other people's lives. And second, that the course seems logically necessary is a *compelling* argument. It may be that you choose to commit suicide, but it *feels* as if suicide chooses you. In effect, someone hands you a knife and says, Here, cut your wrists; or someone tells you to face facts and jump off a bridge, and you don't feel you're expressing "hostility" but just good sense considering the way things are—the way they look *to you*. You feel you are merely intelligently renouncing the claims that you made on the world out of sheer stupidity. If you could make that renunciation out of love, you'd be a saint and a martyr, but if, like me, you want to make it because it seems logically necessary, then what you are is only unhappy.

God—to use a metaphor—surrenders his body not because it's logically necessary but because for him to do so is a sign of grace, freely willed.

You and I, being earthbound, must seek a less ethereal raising of the body. Our immediate problem is not how to ascend to heaven but how to get out of bed in the morning.

The problem's only aggravated by comparing it with other people's problems, namely, death, disease, famine, injury, persecution, imprisonment, humiliation; in short, poverty and desperation, and in shortest, pain. If you are going to say that the hurt you feel is minor compared with someone else's, you have to decide where you're going to draw the line between pain worth crying over and pain that's tolerable. Governments speak of "acceptable" losses. Are you going to draw the line between the war dead and the bereaved? Between physical paralysis and psychosis? How do you draw a line and say, All the suffering on this side is secondary to the suffering on that side? I said it before: anguish—the subjective sensation of suffering—is infinite.* The sufferer's wounds seem to be exactly congruent with the whole universe, because pain, while it lasts, usurps the perception of pleasure. *What* one suffers can be greater or less, deliberate or accidental, necessary or gratuitous, and as individuals and in groups, we have to assign priorities to our grief and rage as best we can, but we will not take even the first step toward moral responsibility if we don't respect our own capacity for pain, since we move and are moved by metaphor.

Pain hurts. Nothing could be more of a truism—or more easily forgotten. In a way, even Solzhenitsyn forgets it when he says, "To do evil a human being must first of all believe that what he's doing is good, or else that it's a well-considered act in conformity with natural law." Some people may feel a need to justify their actions according to some scheme, but lots of

---

* As Wordsworth said, suffering is "permanent, obscure and dark."

others plainly don't, and many others don't even imagine that people might respond to their actions with pain. So we speak of "gooks" and "body counts" and "escalation," rendering the palpably live into the abstract inanimate. In lieu of law, natural or otherwise, we have directives.

The question on the floor is, Why must people suffer? The answer from the back of the room is, Because other people insist on it. And as for the rest of it, it could just be that an all-good God would want to exercise every scrap of his ingenuity *not* to perform miracles. Didn't Jesus tell the tempter in the wilderness to be gone? "Thou shall not tempt the Lord thy God." We tempt him at every turn.

If by and large God manages not to interfere with birth and death, we still test his will to the limit every minute of our lives. We're not all, thank God, as spectacularly evil as Hitler and Stalin, but most of us devote a good part of our lives to attempts to inflict our will on someone else.

Mostly, of course, our demands seem, to ourselves at least, reasonable. We negotiate. And this complicates everything. Solzhenitsyn makes the same complaint: "If only it were all . . . simple! If only there were evil people somewhere insidiously committing evil deeds, and it were necessary only to separate them from the rest of us and destroy them. But the line dividing good and evil cuts through the heart of every human being. And who is willing to destroy a piece of his own heart?"

Who indeed? We seem in our twentieth century to be showing signs of a very disagreeable "natural" law, one which more and more people are acting in conformity with. Let's hope it's not so much a law as a mere trick reflection of history, like looking through a glass into the dark from a lighted room and seeing your blind face superimposed on a tree, wet laundry, Orion's knee. . . . But from where I stand in time, it looks for all the world as though we're subject to a kind of moral entropy. Kant had said, "Two things fill my mind with ever-increasing wonder and awe, the more often and the more intensely the reflection dwells on them: the starry heavens above me and the moral law within me." But the universe is running down. Soon the whole shebang will be a cold black stillness, a thick, tasteless soup, and the heart's own world, where kindness and consideration hang in the heavens like a greater and a lesser light, is already chill.

The curtains stayed drawn, so I don't know what kind of day Saturday became, but it turned into a night as black as any I have ever gotten through. My "plans"—New York, hotel, wrist-slashing—having been arrived at, I had only the past to think about. And I thought about it, over and over, obsessively. I'd start from a given point, review all the effort expended from there to the present, and end up, in my mind, against a blank wall that seemed to make the whole long, wearisome, difficult journey pointless. Riga, China, Calcutta—sure. But who willingly travels half the world to see a blank wall?

Here I am, up against a wall, and I have to make it mean something, this wall. I call it a wailing wall.

I lie with my face to the wall. On this particular wall I have taped two items: a map of Europe and the Soviet Union, and a black-and-white postcard of Riga's sweetly unpretentious skyline viewed from the Daugava. The Daugava sparkles so brightly you could think it was mineral water instead of run-of-the-mill river. I flatten my palm against the wall like the third panel in an altar painting and study the back of my hand. This, even before her face, is where a woman first reads a certain fear. The back of the hand tells its own story, the conclusion of which, I was thinking, is uselessness and rejection.

But at least I could still shake hands, if I was willing and met a body coming through the rye. At the college where I taught in Minnesota, a percentage of the students were physically handicapped. They could not all shake hands with me.

I used to eat in the cafeteria with the students, and just watching the way a kid whose fingers are paralyzed manipulates his knife and fork is an education. Sometimes a kid's hands are bent permanently over and under, like paws. The wrists are encased in metal, like silver bracelets. A fork is fitted to the metal cuff, and the kid eats, in effect, with his forearms.

The wheelchair kids balanced their trays on their laps, but some of them needed helpers to lift the trays to the cleanup counter. The helpers were other students; their jobs included getting the handicapped kids from one class to another on time if the classes were scheduled close together, or over to the Chalet for Happy Hour. The entire school had been designed with the problems of the physically handicapped in mind, and in town there were special sidewalk curbs.

There was in general an extraordinary niceness about all the students, as if the experience of helping those so guiltlessly shafted by fate spilled over into their dealings with one another. Nevertheless, though we all benefited, the handicapped students did need extra attention. They were tough—they had to be tough to be in college in the first place—and sometimes the rest of us forgot that toughness is not enough. On the other hand, it is very difficult to remember to be gloomy about the human condition when the specific condition you are observing is that of one college kid's having hooked his electric wheelchair onto the back of another's: this Siamese contraption careens down the hall like a two-car train with a likkered engineer and a drunk in the caboose.

One member of this pair of cards, the back half, was named Wayne Thomas. I had Wayne in my fiction-writing class, and I regret to report that he was a joker only in tandem; left to his own devices, he couldn't cut up much, because he lacked the requisite physical ability. I've been calling him a kid because he was my student, but actually he was thirty years old. There was no saying how long he could expect to live: people in wheelchairs may suffer, in addition to their primary affliction, from atrophy of their internal organs, so that their life expectancy is curtailed. Wayne looked younger than his age, the way people whose lives have been circumscribed often do. He had not the look of young adulthood's sharp-edged intensity; it went deeper than that, farther back into the beginning, something soft and nonresistant, something receptive. He looked as though he could absorb a great deal of love.

Wayne had been in a wheelchair all his life; he had as bad a case of cerebral palsy as I have ever seen. I am no specialist, so there may be worse. His legs were so thin they looked vestigial, and his back and neck curved forward as if some huge, invisible weight lay across his shoulders, so that his nose nearly touched the book tray across his lap. He could hardly move his hands, and as for his head, it was more or less locked into a horizontal position that gave him, when he looked up, a painfully quizzical air. It took me a couple of weeks to learn something about his speech patterns, but in class, if I didn't understand what he wanted to say, the other students would volunteer their translations, and somebody finally would get it right—if Wayne hadn't dissolved into guffaws first. Some of our stabs at what he might be saying really cracked him up. When he came to my office, communication was up to the two of us. A stream of green sputum flowed from the side of his mouth; it was thickish, like pea soup, and could hang on the air. Sometimes he would take a swipe at it with a handkerchief, but this effort exhausted him.

One day I had a call from a colleague. I was still at the trailer, groggy in my nightgown, putting the coffee water on with one hand while I answered the phone with the other. My roommate had opened the living room curtains and I could see blue sky, white snow, and golden sun. Suicide attempts may take place during the dark night of the soul, but they tend to be broadcast in broad daylight, with Bach on the radio and the relentlessly energetic whine of a snowmobile in the distance. Wayne had tried to kill himself with a gun. True, the shot had never been fired, but only because when he was drunk he couldn't muster sufficient coordination to work the trigger, and he'd had to get drunk in order to try to pull the trigger. It turned out, though, that Wayne got smashed a whole lot oftener than anyone suspected, and furthermore, he'd attempted suicide, in different ways, on at least two previous occasions. If he'd had keener muscular coordination, he almost surely would have succeeded. This time he had taken both bottle and gun into the school library. As he struggled to squeeze the trigger with one hand, the gun slipped from his other hand and clattered against his metal book tray, loud enough to wake the living. Among the whispers, the page-turnings, the muffled footsteps, the throat-clearings and note-passings, the soft whap of the rubber date stamp against past-due notices, that sudden jangle of iron on aluminum must have sounded like an alarm, an air-raid warning, disaster. The librarian found him, parked in one of our more isolated carrels, with the barrel of the gun pressed— if at first you don't succeed, try, try again—against the temple of his side-bent head.

I went up to the school, but Wayne was nowhere around. I thought he must be in the hospital and assumed I'd go see him in the evening, but at three o'clock he turned up in my class, the same old sad-eyed wisecracking sad-sack Wayne Thomas. He looked a little hung over, that was all. A little tired, a little sorry—because he'd tried, or because he'd failed? A parent, but not a teacher, might have said a few foolish words in the right tone of voice and wiped away his spittle. I don't know whether his parents were notified. My colleague and I tried to find out his background from the Rehab Department, but we were told that, as we were teachers and not therapists, we shouldn't "interfere."

Wayne Thomas wasn't one of the lucky ones. He is not to be listed among those well-integrated individuals whose glad for-bearance of the world's pain and in particular their share of it is a sign and an inspiration—and a pain in the neck. As pneu-monia complicates an illness, self-pity complicated Wayne's suffering. If he had been someone else and not himself, he might have thanked happenstance for his intelligence, his spe-cially designed school, his electric wheelchair, his limbs which though not the most functional numbered four. But the way I look at it, Wayne Thomas was exactly right to pity him-self. I see nothing acceptable in Wayne's pain. It might be, it had so far been, if only by a hair's breadth, endurable. That didn't make it acceptable. I root for Wayne; I hope he makes it through a long life; if he killed himself, everyone who knew him would, as the poet said, be diminished, but how could any of us ask him to go on hurting simply in order to spare *us* pain? Wayne Thomas couldn't teach me how to live in the world. He could only break my heart. But a broken heart is a book, a book which I will attempt to summarize here.

When the Rehab Department closed its doors, my colleague and I worked out our own theories and procedures in the snack bar. Meanwhile, by this time, Wayne was sitting with a group of students at a round table in the center of the floor, slurping up a milkshake through a bent straw. A bent straw is a standard piece of equipment for the handicapped. When I was a very young child, I had a book about Tibet; it said that the people there, when they go visiting, take along their own teacups tucked in their shirts. Wayne brings his bent straw.

But my colleague took one bite out of a jelly doughnut and shoved it to the wall end of our table. His face was as white as bond paper, and when he took off his glasses for a minute to rub the bridge of his nose, angry red imprints were briefly visible, like commas. Turning my attention from Wayne to him, something I had scarcely thought about before became all at once the center of everything, the point to which the whole story led. All at once, I realized how involved in it *he* had been, and I thought: If only Wayne could know how important he is to this person! Wayne would never know, but I couldn't help but know. Now when I want to kill myself I think maybe there's someone who would be shattered by it, someone whose existence I don't even suspect.

A Jewish legend says that God endures the world for the sake of thirty-six just men. So, I guess, if one morning we should wake with only thirty-five, we can start saying our prayers, fast. The thirty-six just men, in other words, redeem the world. The world has been sold to death and destruction, but they buy it back, and the price on the pawn ticket is a measure of the world's worth: one man.

One man with his sense of outrage and grievance and fair play is the thirty-sixth man, but we never know who he is. The only way we can ensure the world's survival, then, is for each of us to act as though he might be the thirty-sixth man. Call it the responsibility for redemption. It's a responsibility no one can charge *another* person with, since another person might be, at best, only the thirty-fifth just man. But it's a responsibility none of us can escape. My colleague couldn't escape it, Wayne Thomas couldn't, and now I was smack up against it too.

It was Sunday afternoon. Cold sunlight crept in through a crack in the curtains. Already the days were longer than they had been. A parallelogram of light fell across the bed and extended up the wall to the map of Europe and the Soviet Union, and I knew my three-day night was about over. The answer is that you *can* get there from here, but when you are "there," it is "here." There is no clear line dividing light from dark, good from evil, pity from self-pity, or martyrdom from suicide, but the one is as different from the other as love is different from the will to power. We are like travelers between two continents, and if we aren't headed one way, we're headed the other. You know when you get there.

I read again the letter from America. It could be wrong; as my parents said, "If you leave here now, he won't be able to reach you, and you'll never know." I didn't hope for any miracles; I just don't believe in miracles. In fact, as an incorrigible skeptic who'll go on doubting the resurrection until such time as I'm permitted to touch it, I suppose that if I'd been dead I would not have heard the telephone ringing a week later. It was Imant.

CHAPTER 7

Espionage

I

"Is nonsense!" he said. "Who tells you this?"

Talk about words being music to the ear. "Is nonsense": that sentence was a symphony.

I didn't want to name names. "It doesn't matter," I said. "It must have been a rumor. But it's been so long since I heard from you—"

"Kelly," he asked, "when came the last letter you got from me?"

"November the eighteenth."

There was a prolonged silence from the other end of the line. "Kelly, listen," he said, slowly and distinctly. "I have been writing to you all these weeks. This information you have received is nonsense."

"Do you get my letters?"

"Yes, yes. And the books about Russian composers you have sent."

In my letters—the many I had sent up until the last, farewell letter, which I'd sent in care of Frederika—I very carefully did not refer to the absence of his, since then the censors almost certainly wouldn't let mine go through to him. Imant hadn't even known anything was wrong!

I warned him that I'd already mailed him a farewell letter in care of Frederika. "I do not see her," he said; "I will not get."
I do not see her.

"I am in the farmhouse. Kelly, it is very nice! I sent you some photographs, did you get?" I had to tell him no. "I do not understand why this is happening— Kelly," he said, "I call you in a week or two weeks, okay?"

"Oh yes," I said, happily, "okay!"

Then the operator cut us off. My watch—Imant's watch, the watch he had given me so long ago—said it was eleven o'clock.

I had closed the curtains in my room against the streetlamp, and the only light inside my room was an unshaded bulb near the ceiling: it was attached to the ceiling by a chain and, to all appearances, a cobweb.

I had been working in my room when the telephone rang. The sudden noise had startled me out of deep concentration, and now I returned to the night's taut stillness. The only interruption was the cooing of the doves, long, hollow notes mournfully rendered. Do doves suffer from insomnia? They seemed to be up half the night, grieving. But they were outside. Nothing in the room stirred. The curtains were as motionless as draped iron, and the light cast by the ceiling fixture stuck to the walls and desk as if glued. I sat on the bed.

A moment ago Imant's voice had filled my heart; now there was only this quiet emptiness, and I wondered if I'd been dreaming. The experience of unreality persisted through the following week. Then there was another call.

It came in the late afternoon, and it came from Karl. My mother had sent a letter to Karl, at about the same time I had sent the one to Frederika's apartment on Suvorova. What it said was, If Imant has gone back to Frederika, why hasn't he told Kelly? Karl was calling to assure my mother that we had been misinformed. "Imant is waiting for Kelly," he said. Then Karl handed his end of the line to Imant, and my mother handed me hers, and Imant told it to me, again, and finally, with the dog rolling over on his back and waiting for someone to rub his belly, with the chrysanthemum petals drifting onto the polished wood like gold snow, with our neighborhood tricycle addict zipping back and forth in front of the window as if his life depended on it—with the new spring air filling up the living room, as if we were changing the air in the room like we change the oil in the car—with all these goings-on to tie me to my senses, the dreamlike aura dissipated, lifted like fog.

II

I kept on posting my letters to Imant, and I sent records and poetry books as well. I also wrote to the Universal Postal Union in Berne, which informed me that, regretfully, they could do nothing to stop the Soviet Union's interference with our mail.

A congresswoman proposed a bill to monitor Soviet compliance with the Helsinki Accords; I wrote to her, detailing what I knew about Soviet *lack* of compliance. The newspapers said that Henry Kissinger opposed the formation of this committee as "counterproductive" to Soviet-American relations. Not being, as the woman at the U.S. embassy had been so quick to point out, an expert in international law, I can't comment on this; but I can certainly say that the committee was a terrific idea for American-American relations. It gave me, at last, a place to turn to, and some hope of political sympathy.

The newspapers also told me that the West German courts had recently ruled that their post office was legally obligated either to pay compensation for "lost" registered mail or to intercede with the Russians and that certain groups were arguing that the same should hold for England. I now always attached an Advice of Delivery card to my letters to the USSR. I read that one man, a member of the Committee for the Release of Soviet Jewry, had sent 322 registered letters, of which 188 disappeared without a trace. The remaining 134 Advice of Delivery forms were reportedly returned to him—signed not by the addressees but by Soviet officials.

Meanwhile the papers were full of the Soviet Union's accusations about the West. The West was "contradict[ing] the elementary principles of noninterference in the affairs of other countries." The West was the toxic source of "snide comments, all designed to poison the atmosphere." But in May, when nine Soviet citizens banded together to form the Public Group to Assist the Fulfillment of the Helsinki Accords in the Soviet Union, they were promptly informed that they were breaking the law. (Whose law? Stalin's?)

A Soviet representative reportedly explained that détente "does not mean the U.S. and the Soviet Union must have an identical approach to problems. It does not mean that we stop the war of ideas." There was that war of ideas again. But clearly, the simple fact of the matter was that the Soviet Union, which was understandably determined not to fight another war within its own boundaries, was equally afraid of waging the war of ideas on its own ground. It might lose.

At the same time, the papers—for the time being, my only social life—were rife with stories about the CIA, the FBI, the NSA, exposing one dirty trick after another. As a child of the fifties, I had been a loyal advocate of the American system of checks and balances. I studied the Bill of Rights and the amendments. In high school, which was of course a southern high school, every day began with the Pledge of Allegiance; and when at sixteen I went off to college, I went clutching a five-page government-printed list of subversive organizations which I was not, under any circumstances, to join, in case I imperiled my relatives' jobs. I remember one was something called the Chopin Society. There may be legitimate Chopin societies; for all I know, this one was legitimate, but it was blacklisted. In any case, I thought it was pretty funny. I didn't think I wanted to be a Communist, but I knew for damn sure I didn't want to belong to the Chopin Society. Beethoven, yes. Chopin, no.

I no longer knew what to believe or whom to trust. In England I read dozens of publications from all over, following a dozen different accounts of each story, piecing them together in some way that I hoped approximated the truth. Diving into the newspapers every morning, I felt like Alice down the rabbit hole. Sometimes what I met with was the course of world events as seen by the March Hare. I read that the successor to Brezhnev might well be Yuri Andropov, head of the KGB. I was informed that in the event of a brokered convention, the Republican presidential nominee could conceivably be George Bush, then head of the CIA. What kind of a scenario for the future was this? And why didn't anyone else remark on it? Maybe the KGB and the CIA were keeping an agreed silence. One morning I woke up with an answer: Yuri Andropov and George Bush were one and the same. (And he lives in Sicily.)

I thought this was hilarious. How was I to know that, a few years later, Bush *would* be president?

III

Clearly, I was not cut out for a life of espionage. And why should I be? What had the world come to, when someone whose most revolutionary aim was to become a bride had to regret that she and her fiancé had parted without first devising a *code?* How cryptic must a love letter be, in this day and age?

What I knew about codes: I had a book on codes in the sixth grade. The best code in the book involved wrapping a strip of paper around a pencil obliquely so that the edges slightly overlapped: this gave you a series of tiny squares to write in. In each section you wrote a single letter with a pen—invisible ink was good if you could get it—and then you slipped the pencil out and smoothed the paper flat. What you were left with was a line of letters that looked satisfyingly mysterious (unless you happened to view the paper vertically).

Codes were vital. As a child, I didn't doubt that we were going to blow up the whole earth very soon, and I tried to plan for a devastated tomorrow. I remember an old movie; it turned up again on the late show a while back.

In the movie, a small boy, son of a Los Alamos scientist, is kidnapped. His abductors hold him in a cave in the desert; they use tapes of his voice to try to persuade his father to reveal the "secret formula." But what I remember most about the movie, the thing that wowed me when I saw it as a kid, is that the boy, whenever he's asked what he wants to be when he grows up, says, "*If* I grow up . . ." His mother tries to get him to say "when," but he always wisely says "if."

At least in my mind, the threat of nuclear attack was never associated with the Russians. I simply assumed that someone somewhere was sooner or later going to slip up, and bang, that'd be it for everyone who didn't have a shortwave radio, a compass, two weeks' supply of distilled water, and a flashlight with EverReady batteries. This included our family, since my father was more worried about meeting payments on the shelter we had than about building a fallout shelter. I was convinced we were living in a fool's paradise. I look out my window this evening, see dark green treetops against a watercolor sky, and I still think that's where we're living—in a fool's paradise. I am surprised that it is all still *here, that* we are all still here.

In the ninth grade, or maybe it was the tenth, I was a lieutenant in the Civil Air Patrol. Now the purpose of this quasi-military outfit was to keep an eye on the sky; the minute we spotted a suspicious aircraft, we were to inform our commander and place the troops on alert. At first we met at night on a playground; later we were allowed to hold maneuvers in a vacated army barracks on the outskirts of the city. I wonder now who the grownups were who organized these meetings; they told us we were doing our country a service. That was all right, but it wasn't why I joined. Our chief activity was marching. We also looked at pictures of planes. Unfortunately, I never was able to distinguish one plane from another; all I ever could make out, skygazing, was a flying wedge of lights, and the following year, the school doctor discovered that I was myopic. In the meantime I simply pretended to see whatever the others saw. It was a great way to meet boys.

About spying, though: we all took it for granted that it was very cloak-and-dagger, not knowing that much spying is conducted as a kind of gentleman's agreement—we'll post this ambassador here, and you can station your undersecretary there—and most of the rest of it is carried out by dullish bureaucrats putting in time toward their pensions. Even technology defeats itself, and technology is the guise the most sophisticated espionage wears. The Russians bombard the American embassy in Moscow with microwave radiation, and we counter with window screens to reduce the signals, but we don't dare raise a fuss. The West Germans televise film of KGB agents "secretly" attached to the Soviet embassy there, and the Soviet Union counters by filming German diplomats in Russia. Do they show the film during prime time? The tiny country of Luxembourg is crawling with KGB men. Radio Free Europe used to be illicitly funded by the CIA; according to "a captain in the Czech Intelligence Service," it still is, but Radio Free Europe strenuously denies the charge, and indeed, someone has suggested that the KGB planted the Czech agent to undermine Radio Free Europe by falsely implicating the CIA. My head spins. The KGB—and for all I know, the CIA as well—has a "disinformation" department. "Disinformation" is purposeful misinformation; it is the deliberate introduction of inaccurate propositions into a factual situation, so that people in that situation will seek to alter it one way while unintentionally altering it another. There must be instances where espionage by disinformation is performed in the service of some high cause, patriotism or personal loyalty, but an awful lot of it is nothing but a kind of bureaucratic bullying, an institutionalized version of the gangster mentality: I'm the boss, and if you know what's good for you, you'll do what I say. It usually seems reasonable to do what the man says. It seems so, because how can you ever know when it's unreasonable, if you can't distinguish false information from true? A Rumanian manages to get to England, achieves British citizenship, and makes every effort over a period of years to bring his widowed mother to England, but the Rumanian authorities demand hard currency, and a train ticket which, like Imant's and my letters, is inexplicably "lost" en route. At one point the Rumanian authorities "inform" the elderly widow that her son has been killed in an automobile accident; there is no reason for her—they can now explain, sadly but firmly—to persist in her applications for emigration. Should she persist in believing the incredible (which in this case happens to be true)—that her son is alive and well and living in England? And should I not wonder, from time to time, exactly where the rumor about Imant originated?

IV

John le Carré has invented a term for "a sexual enticement operation": *honey trap*.

Imant and I knew our respective countries had a history of setting honey traps, and we might have been slower to trust each other except that there was no earthly reason for either country to want to entice either of us. Nevertheless, when Imant jokingly asked if they had sent him the real Kelly Cherry, his question resonated on several levels. Obviously, I could never prove I wasn't someone else. In the Soviet Union especially, you learn to wait for the other person to reveal himself first. I knew that Imant's trusting me was courageous. And suppose the KGB did have photographs of us? Imant had a plan. He said he would hide inside me. I could smuggle him across the border inside my body. He would be reborn free.

Well, maybe. Back in England, I read a story about a policeman. A twenty-one-year-old policeman went to Russia on his holiday, and while he was there, he sent postcards to his friends back home. "Come and join the revolution," he scribbled, as a lark. When he returned from Russia, the Special Branch questioned him; my newspaper said he said it was a "nightmare grilling," and "details of the holiday" were noted in his file. This policeman is supposed to have reported that "they asked me if I had sex while I was there. They were convinced that the Russians had compromised me in a sex trap and forced me to send the postcards." Here was a new way to make a revolution, via airmail. The Special Branch had more faith in the Soviet post office than I did.

Two months went by. There were not only no letters—there was no word of any kind. I was frantic. Were the Soviet authorities stopping telephone calls, the way they stopped letters? As I say, poetry, not espionage, is what I know, and I hadn't a clue how someone might go about blocking a call. Did a KGB agent clap a hand on Imant's shoulder as he dialed? Did the operator check my number against a blacklist? Did some sinister device of the twentieth century automatically break the connection?

By now I could speak a little Latvian. I got out my Latvian book and carefully wrote down the words I thought I might need, and then I gave the operator Emil's number. And what happened next? I still don't understand.

Even after the operator at my end connected me with an operator there, I had a strangely long wait, and then the operator there refused to let me speak with anyone. I could hear the phone ringing in the house with the many paintings. A young woman answered; it might have been Olga, or Annele, or Ilze. She gave Emil's last name. I couldn't hear what she said.

The Russian operator then said to me: "The people in this house do not know anyone in England."

I tried to give my name, but she wouldn't pass it along to the young woman. "Please!" I said.

"Do you speak Russian?" she demanded.

"No-o-o . . ." (wondering why she should ask this question and if there was a trick to it).

"The people in this house speak only Russian!"

She was barking at me, and I barked back. "No, they speak Latvian! I'll speak Latvian!"

"They know only Russian!"

I knew everyone in that house; they were all Latvian and spoke Russian *and* Latvian (and any one of them certainly would know that I was the party in England). Had something happened to cause them to be fearful of accepting a phone call from me? I had sent Emil a couple of letters and never got an answer: maybe the Soviet authorities, intercepting the letters, had put his telephone number on a list so that incoming calls would be intercepted too. Or maybe he had got the letters and was afraid to answer them, or maybe he had answered them but *those* letters were intercepted. I was persona non grata with somebody, but there was no reason for it to be Emil or Bruno or Olga or Annele or Ilze. Unless, taking a cue from certain Rumanian authorities, the Soviet authorities had given them a reason after I left. What was Imant going through on the other side of the Iron Curtain?

A report was smuggled out of Russia to Paris. It named twelve hard-labor camps in Latvia alone. According to the report, the prison in Riga had five thousand permanent inmates, and the "psychiatric" wing was under the direction of the MVD. There were special camps for women, children under eighteen, and invalids. They were all under the Department of Rehabilitation Through Work, a rubric with telling echoes, and I noted the address of the one in Riga in case I ever had to go there. After all, I wouldn't be able to look it up in a phone book, inasmuch as there were no phone books.

More weeks passed. It began to be definitely spring. I wrote to Imant in my elementary Latvian: "Grass is becoming green, and leaves are growing so rapidly it is almost possible to see them at it. I look at the tree, and then away for a second, and then back, and a new bud has begun in a blink.

"If I look inward I see your yellow Fiat, rain at the sanatorium in Jurmala, the white table in Indra's garden, you. These pictures I have stored in my heart.

"Sometimes I look at the world map on the wall in my small room, and I think, What a big world, how far Latvia is! On my wall there is also a postcard which shows the skyline of Riga on the far side of the Daugava, and when I look at it, I feel homesick. My home is with you."

Whenever we had a really warm day, I felt transported to Latvia, or Moscow or Leningrad. The smells came rushing back—cheap tobacco, so sweet a westerner could mistake it for marijuana; dirt lanes and wild flowers; butter sautéed in an iron skillet; the smells of cooking caught in lace curtains. And with them came that paradoxical sense of exhilaration, the inspiriting knowledge that each moment of friendship or communion, no matter how brief or simple, is a felt triumph of the soul over the State.

If I was working in my room, I watched the changing view from my window. I could sit at my desk, and the view in front of my window changed like painted scenery pulled past a stationary movie-set "train." Though the trip was a pleasure, the only place I ever seemed to arrive at was the present.

A high school habit stayed with me, and at night, looking out my window, I instinctively turned my gaze upward. Orion strode out of sight as the seasons turned. The low moon of streetlamp and the high moon of spacewalk made circles of equal size, like paper cutouts pasted to the windowpane. Sometimes you could hear Concorde taking off from Heathrow, but now it was dead silent. No unidentified flying objects in the upper right quadrant—only a large white-winged moth in the lower left.

I tried to second-guess Imant's view from the farmhouse. He had rolling country to look at, a lake, trees in the distance. Before a cloudburst, sheet lightning would score the sky like a photographer's flash, brilliantly exposing rivulets beginning to fill up the ruts in the clay road, woolly caterpillars clinging to the underside of leaves, the anthill washing away in the first fresh fall of rain, but thunderbolts would pop safely far out in the lake. He could see mist at dawn, fog at dusk, and, in the cool of the day, our cow. Could he also see spies in the shadows of the ditch?

Here in Burghfield Common, we had our very own spies. They were Hungarian.

If you drove down the road a piece and turned right, you came to the Royal Ordnance Factory, which makes Polaris missiles. (On our other side, there was the Atomic Weapons Research Establishment, so we were well protected, or endangered, as the case may be.)

I am, as I have explained, a member of the first generation to grow up with the threat of thermonuclear war hanging over our collective Damoclean head. For a short time when I was seventeen, I was a student at the New Mexico Institute of Mining and Technology. I plotted my vectors in physics lab and read *Dr. Zhivago* on the sly. There was an R&D—research and development—center connected with the school, and I used to study there, in a seminar room, instead of in the library. Some of the scientists and graduate students used it too. One of the engineers who hung out there was a Hungarian refugee; he'd gotten out at the time of the uprising.

So unlike some people, I have a persevering affection for mathematics and the physical sciences, but I always associate them—and Hungarians—with the majestic country of the Southwest. I remember the scratchy sound of sand blowing over rock, the sense of self-importance you used to get from the smell of a new slide rule, how the sharpness with which you perceive the elements out there—the air's clarity, the earth's solidity—can convince you that you are just before learning something big. Socorro is dry, open country the color of the sun; farther north, around Los Alamos, snow lies in blue patches on green uncluttered mountains, but here in Burghfield, spring lambs cavorted alongside the M-4, and a single meadow would be packed with mustard, May trees, and flowering chestnut. What were Polaris missile plants doing here, or Hungarians?

They were spotted taking photographs outside the factory. Since they weren't *in* the factory, nobody could imagine what they thought they were accomplishing, unless perhaps they were concerned not so much with the missiles themselves as with the way they are conveyed from place to place.

The Hungarians—a lieutenant colonel and a captain—had stationed their car on the lane leading to the factory. Approached, they panicked, and took off on an insane ride through the countryside, but as I say, this is not the most appropriate landscape for this kind of thing. Every few yards you come to a drawbridge over a canal, a railway crossing, or a solemn cluster of very intent birdwatchers. After a couple of hours the chase ended abruptly, and our Hungarians were taken to the

Basingstoke police station, but they were released when they claimed diplomatic immunity.

Soviet Russia restricts British and American diplomats in Moscow to a radius of forty kilometers, and Britain retaliates by doing likewise to Russian diplomats, but the Russians have a way around this: they simply assign certain of their espionage missions to diplomats from the satellite countries. The Hungarians weren't even made to leave, but everyone in England was laughing about them for days afterward.

One night in March, Imant called my sister. He told her to let me know that the second trial for the divorce would be held later that month. My sister believed in coming to the point. "Do you still want to marry Kelly?" she asked. "Yes, oh yes!" he said—like that. "Tell her I love her!" But then he also said, "Is not possible to talk long. Tell her I try to call her." But still no call came, and I couldn't know why his call to my sister was cut short or even if the reason was significant. When anxiety keeps you awake at night, you first check out the loose board banging against the barn, but if, after that's secured, there's still some unaccountable noise and fear, I guess you've got a right to look for reds under the bed.

V

Arriving in England, I'd been given the usual six-month tourist visa. I now applied for an extension, thinking the procedure routine. My request was denied.

I filed an appeal. Where was I going to go, what was I going to do? I remembered the man in the Moscow bar, with his friend's cigarette lighter that was a camera, who'd said he was without a country. I could have told him he wouldn't know what confusion *was* until he was a citizen of one country, living in a second country, trying to get a visa to marry a citizen of a third country.

There was nothing more I *could* do, no place I could go. I

wrote, just sat at my desk and wrote, from nine in the morning until eleven or twelve at night (with time out for "The News at One" and dinner at six). And while my appeal was being considered, I at least got a good look, from the window of my waiting room, at the country I might have to leave: England.

The light skips across this island like a flat rock over a river, sending out ripples of wind and shadow. The older I get, the better I like every part of the world, but I don't love, I do not admire, what politicians do to it. An East German athlete sought asylum in Austria. He had met an Austrian girl there and wanted to marry her, but there was "little hope of getting official permission in his country for the wedding." What about my wedding?

I had not heard Imant's voice since the middle of January; it was now May, and when Imant's call finally did come, he said he had just received the first letter from me in *two months*. For two months, I had been writing registered, tracered letters to a stranger, a nameless, faceless clerk in the infinite Soviet bureaucracy.

"I do not trust," Imant now said, about the mails, and there was hurt in his voice, as if he'd been wounded. If a citizen betrays his country, he is accused of treason, but what is the word for the country that betrays its citizens? "Do you get *any* letters from me?" he asked.

"No."

"Not any?"

I didn't understand that this time he was making a specific reference, which he couldn't explain over the telephone. "No," I said. At least, after the long hiatus, he was now getting some of my letters again. "I like these Latvian letters!" he said.

At the beginning of the call, Imant had told me that the second trial for the divorce had taken place on the twenty-seventh of April and that Frederika had not shown up for it; this meant that the third trial would be scheduled for within the coming month, instead of half a year off. In other words he would be divorced in a bare few weeks.

"Kelly," he said, "this house is a wonderful place to live!

You will like *very* much, I am sure. It needs much of work, is true. Also much of money. But all is beautiful around, and there is great peace." But he had gone through the whole winter in that farmhouse alone, gone through weeks of it without letters, with the snowy silence broken only by the wind whistling in the attic. How many hours of televised ice hockey had he watched? His father wasn't speaking to him, his children were in the city, and he was evidently under surveillance—and even if you would like to, you can't invite to dinner a secret agent who, ostensibly, doesn't exist. The operator made us hang up, but a little later he called back. "Kelly," he said, almost guiltily, "I feel very lonely."

Le Carré says that "lamplighters were the courier service which serviced agents abroad, and stepped into areas where the local Secret Service resident couldn't handle the job for himself." The lamplighter is a le Carré fiction, of course, but I sometimes think we are all living in a spy novel.

I sat down in the green chair in the living room to go through the mail. Some lamplighter had brought a letter from Imant out of the Soviet Union, cut out my address, which Imant had written at the bottom of the letter, pasted it onto the envelope, and mailed the letter, dated the fifteenth of April, from inside England. Philby, McLean, Burgess & Co. could examine that envelope with a fine-toothed comb, if fine-toothed combs were part of their government issue: nothing on it revealed anything about the sender. But I had no trouble cracking Imant's code. "I love you very much," Imant wrote. "I am working very much and this is the only thing that keeps me away from sad and black thoughts." "I love you" means *I love you* even, or especially, under cover.

This was the letter Imant had been trying to ask about. As for my lamplighter, he—or she—brightened my day. And not only my day: it was the first letter from Imant in half a year.

CHAPTER 8

What Good Is Poetry?

I, too, was "working very much." I didn't want to leave myself any time for thinking about Imant and how I missed him. But this is the Catch-22 about being a poet: much of my work consisted in exactly that, in thinking about Imant and how I missed him.

Reaching for some sort of larger, more general view, a way to make philosophy out of my personal obsessions, I might compose essays about "love" and "pain," but at three in the morning, with the unforgiving future bearing down on the present like a truck, pain and love come to the same thing: despair. In a song, then, I outlined the themes of despair: *God is dead, having been stuffed into an oven like meat. God is dead, having been eaten. Blood is what we batten on. Therefore, love is lying, light is scattered like bread crumbs at the creek's edge, and free will is the reflection of time's wings in water. My heart is shattered in the pebbled shallows and lost in the sedge. People are dying.*

Imant was setting the songs to music. When I listened to Imant's music, it spoke to me. More than that. Somewhere I wrote, "If sound could grow a body I would be its lover forever, and never need another." Imant made sound real; his work touched me.

That, of course, was the real basis for our relationship, and

the reason it had survived—our shared work. It's so embar-
rassing to talk about one's work. Sex is easier to talk about.
But for Imant and me, the sharing of work was as intimate as
the making of love. When the Soviet government stole our
letters, they also stopped us from working together—another
contravention of the Helsinki Accords. (Is détente a tease? Are
politicians *intellectual* prudes, afraid of losing their ideological
virginity in international relations?)

"I know who you are," Imant said, looking at me and quoting me, "dragon dragging your muffled fires." After a few
days I got used to this Soviet capacity for quoting poetry, but
I never got used to hearing my own poetry quoted. The Daugava became "cool" and "tangy," forsythia hung "over the
bank in bright clumps of light dripping petals.like water," and
in Leningrad, when Imant wanted to know the name in English for a certain tree and I wasn't sure, he insisted, "You
know what is this. Is the tree with the owl in it!" *The owl lights
on the oak.* I have been married to a critic, and one thing I
learned: better a fan.

Once, at a party after a poetry reading I gave, I bumped into
a famous poet who, it seems, had not reckoned on bumping
into me. Blurting out what he had thought of the reading, he
said, "Your poetry is very . . . peculiar!" I was equally taken
aback. "Peculiar? What does that mean?" I wouldn't have dared
to ask if I hadn't been surprised into it. Famous Poet stopped
and reconsidered, and then he said, slowly, "I guess what I
mean is, original," and then, looking as if he'd surprised *himself,* Famous Poet wandered off in deep thought, entirely forgetting that he was supposed to be headed in the opposite direction, toward the bar. I told Imant this story. From there on
out, whenever I asked Imant if he liked something I had written, he would say, "Well! Is very—"

Original?

"Peculiar."

Art is the achievement of peculiarity, is self-definition, and so
is love. When people love each other, they agree to be the occasion for each other's self-definition. This is the first clause in

the treaty they signed when they agreed to love each other. All is *not* fair in love (or even war).

As an artist establishes himself (or herself!) by making art, the lover, by loving, performs an act of definition which determines *that* he is as well as *who* he is. The writer who always talks about writing and never does it is no writer. And if there is a God, he surely sits at his desk in the great study, eternally scribbling his one word, the Logos. But this one word, being metaword, contains beginning, middle, and end, and so he never writes a second word and therefore is always beginning to tell the story. He creates himself anew every morning. At least so far as *poetry* is concerned, whether philosophy could concur or not, the answer to the old question, What came before God?, is God.

(But musicians understandably have a different theory. To them, God is a cellist who plays the same note over and over. Why doesn't he change strings and go up and down the fingerboard like other cellists? "I've found the spot," says God the Cellist, smiling beatifically. "I've found the spot.")

Here below, we are stuck with sequence, endings and death. No one word is ever enough: we need billions of words, a nonstop literature that propels us through time along vectors parallel to our experience. The moral dignity of a writer's work consists in this: by exploring in his own life or the lives of his characters the phenomena of motivation, feeling, and idea, and their interlinkages, he gives his reader *source* for metaphor, and metaphor. Knowing Grushenka, say, or for that matter Prufrock, I not only know myself better—I know you. I know you from the inside out, more thoroughly than I ever could from sheer observation and a report of your behavior; I know you by analogy. (Analogy is knowledge predicated on a leap of faith.) In a world where one-fourth of the people—not to mention animals—go hungry, this is the only moral claim the imaginative writer can make, but it is a rare and distinguished claim. Of making many books there *must be* no end.

Or so I lectured myself, but still I spent much of my time in my room, when I intended to be working, looking idly out the window. *My* oak tree was putting out new leaves like yellow-green dablets of paint, a kind of real-life pointillism. It was summer. The sky was as clear as cellophane.

Funny, how the weather is different all over the world. A North Atlantic cyclone was making its way into the Baltic States.

I wondered if Imant, in his room in the farmhouse, was working on the songs. A nationalist I know had suggested that the songs should be designated for a *Latvian* composer. (I preferred *Soviet* because it made clear to an American reader the reality of foreign occupation.) About Latvia, I read in Bilmanis, "The lyric melancholy of the music and poetry is derived partly from the northern poetic temper, determined by the contrast of harshness with sudden exquisite moments in nature; and partly from centuries of suffering in whose darkness was called up the remembrance of past dignity and peace."

Could Imant make a song out of a cyclone? I pictured him in his old brown slacks, sweater, and suede jacket. He looked Western, at least sartorially—the heavy eyebrows and long face and prominent cheekbones were East European—except for his sandals, which must have been intended for the tourist trade in Odessa.

My *southern* "poetic temper" languished on Auclum Close. Sometimes, if you look out a window without thinking about it first, you forget to place the correct scene in the frame. You look out of a window in Berkshire and see southwest Minnesota, or upper Broadway, or Richmond with its azalea malls, even Moscow. You have to remember which tree goes where.

That summer, the view from my window was endlessly sunny. It was so sunny I could hardly look up to get a fix on my location; the glare was that great. Some days I felt like the lone survivor of a shipwreck, adrift on a raft in the wide, sun-speckled, unspeaking sea. This was romance? This was monotony. Somebody suggested to me that a certain glamor attaches itself to these marriages between citizens of East and West. Maybe. I didn't feel glamorous; what is glamorous about being alone in the middle of an ocean, not knowing whether you're ever going to make it to shore? I suppose having the time to think about poetry could be considered glamorous.

We were having a major drought. (You would never guess

that we *were* in the middle of an ocean.) When I could face the glare, I saw what looked like "the Continent"—France or Italy. The new green of leaf looked English enough, but the old green of grass was already browned, dulled, blotched. The CIA says the world's climate is changing: Russia will lose its northern wheatfields and turn to us for help. The CIA has the future all doped out. They could be right. Even as I read this, restaurants in Russia, because of the grain shortage, are promoting "meatless Thursdays." Someone in the Kremlin must have figured meatless Fridays would be too tricky.

The whole world is hot and hungry and hurting. There was an earthquake in Italy near the Yugoslav border. You must have read about it. It happened in the evening. The shock waves reached into Germany and Belgium. I heard later that the Red Chinese predict earthquakes hundreds of miles away partly on the basis of animal behavior. Snakes will come up out of the ground in the middle of winter.

I found myself asking myself, when that earthquake happened, causing people to suffer while I sat in my room writing, what good poetry is. Because I don't believe *good* is a word that can be seriously used of anything without making a moral claim about it; if you want to steer clear of moral questions, you'd simply better use another word, maybe a descriptive term like *exhilarating,* or *inspiring* or *serene* or *thoughtful.* But is poetry any good, and if so, which poetry?

What good, when countries everywhere collaborate in the infringing of people's freedoms and opportunities, when the earth opens up in all kinds of devastating ways?

You may come to terms with your own suffering. You may even succeed in rationalizing your fellow's suffering, though I don't know how. (Does each of us, then, suffer in order that his fellow souls may be tested to some unfathomable purpose? I doubt it.) What you probably won't find is a way to feel intellectually good about *his* suffering on the account of somebody *else's* suffering. You'll tell yourself that it is better for people to respond to others' pain with pain than with pleasure, and that's the truth—the awful, ironic, important truth—but it's not a truth you'll feel intellectually *good* about.

You can't feel intellectually good about others' suffering,

but you can feel *bad* about it, and that is where the writer comes in. He does his best to remind us that the world qua world—a collection of entities—exists for us only as we become convinced of the existence of entities outside ourselves, and that in the eyes of many of these entities, we may or may not be seen as fellow entities. The writer is by no means the only person who does this; every man or woman who loves arrives at the same conviction, but the writer tries to do it *for* other people, namely, readers. That is to say, he makes metaphors, or he sets up terms out of which his readers can make metaphors, and this is what morality is all about and what art and poetry are partly about. It comes to this: sympathy is the human dimension of metaphor. What is the Golden Rule, if not a metaphor?

I don't know how—maybe Imant knows how—but music has that same ability to unite. Lenin recognized it, reluctantly. "But I can't listen often to music," he is reported to have complained, thinking about Beethoven; "it affects my nerves, makes me want to say kind stupidities and pat the heads of people who, living in this dirty hell, can create such beauty. But now one must not pat anyone's little head—they would bite off your hand, and one has to beat their little heads, beat mercilessly, although ideally we're against any sort of force against people. Hmm—it's a devilishly difficult task."

The poet's difficult task, then, is to make Lenin's task as difficult as possible. Make him want to pat the heads of people. This is what gives you a justification for your work even when there is an earthquake in Yugoslavia. This is why it is moral, a moral act, to record even the quiet weather of your poem, the singular historical reality of it, the reckless, silent sunlight skidding across the lawn and slamming into the oak tree, angling off and back into your eyes when you look up from your work at your desk. Yet at this very moment a cyclone was making its way into the Baltic States. I wouldn't know it if I didn't *read* it.

I thought how far away Imant was. If I knew how, I could buy a fake passport, fast-talk my way past the guards at Checkpoint Charlie, and hitch a ride with a truck driver. The truck drivers in Russia never have enough to do anyway—trucks that are supposed to wash the street go right on washing the street in the midst of a torrential downpour, simply because they have to report that they've used up their prescribed quota of fuel. So much for a planned economy: who plans the planners? But I could hitch a ride with one of those lonesome, redundant trucks, travel east to the sun, and north, and be in Latvia. . . . I knock, and Imant comes to the door. When he asks my name, I answer: Despair. I am the lonely music. But I am sound that has grown a body, and for every body there is a "Body Song." It goes like this: *Put your mouth on mine and make music with my windpipe: my throat is a thirsty flute only sound can slake. Each heartbeat is a note: draw your art from my body like blood, teach spine and sinew song, and play me all night long.*

CHAPTER 9

The Silenced

I

On a day in summer, I scooped up the morning's mail from the floor by the door. One of the envelopes bore no return address.

There were two letters inside. The first letter said, "A pleasure to be forwarding this letter to you. It seems like the very least I could do for the wonderful people of Latvia. . . . My warmth and best wishes come to you though we have never met. . . . You have Karl to thank." It was signed, "Yes, A Friend."

The second letter was from Imant. "The long time we were to wait is over," he wrote. "The trial took place 31st of May and I got divorced. I did not write to you, because I knew, that my every letter will be stopped. Now that I have a possibility to reach you with my letter I want you to know, that all this time was rather terrible, but more details about all I will tell you when we meet. Now, dearest heart, you should apply for visa on grounds that we want to get married."

The divorce was final. These months of waiting, instead of accustoming me to that idea, had gotten me used to the divorce's *not* being final, and now I had to ease this brand-new fact into my consciousness, find a place for it in my view of the world. Imant was divorced. I turned it around to look at it from every side. Imant was free—of Frederika, anyway.

It was too hot to stay in the waiting room, and anyway, the waiting—I thought—was over. "The long time we were to wait is over." I went out back and turned on the hose; I thought watering the lawn would calm me down.

The omnipresent pigeons were cooing, and bright-eyed blackbirds (they were all Bertie Blackbird, a neighbor's daughter informed me) watched me from the high fence and the gutter over the garage. A white butterfly danced around the stream of water issuing from the hose, but the water pressure was low. It was Great Britain's worst drought in two hundred and fifty years. Despite the exaggerations of U.S. newscasts, the Thames had water in it, but Wales and East Anglia were drying up. Right here, over on the common, we had fires every day. If kids didn't start them, the sun would, by striking a shard of glass.

Suddenly I passionately resented the whole complicated and fragile framework that the Soviet Union had boxed us into: why couldn't we write "I love you" without being censored? Was love really so subversive?

I should have been happy, but I wasn't. Maybe I was "too excited." Maybe it was just the heat that was making me gloomy. I dragged the hose off the patio and aimed at the azaleas. Then the rhododendron, then the lilac and the laurel, and I sprinkled the grass to make the ground spongy. My toes sank into it, and I felt better. Everyone needs a bit of a mudbath now and again.

The dog, Beauregard, was hiding in the cool shade of a bush, resting after a bout of bird-chasing. I read once that one dog year equals seven person years. By that reckoning, our dog was forty-nine. By the time I came back out of the Soviet Union, he could be dead.

I figured that when I came back out from the Soviet Union, five or ten or twenty-five years from now, I would find our dog's grave and lie on it, waiting, and baying. My tongue would swell and blacken. After a while I would die of heartbreak.

I filled his water bowl with clean water—a ladybug flew off from the rim—and turned the faucet off. The hose lay sprawled on the lawn like an overgrown green snake.

Everything (except the dog and the birds and the butterfly)

seemed motionless. Dust lay on the leaves; the leaves were half dead, browned by drought and eaten by insects. The butterfly coasted out of sight. A bee nosed its way in and out of a honeysuckle blossom and then hovered hypnotically in one airy spot. The whole world had fallen asleep, but I was as wide awake as you always are in your worst dreams. My heart was pounding. And here I did a terrible thing: I began to lose my nerve.

II

I thought I would present myself on Monday at the Soviet consulate and they would say, Fine, wonderful. Russians are human too, they would say, even we know what it means to be in love! They had no grounds for keeping me out, and now that the divorce was final, I'd have to make good on all my claims to bravery. I might even have to use my doomsday weapon—offer to immigrate.

I wasn't the only one with apocalyptic forebodings. Throughout the weekend, my mother would come up behind me while I was sitting in the green chair in the living room, or at the table, and under the guise of some question or comment start idly twisting my hair around her finger. This hair-twisting was as expressive as any words. She had been twisting my hair around her finger at moments of crisis ever since I was three. I knew she was remembering beginnings and wondering how anyone ever dreams what they will lead to. I knew she was wondering if she'd ever see me again.

As we set off for London on Monday morning, she looked very pretty, in a pale blue dress, and I felt proud of her. I think that in back of this there was a feeling that we were going to be judged. Was I a desirable alien? Just then, neatly painted in tall white letters along the length of a fence on the outskirts of the city, this message manifested itself to our passing window: FAR AWAY IS CLOSE AT HAND IN IMAGES OF ELSEWHERE.

We pulled into Paddington.

There was talk in the papers that the Russians were going to build an enormous new embassy and consulate in London, with private apartments, and public billboards for propaganda. The current consulate in Kensington Palace Gardens was a fine old house with ornate moldings, but the appointments shouted poverty—of the spirit, and, for that matter, the bank. The staff that greeted visitors was minuscule, but maybe they didn't get many visitors. The rest of the staff were in offices hidden behind drapery on the other side of the hall. Although a job at the consulate in London must be a plum assignment for a Soviet citizen, the doorman qualified for it by being apparently, unable to speak English. He smiled a great deal, but he didn't stand by the door; he stood at the entrance to the main room, and watched. Occasionally, he answered the door; but he came right back and got on with what was either his chief avocation—or his chief vocation. Was it a way to pass the time, or duty? At any Soviet embassy or consulate the top KGB man is just as likely to be the doorman, or the chauffeur. (In Norway, it was a chauffeur.)

We sat there, my mother in pale blue and me in fear and trembling. A sexy but sullen blonde gave me forms to fill out, for an Ordinary Visa. The Ordinary Visa, which is the visa for relatives and friends wanting to visit Soviet citizens in their homes for extended periods, is so seldom granted that the U.S. State Department issues a statement warning U.S. citizens of the odds against their receiving it. It does exist. It was what I needed in order to stay in the Soviet Union long enough to get married. To apply for one, I had to return one filled-in copy of the form to the Soviet consulate and mail the other three to Imant, who was to submit them to the authorities there. But how could I even be sure he'd get them? The doorman ushered us out. He smiled. I was no closer to Imant than when I went in. Images of elsewhere were still far, far away.

Our next stop, after the Soviet consulate, was the American embassy. At first, we thought things were looking up—the people downstairs seemed to think the forms could be sent to Imant via diplomatic pouch. A man upstairs in the Political

Section squelched that. "Impossible," he said. He smiled benignly, as if there was no connection between him and the words that came out of his mouth. These words—they were just givens, part of The Way Things Are. They had been put in his mouth by someone else, by the Bureaucrat of bureaucrats, from whom all mandates flow. He was not himself responsible for them. At this, he smiled sadly.

"But you see what I'm fighting," I said.

"It looks like the Russians are up to their old tricks."

"Well, what can I do?"

"I'm afraid I don't know."

"Can you do anything?"

"I'm afraid not."

"Shall I write to Congress?"

"I suppose so."

"The president?"

"I suppose so."

"Don't the Helsinki Accords mean anything?"

"Not really."

"Should I seek publicity?"

"Perhaps."

"Should I, on the other hand, not seek publicity?"

"Perhaps not."

"Can't the U.S. government do anything?"

"I'm afraid I don't know."

"But you see what I'm fighting," I said.

"It looks like the Russians are up to their old tricks."

"Yes," I said. "Thank you for your help."

And he said, "You're welcome." He really did! In that same bland, unctuous tone of voice that disowned any liability for the words he was uttering in it. But these words—they weren't merely the immovable facts he seemed to think they were; they weren't inorganic at all; they were live. It was as if a swarm of bees poured out from his mouth every time he opened it. Each word stung like hell. The Helsinki Accords were a pack of lies, a deal done on millions of innocent people by the powers-that-be! I thought that as a representative of a signatory country this gentleman should at least feel some compunction to lie.

He didn't. At the end of this utterly unenlightening conversation with someone who, if he was not with the CIA, certainly ought to have been, it was gently suggested that carbons of any letters I might write ought to be forwarded to him. Why? I didn't bother to ask.

It was now four or four-thirty in the afternoon. We were in the office of an editor who published a continuing record of censorship in all countries. There were hundreds of magazines stacked in cartons against the walls and, on the walls, photographs of Victor Feinberg and other exiles and dissidents from the Soviet Union and East Europe, Latin America, Africa. The office was several flights up over what appeared to be a deserted downstairs, and with each step we had climbed, our hearts sank. But this is one of England's quirks: in England you can never form an accurate judgment about the inside from the outside. The best restaurants can have the dingiest windows, and here, at the top of this forbidding staircase, we found the only genuinely accessible person we'd met all day. Besides, the office smelled of printer's ink and new paper. Instead of a wide expanse of desk top graced with only a manly ashtray, a carved "folk" figure, and two or three telephones—the kind of desk that lets you know its owner is too important to need it—we were facing a reassuring chaos of clippings, file folders, and, I suppose, production schedules. I felt I was in familiar surroundings—a place I could understand. The sensation we had had, of being on a treadmill, slowed. We were safe in this room. Outside, rush hour was beginning, but the street noises were so muted by the time they drifted up to us that there seemed to be an almost languorous quality to the flow of traffic below.

"If the Soviets would do what they agree to do," the editor said, "I could fold up shop. But the human rights provisions of the Helsinki Accords *don't* mean anything to anybody—except of course to the people to whom they are denied."

"Then why did the U.S. sign it?"

"To sell tractors." Then he said, "The Russians always act like this."

"They're stopping the mail."

"Oh, the mail," he said. He waved his hand at the desk. "I've got a file here about a mile thick documenting Soviet abuses of the mail."

"I read that England wasn't even going to try to do anything about it."

"It's the same with America. They don't do anything either."

"Then what should *I* do?"

"Well, we can help you with publicity if you decide to go that route. Only it should be a last resort, for your fiancé's sake. Meanwhile I can give you the names of a couple of couples who've gone through something similar." He wrote the names on a piece of paper. Everyone else in the office had gone home, and the scratching of his pencil on the memo pad was magnified by the silence. A chute of dim light fell from the window onto the desk, spotlighting his hand on the pad. We thanked him and got up to leave, but he walked us to the door. "How do you like living here?" he asked my mother. My mother told him. "I used to live in New York," he said; "I was in school there." I said, "Really?" "Yes," he said. "The great day in our lives"—meaning himself and his family— "was the day we found out where to get Hellmann's mayonnaise over here."

Galina (one-half of one of the couples) promised me that Imant wouldn't be expelled from the Union of Composers for wanting to marry an American. I had been afraid that Imant might not be aware of all the risks he was running on my account, but Galina said any Soviet citizen would know the risks. When Soviet authorities want to silence someone, they can have him dismissed from his job or union. Then he can't find work. If he's young enough, he's made eligible for the draft; if he's older, he goes into debt, and that makes him eligible for jail. But Galina said they'd never resort to such tactics simply to stop a marriage. "They are only playing with you, do you understand? You must understand this—it is essential. Threats are nothing. It is a cat-and-mouse game. Everyone gets threats."

It had taken her six years to get out. Her husband was English.

Later, in the reverberating soundlessness of the room in Burghfield Common, I tried to think what it meant: everyone gets threats—it is nothing. What was something? Everyone gets threats. That must mean that their treatment of Imant and me was—normal.

I thought about the dissidents who can *expect* to have their mail tampered with—and worse. As Galina said, Imant and I didn't have anything like the worries of dissidents to contend with. And so bit by bit I regained my nerve. Not because I felt things were any better or safer—far from it—but because of Imant. If he could endure that regime and felt I could, then I could, and would. The question was not, Would I live in the Soviet Union? but, Would they let me?

III

Once you start any publicity, it has to be sufficient for the Soviet authorities to let their citizen go; they won't let you in, and they'll make his life there a misery. I didn't know if I could drum up that much publicity. And if I got publicity and it worked, would Imant now be willing to come to the West? If only we had known enough to discuss these contingencies when I was there, but we had believed the Helsinki Accords.

Once again I fired off letters to everyone I could think of. Sometimes the people I wrote would make promises they never kept. Sometimes my letters went unanswered; I couldn't even be sure they had been received. Sometimes I received conflicting advice. Sometimes I stumbled quite by accident in the right direction. My parents' congressman forwarded a State Department memorandum titled "Marriage to a Soviet Citizen." I learned that the very necessary but elusive Certificate of No Impediment could be obtained only from the U.S. embassy in Moscow or the U.S. consulate in Leningrad. I learned how to get my personal documents translated and certified; it took over a month and cost two hundred dollars, but when it was done, the United States, the Soviet Union, Mexico, and the United Kingdom were all agreed that I had been born and was divorced from my first husband. An Englishwoman married to a Moldavian tried to cheer me by saying the Russians could be fooled: "They don't always know what they're doing," she said. "When my husband applied for an exit visa, he was told to bring a letter of permission from his father. His father wouldn't give it, so my husband asked him to write a letter *refusing* permission. This the old man did, and it quite satisfied the officials. They didn't care what the letter said, they just had to have a letter for their files."

"Imant's father is against us!"

"They all are. They're afraid."

"But Imant said nothing could happen to his parents, because they're pensioners."

"But certain friends will stop speaking to them. They won't want to be seen speaking to them."

I remembered that under Stalin it had been against the law for a Soviet citizen to marry a foreigner. It wasn't against the law to marry a foreigner now—only damn near impossible. At once, the letter Imant's father had sent me the previous fall made sense. Imant's *father* had lived under Hitler's occupation of Riga, and under Stalin's no less brutal forced rule. Suddenly I had a startling vision of an entire nation inhabited by thousands of subdued fathers, all fearing for their sons. *Be meek,* they said; *inherit what you can.*

IV

Because of the drought, there was now a ban on garden hoses. Two of the azaleas died. They hadn't grown big enough to die very noticeably; they simply folded back into the earth, and the dog trampled them underfoot. The birch tree in the backyard turned a not-good brown. But over at the Soviet embassy, roses were in bloom. The British government had had to reprimand the Soviet embassy for watering the roses in defiance of the ban. The soil may have been Soviet, but the H_2O was British. What I wanted to know was, Who snitched on the Soviet embassy? Was there a CIA or MI-6 man hanging out on the Kensington grounds, a bunch of oak leaves and hickory twigs tied to his close-cropped head, spying on the gardener?

About the KGB, Imant had said, "They are just people, and not always very clever people." They were all playing an elaborate game of hide-and-seek, and the prize was a little something extra now and then and a pension at the end, and the penalty was paid by the rest of us. What's at stake isn't "just" nuclear warheads and human rights: it's money too, and no one's ever going to reduce the espionage network in any of our countries until someone figures out how to disentangle it from the economy. Think of the jobs that would be lost, the bureaucratic kingdoms depleted, and budgets cut! Every civil service perceives that its first duty is to the departmental budget. If you don't spend what you've wrested for this fiscal year, you won't get as much next year, and a step backward is a step down. Each budget has to keep pace with all the other budgets, and if this means buying more arms or training more spies, so be it. A military installation in Virginia, during the Vietnam War, had a contract to buy empty boxes; pilots in training were to drop these boxes from airplanes, learning how to hit targets. The department, not having used up the greenbacks allotted to it, ordered boxes made of *oak*. When these boxes made of oak were dropped from the skies, they did what boxes made of plywood would have done. They smashed to smithereens.

Our rhododendron was blooming, sort of. It was almost the time of year when I had last been in Riga. On certain days, the weather seemed so like what I had known with Imant that the ache in my heart was physical. I watched a small gray and olive bird scratch for worms, and I almost started to cry. Not, I admit, because I felt sorry for the bird or for the worm it eventually caught. What I found hard to handle was that the bird was *here* while Imant was *there*. Imant's absence weighted the world with such reality that I could hardly bear it. The more the little bird's beauty filled the world, the emptier my world became.

I made myself a gin and tonic and returned to the back stoop. Beauregard was playing with his pink elephant. He also owned a blue elephant, a gray rat, a yellow hammer, and an orange man with a black derby. Each of these toys originally possessed a squeaker, which Beauregard destroyed with about seven good squeaks. Now he squeezed and squeezed, doggedly, but the toys wouldn't squeak anymore. He didn't understand he'd punctured the toys with his teeth, and he looked up with a baffled and hurt expression. Nevertheless, the broken toys were his, and he protected them fiercely. If you looked at the backyard from the upstairs window, we seemed to be growing some colorful variety of plastic flower.

There was an oak tree here in the backyard too—an immense oak tree, much larger than the one I watched from the window of my waiting room, with a top that seemed to spread over half the sky. Behind the oak there was a factory.

A flock of silver gray doves flew over the factory in formation, like a fleet of miniature B-57's. Autumn was coming, even if it still felt like summer. And maybe, I thought, I would soon be in Latvia with Imant after all: I knew that Imant had gotten the three copies of the Ordinary Visa application, but even if all went well, it could be months before the Soviets replied to my application. Since Imant was now divorced, I'd decided to apply for a Tourist Visa. With a Tourist Visa I would be limited to a few days, we couldn't get married, but it would be better than nothing. I had called American Express. They would schedule my itinerary with Intourist to give me time in Leningrad, where I could obtain the Certificate of No Impediment, and from there I'd go to Riga for five days.

When Imant telephoned in response to the cable in which I told him what I planned to do, he was so excited he could hardly talk. "Yes, yes," he said, "when I got this news it was simply marvelous! I will find you at the airport. Kelly, you must bring all your documents. I have found people here who will help us."

All at once the world was right side up again. People who will help!

American Express had said I would have my visa on a Friday, but when Friday came, they said the Soviet consulate had told them to pick it up on Monday. Immediately, I began to worry, but the man at American Express said it had *never* happened—he swore to the *never*—that a visa they'd actually been told to pick up was denied. I knew from the tracers that Imant had been getting all my letters recently. And he had found people who would help!

So I bought a bright red Shetland wool crew-neck sweater for Imant. Trying to plan for every contingency, I even managed to buy a map of Riga, though it didn't show any of the streets my friends lived on. The only Soviet maps made available to foreigners by the Soviets are deliberately sketchy; you are not supposed to want to go anywhere except museums. Maybe I could fill mine out while I was there, and then other visitors could find their way around without having to reveal every move to their Intourist guides.

Then, on Monday, American Express said the consulate had told their messenger that the visa still wasn't ready; come back on Tuesday. Was anything wrong? No, the Soviet consulate was just short of staff, like everybody else during the summer.

But of course something was wrong. How could something not be wrong? Something had been wrong for over a year, issuing threats, postponing the divorce, hassling Imant, stopping the mail. Something was wrong, and that something was the KGB.

Tuesday morning, I was trying to read a magazine, trying, that is, to fool myself into thinking I was reading a magazine and not simply gazing at a lot of meaningless print. I was to call American Express at three, but the telephone rang at eleven-thirty, and I had the receiver off the hook before the double brr-ng had run its course.

I was quite calm when he told me—calm with that formality that comes to your aid at the point of dead reckoning. Just before the blindfold is lowered over your eyes, you blow smoke in the commander's face. Just before the order to fire is given, you go numb, and you are "dead" even before they shoot you.

The trouble was that the minute I hung up I came back to life—or to the real dying. I couldn't breathe; it was as if I had a bullet hole in my heart and all the air had whooshed out.

The visa had been lying on the counter—and then they'd snatched it back.

All I could think was that I would never see Imant again. He couldn't write to me; now I couldn't visit him. If there was anything to be done for us, it had to be done right away. I called the Soviet consulate and set up an appointment for the following day with one Mr. Pribanov, the man apparently in charge of visas.

In the morning, both of my parents and I caught a train into London. FAR AWAY IS CLOSE AT HAND IN IMAGES OF ELSEWHERE. I couldn't look at it now without feeling bitter.

Pribanov was a nasty-looking functionary of medium height with a Teen Angel hairdo and an uncontrollable smirk. I should have thought he wouldn't have got his job unless he could bring that smirk into line, like an upstart subordinate, but it seemed to be a kind of tic, true colors outing. He ushered us to a lounge in the lobby. Our friend the doorman smiled at us, profusely and omnipresently. The blonde bombshell, on the other hand, as before, scowled. My mother's theory was that the bombshell was married to the doorman, and that's why one smiled and the other scowled. It may even have been why Pribanov smirked.

This lobby, or discussion area, was at the back end of the hall in between the main room and the curtained-off private part of the house. My father and I sat on the couch; my mother and Pribanov were in chairs. Slightly behind us, there was an enormous old-fashioned radio, the kind you are supposed to listen to "The Lone Ranger" on. It was similar to the radios in Russian hotels. I don't know if there was a microphone in it, but why not? The history of Eastern Europe since World War II indicates that the Soviet Union, like nature, abhors a vacuum.

Pribanov insisted that he didn't know why the Tourist Visa was denied; he suggested that possibly a Tourist Visa couldn't be issued while an application for an Ordinary Visa was pending. But none of their brochures mentioned any such regulation, and if that was the case, why had the Tourist Visa been drawn up at all? Surely the Soviet officials who drew up visas were familiar with Soviet regulations regarding visas? He smirked.

There was no way I could stay silent in the face of that smirk.

Pribanov left us for a moment, and at once we began to talk among ourselves, until my mother reminded us of the radio; then in a terrific non sequitur my father began to rave about the molding along the ceiling. When they gave this up for the new complex, would they bring in their own architects? Architecture, as Imant had pointed out in disgust, is one of the least inspired themes in Soviet history; the beautiful buildings in Russia are nearly all copies of developments in the West or the farther East. I wondered if Pribanov ever looked at the molding.

When Pribanov returned, he merely gave us the same spiel as before. He had nothing to do with anything: the visa—"the weeza"—was denied in accordance with instructions from the Ministry of Foreign Affairs in Moscow. I asked for the name of the minister of foreign affairs. "But you cannot write to him," he said, sneering at me.

"Why not?"

Smirk.

I said hotly, "You don't leave me any choice. I'll have to go to the newspapers, so you'd better think out what you want to say before you say it. I'll quote you."

Smirk.

My mother punched me on the arm, but I couldn't help myself. I asked him to call Latvia to find out what was happening with my other application, the one for an Ordinary Visa, but of course he refused. At last I announced I wanted to file an application to immigrate. "Then," he said, with a relief he didn't trouble to disguise, "you want to see Mr. Nepesov."

Indeed. We had wanted to see Mr. Nepesov weeks ago, but he had been out. He was out now. He seemed to be very seldom in.

We said we would wait.

We had our various ways of doing this. My father more or less vacated his body. He had been known to do this while driving. If you were in a car with him and found that it was decelerating when it should have been accelerating, it was because he was working on the slow movement of a string quartet. Since here he was only sitting, not driving, his body stayed behind in this unpleasant place, but *he* traveled back to better times, probably to his violin lessons with Hugo Kortschak in New York in 1930.

We all knew when Nepesov entered. He immediately went into a huddle in the hallway with Pribanov—and the doorman. (No doubt they needed a worker's point of view.) Pribanov left the group for a moment to pull out my visa application—from where we sat, I could see my photograph stapled to the form—and then the discussion—or briefing—resumed.

Nepesov detached himself from the group and came forward. He was dark, with shiny, black, delicately slanted eyes and a middling build. He wore an Ivy League vest; in fact, he looked like a college man from the fifties with just an aura of something unexplainably exotic about him. But the moist eyes were attractive. He seemed—did I dare to believe it?—kind. Or almost kind.

Pribanov was behind him, at his elbow, and at first Nepesov merely repeated what Pribanov had said. My anger had been defused by the sympathy in Nepesov's eyes, but at this inane parroting of what could only be a lie—that you couldn't apply for a second kind of visa while the first was still under consideration—I began to reseethe. If this was the case, shouldn't someone at the Soviet consulate be aware of the fact? Why did they all keep saying "perhaps," if it *was* the case? "Well, I think it may be a new regulation," Nepesov said.

"How new?"

"Very new."

Pribanov ducked out to resume his conversation with the doorman on the other side of the room.

"Like since yesterday morning?"

But before I could get sidetracked back onto that fruitless path, my mother broke in and told Nepesov the whole story:

how Imant and I only wanted to marry and live in Latvia, how we planned to work on an opera, and what a shame it would be if my writing—which of course would have to tell it like it was—if my writing couldn't reflect Soviet adherence to the Helsinki Accords. A pragmatic glint came into Nepesov's moist almond-shaped eyes, but he insisted that the refusal of one kind of visa didn't at all mean I wouldn't get the other kind.

I pointed out for him that the other kind was issued so rarely that the U.S. State Department put out a printed memorandum cautioning applicants not to get their hopes up. Nepesov shrugged, as if he couldn't possibly account for the vagaries of the U.S. State Department. "Half the time," I said, "the Soviet Union doesn't even *acknowledge* applications."

Nepesov shrugged again; he wasn't responsible for the Soviet Union, either. But he did volunteer to give me the information on how to apply to immigrate. This information consisted of a half sheet of paper naming the required documents. I said I wanted to apply right away, but Nepesov wouldn't have that. He laughed softly: "It is premature. Wait until you have heard about the visa."

"But that could take months. And I told you, they may never reply."

"Of course they will reply. If they say no, then you can ask to immigrate. But I hope they will say yes." He really did look as though he hoped that. "I have twenty-five such applications on my desk right now," he said.

I was excited, waving my hands as I talked, and I realized only belatedly that I was holding the paper about immigration. I read it. "But this says"—if I wasn't actually wailing, I was wailing inwardly—"that I have to have a letter from Imant!"

"That is right. He must say he will support you and give the address where you will live."

"But Imant can't get a letter to me! The Soviet Union has stopped all his mail."

"But this is not possible." He laughed again, the gentle laugh a doctor uses to humor a hysterical patient.

"It *is* possible. They have done it."

"No, no," he said. "It is against the law."

There was a hush. It was my moment. "I *know*," I said.

The hush lasted. Then, more laughter, oddly damped. Pribanov in the distance, smirking.

The American Express agent had told us that when the messenger went to pick up my visa on Tuesday morning—and it was lying on the top of the counter, ready to be signed—a violent argument had ensued between two men. Then one of the men came forward to tell the messenger that no visa would be issued. When we had asked Pribanov about this, wondering why there should be any argument, he'd dragged himself dramatically over to the counter, asking the girl behind it if there'd been such an argument, mouthed the word "vi-o-lent," exaggerating syllables as if this were a silent movie, and then had slunk wearily back, as if his point was proved. The point being, I suppose, that American Express messengers are given to fabricating wild stories about arguments in Soviet consulates. Now he was caught up in the same Grade B flick, watching us out of the corner of his eye less like a KGB man than a Chicago dick.

Nepesov went on: "This letter can come to me. But tell him to send it to you. Then you will see that the Soviet Union does not stop the mail."

"The Soviet Union not only stops the mail, they are trying to stop us," I said. "When I was in Riga, the Latvian Central Committee called my fiancé's union twice, warning him to quit seeing me."

"Oh," he said, "this cannot happen."

"Don't tell me it can't happen. It *did* happen. I was there when it happened."

Instead of responding directly to my statement, he said, "Then have the letter sent to me."

But how would I ever prove that he'd got it?

"All Imant and I want to do is get married," I said, feeling hopeless again, all my anger momentarily gone.

"Of course, you have every right to get married. This is in the Helsinki Accords."

"Then why have we been threatened? Why is our mail being intercepted? Why was the Tourist Visa denied?"

Finally Nepesov looked genuinely perplexed. "I don't know,"

he said; "perhaps the other visa will come though. You must trust—"

"Trust," I said. "I don't trust the Soviet Union *in anything.*"

And the minute I said that, I was ready to hang myself. It was true; it wouldn't hurt the Soviet consulate to hear somebody say it; but it might hurt Imant. And it killed the conversation.

V

Down the street from the consulate, I found a post office, where, wasting no time, I sent a detailed cable to Imant, asking him in turn to cable Nepesov. I explained that he was to say he intended to marry me and could support me, and I told him to give the address where we would be living. I told him to follow this up with a registered letter to Nepesov and also with a registered letter to me, saying the same things in all three communications. And when he had done all these things, he was to let me know by telephone.

Another short distance down the same street, my parents and I stopped at an Italian restaurant, but I couldn't eat much. My parents were cheerful—they said they felt encouraged by Nepesov's niceness—but I wondered if the Latvian Central Committee or the Ministry of Foreign Affairs in Moscow would be moved by niceness.

I drank a glass of wine. My parents were smiling at each other over the lasagna. I was positively amazed at their bright faces and forward-looking mood.

I thought of what could account for their optimism, a source for optimism which couples, happy or not, take for granted: they could touch each other. I was thinking of the most elementary connections—a hand on your arm or back. A hug. Feeling a kid's forehead for fever. This must be one of the reasons people keep pets. It may even be why pets keep people.

Letter-writing had become my chief activity. I wrote to Nepesov, confirming our conversation. I thanked him for his help, said I was glad he had pointed out that the Helsinki Accords specified the right of people like Imant and me to marry, and expressed my hope that I would be allowed to visit Imant soon, as, according to the Helsinki Accords, I had the right to. I sent him a Xerox of the letter so he could forward it to Moscow.

The congresswoman had forwarded to me a letter she had received from an official in the State Department. The State Department said that Imant and I had every right to get married and that the State Department would support me in our efforts to do this. It also suggested that I write to the U.S. embassy in Moscow.

I couldn't mail a letter to the U.S. embassy in Moscow because the Soviet censors would intercept it, just as they intercepted my mail to Imant whenever they felt like it. But this letter, I thought, should be eligible for the diplomatic pouch: since it was addressed to an embassy, it was mailable by an embassy. This time the embassy cooperated. In fact, the embassy seemed to have done an about-face. We were put in touch with the first helpful official we encountered at the upper echelons of the embassy, the man we were to be in touch with from here on out. He couldn't have been nicer, though he admitted candidly that the letter the congresswoman had elicited from the State Department helped. The signature on that letter, he indicated, was one to which attention had to be paid. It belonged to Senator Mondale, then in the process of becoming vice-president.

What do you know! I hadn't had the slightest notion that the signature on the letter was significant. I didn't find out about it until my mother returned home from another trip to London, on Friday. She went to meet the man at the U.S. embassy. She wanted to do some shopping anyway, and I stayed home in case the call from Imant came. He might have gotten the cable by now.

I had stayed "home" almost all of the past year, fall, winter, spring, summer. The oak tree out back was ripening; blue tits and coal tits and wagtails, stopping over, fluttered in its crown and knocked acorns to the grass below.

And there *was* grass, because the drought had ended. Suddenly it seemed to rain every day, softening the ground. The crate-board table, hammered together for makeshift furniture when my parents first moved into the house, stood neglected on the stoop, supporting puddles instead of plates. I stood at the kitchen door, listening to the slap of rain against leaf. The hybrid hawthorn turned yellow, bearing clumps of red berries. In the mornings, mist hung in the air like a curtain, and each day, dark came earlier. Beauregard begged me to sit in the yard with him, but it wasn't gin-and-tonic weather anymore, wasn't sitting-in-the-yard-while-the-dog-barks-at-the-birds weather. I stayed "home," and indoors.

The oak tree outside my window was doing the same things it had done the previous fall, changing colors and losing its leaves. It gave me a *déjà vu* sensation: I had been here before. I wished it would do something different—grow apples, or dance. But the only difference this time round was that now I knew the word for *oak* in Latvian. The owl lights on the *ozols*.

Words! Had I, in my determination not to be silenced, said too much at the Soviet consulate? You are supposed at least to pretend to trust the Soviet Union. If *you* pretend, *they* may even pretend to abide by a law or two.

I called American Express and Cook's. The State Department memo about marriage had said that if the visa was denied, the applicant should try for it repeatedly, but both American Express and Cook's refused to file an application for me. They said the denial of the visa meant that I was on a blacklist in Moscow and that any application I might make from any tourist agency anywhere in the world would be denied. They didn't want to fool with me. The State Department memo didn't say what to do in this situation.

But now at last I could begin to feel that my country was on my side: the man at the embassy in London promised that the embassy in Moscow would "get tough" with the Russians. He thought it was entirely possible that the Russians would change their minds as soon as the U.S. broached the matter. He thought I might be married and in Latvia any day now.

My mother looked so convinced that as she recited everything she'd learned I began to toy with the idea that maybe things would be even better as a result of this confusion. Maybe the Soviets, having denied the Tourist Visa, would reverse their decision by granting the Ordinary Visa. Three months with Imant! October, November, December. We would put up a Christmas tree, decorating it with paper chains. We'd have to stamp the snow from our boots when we brought the tree in, and we'd have to keep an eye on the cat to see she didn't pull down the silver ball from the lowest-lying branch. (The cat's name is Princess. *Princese*, in Latvian.) Imant would wear the red sweater I'd bought him and be the brightest spot in the room, not to mention my life.

The next day, the world looked dark again. From the window of my waiting room I watched beads of water clinging to the branches of the familiar oak. I wanted to work, but I couldn't. It wasn't simple lethargy; it was as if an active force had pinned me to the bed and canceled the promise of effectiveness of any action I might wish to take, and the name of this force was . . . I don't know. Fear—but not as in fear of danger. And not fear as in phobia. It was fear of powerlessness. Fear that any action one might take was pointless, because the consequences of it had already been determined, or would be determined, by an altogether different agency. Tyranny's greatest weapon is the paralysis of will which sheer fact induces. It is not merely the odds that are stacked against you; *history* is stacked against you, and the future is being dealt from a marked deck.

I let an entire day go by, lying on the bed, looking out at that oak which, by now, I knew better than my own face. Somewhere I read that there are six million leaves on a standard tree. I don't know what makes a tree standard, unless it's six million leaves, but this oak looked pretty standard to me. I imagined, for "fun," that the six million were people: each leaf was a soul, a living soul. No matter what I did or didn't do, every last one of those leaves was going to turn red and yellow, drop to the ground, dry and die. It was like having the Third Reich for a front yard. If a tree falls in a police state, does anybody admit to hearing it?

If nations can be characterized in psychological terms like

people—and they seem to me to be far less complex than people, policy being less subtle than personality—Soviet Russia is paranoid. The symptoms include xenophobia, the irrational conviction of persecution, and megalomania, but the root cause is a failure of imagination. It is a giving up on the task of making metaphors; it is sacrificing variety of invention to consistency of plot. If you know yourself to be yourself by being defined in relation to others, then a paranoid nation, unable to imagine others, is only half-sure of its own existence and will seek to establish it by force.

The reason this stupidity succeeds—and it does*—is that the machinery of Soviet Russia is *massively* stupid; like true paranoia, it coheres, and coherence—consistency of plot— always gives the illusion of intelligence, as any writer knows. But the needed thing, the majestic thing, is metaphor—the true sign of genius, as Aristotle said—and that is why poetry has had so much to say. All peace talks begin with poetry.

Is love subversive? Yes. What it subverts is silence, and if a state is built on silencing the people, then the state is smart to watch out for love. People who love each other talk to each other; their whole lives become like words, telling their love. The perfect Person says his perfect Word that contains all sentences, word without end. The rest of us babble in our diverse languages, "scattered abroad upon the face of the whole earth," but if we can't climb into heaven, we have not been left without another way of building a tower. Words are the bricks, and the mortar that binds them is metaphor. A tower like this at the very least gets you over the Berlin Wall, *metaphorically*.

Love is metaphor. It links our lives, builds a city, a whole kingdom on earth out of our separate words. We are *translated* into the City of God.

VI

I kept half-waking—at one, two, three in the morning. It was Monday night, or Tuesday morning. I fell asleep again, but I

---

*Or so it seemed, when I was in England trying to get back into Latvia.

woke up a second *before* the telephone rang at five. It wasn't
Imant. It was Karl.

They had returned together to the farmhouse the previous
evening, discovered my cable, and Karl, having to come back
to Riga anyway, had placed the call to me. With the Oxford
accent and foreign-language textbook formality that contrasted so engagingly with his natural manner, he apologized
for calling so late—or so early, as it was in Riga.

Before he asked any questions, he said, "Everything has
been done according to your cable." Did this mean that Imant
had sent a cable and a registered letter to Nepesov? Yes. Had he
sent a registered letter to me? Yes. (But, Mr. Nepesov, *nota
bene*: the Soviet Union intercepted it.)

"What happened?" Karl asked.

I tried to explain, but I thought I'd better not say too much
on the telephone. In any case I couldn't tell him *why* the visa
was denied, because nobody at the Soviet consulate could, or
would, tell me the official reason. I did tell Karl that the U.S.
government was protesting the denial of the Tourist Visa.

"Kelly," he said, "there has been no change of plans here."

"None?"

"None," he said. "Everything is just as it was."

I could breathe again. "Karl, tell Imant I love him!"

And he said, again with that touching correctness, "Yes, I
will. Thank you very much."

One week later, Imant himself telephoned. I was at my Latvian
lesson. In the middle of the lesson, pondering Latvian verbs, I
knew the telephone was ringing back in Burghfield Common.
I don't know how I knew it. I was never one to put much stock
in extrasensory stuff, psychical stuff. If there were spooks
about, it seemed to me they were more than likely government
funded.

When I got home, my mother told me about Imant's call.
She said he had sounded excited and pleased—he had found a
way we could be married in ten days in Riga.

Now to do this, he had worked a minor miracle; marriage
to a foreigner in the USSR normally requires a minimum of

thirty days. This must have been what he'd meant by "people who will help." I don't know whether they were Latvians or Russians, but it was a relief to know that they existed: officials inside the Soviet Union "who will help." Only, what good could they do us if I couldn't get inside too? The KGB handles visas, and *they* were not being helpful.

"Tell Kelly to get a Tourist Visa," Imant kept saying, and my mother had to try to explain again what I had tried to explain to Karl, that the Soviet authorities refused to give me a Tourist Visa. It was not an easy thing to explain because there was no legitimate explanation. I had never been convicted of any criminal activity, I was not in debt, I had never been a source of what the Soviet Union humorlessly calls "anti-Soviet propaganda," I was not acting under false pretenses. What my mother had to tell Imant, without actually saying it, was that the Soviet authorities refused to give me a Tourist Visa because I wanted to marry him. When it sank in, there was a pause. Then Imant said, "I am very discouraged." She told him about the U.S. embassy in Moscow but—she told me—he seemed uncomfortable discussing that by telephone. "We will keep doing everything possible," she said, underscoring *everything*, and he asked her to give me his love, but when I heard this report of their conversation, it was his use of the word *discouraged* that stuck in my heart. What were they doing to Imant? To our future? Would there ever be a Christmas in Latvia after all? Or an Easter? Or a May Day or Fourth of July? I missed Imant more than I could ever have said to anyone; and in any case the only people around to say it to were my parents.

It just isn't good form to tell your parents how much you miss your lover. It was frustrating in every way. On one level, there was the song sequence we wanted to finish and couldn't, the opera we wanted to write and couldn't. On another level, there were the nights. (It is the very ordinariness of what Imant and I wanted to do—"Let's do it in the middle of the road, yeah yeah yeah"—that reveals, if not the brutality of the totalitarian Soviet regime, the *extent* of the brutality.)

CHAPTER 10

Justice

Our man in London rang: the Ministry of Foreign Affairs in Moscow had told the American officials there that they would not grant me a Tourist Visa.

They said I could enter only on a private visitor's Ordinary Visa. And then they said my fiancé had not supported my application for such a visa.

What kind of support was required?

A formal letter of invitation.

Now, the list of instructions which the Soviets issue concerning application for private visits nowhere mentions that such a letter is required. Nor had anyone, on my visits to the Soviet consulate in London, said anything about this requirement.

And naturally, this letter of invitation was not one that Imant could submit to the authorities in Latvia. He had to send it to me, and then I was to submit it to the Soviet consulate in London. The trick here, as everybody knew perfectly well, was that the Soviets still weren't letting any of Imant's mail out.

But there was *something* to show, if it could be brought to light: the cable and registered letter Imant had sent to Nepesov stating his intent to marry me. I was sure Soviet censors wouldn't intercept mail directed to a *Soviet* consulate. They would figure there was no point in it.

So the thing to do was to get Nepesov to own up to the cable and letter. If I could prove that Imant had notified Soviet authorities that he wanted to marry me, they couldn't very well say he didn't support my application for a visa.

I telephoned Nepesov.

After four different people had passed the call along, someone who said he was Nepesov answered. But his voice was higher, his accent thicker, than—

"The first I heard that you came to see me," he said, "is when I get this letter from you." Meaning the letter I had carefully sent, following my meeting with him, detailing, for the record, our conversation.

What? My mother, my father, and I had all been introduced to a "Mr. Nepesov," who, according to Pribanov, "handles immigration," while he—Pribanov—dealt only with visas. Not only that, but the Nepesov we had met said he had "twenty-five applications for immigration on my desk right now."

"That was not me," this Nepesov said.

"Isn't this rather strange?" I asked, with admirable restraint.

"Oh no, is an understandable misunderstanding."

Well, I suppose it might have been, had one of us been introduced to the gentleman under confusing circumstances, but three of us were introduced to him, and under the most precise circumstances of asking for, waiting for, and shaking hands with "Mr. Nepesov," who "handles immigration." It was possible that there were *two* Mr. Nepesovs at the Soviet consulate (but if so, they hadn't met each other).

There was *no* misunderstanding, but I was doing my best not to sound angry. "Then why were we told that we were talking with Mr. Nepesov?" I asked.

"Oh, I cannot say. I knew nothing—" But he didn't deny we'd been told it was Nepesov.

"Well then," I asked, "who *was* he?"

But Nepesov—this Nepesov—never answered that question. I then told him that I wanted to proceed with an application for immigration to the Soviet Union. "You already have the cable and the registered letter from my fiancé," I said, six or seven times, so that he had plenty of opportunity to deny receipt. He never did. But like the Nepesov we had been introduced to at the consulate, he refused to entertain an application for immigration, saying that "the other application must be answered or canceled before a new application can be made."

He admitted that this was a recently inaugurated regulation; again, I wondered if they'd adopted it especially for me. Like the letter of invitation for a private visit, or like the regulation that said I couldn't apply for a Tourist Visa while my application for a private visit was pending, this regulation was mentioned on none of the papers I had ever received from them or from anyone else, and I would bet that it had originally sprung spontaneously from the fertile brow of Mr. Pribanov (beneath the greasy kid stuff that preserved comb tracks in a plaster cast). The Soviets could produce these *ad hoc* "regulations" from now until doomsday, and I had no recourse against them.

I handed the telephone to my mother. I have never come to terms with the instrument where "official" calls are concerned. It's too impersonal for telling the whole story, too intimate for receiving rejections, and too quick to answer—the answers come before you're ready to respond to them. My mother, on the other hand, found the telephone intimate enough for telling the whole story, impersonal enough for receiving rejections, and quick enough with answers—nothing annoyed her more than having to sit around with her responses, waiting to deliver them when she'd had them ready for a week. She asked him outright: Did he have the cable and letter? He hedged; he said he'd have to check if they were on file. But he knew very well what was on file; he had said so at the beginning of the conversation. He informed my mother emphatically that, although he was not the man we'd met, he was "thoroughly familiar with *all* the details of your daughter's case."

He had grown impatient, and there was, in his impatience, a timbre to his tone that echoed . . . someone. But who? Later, drinking hot chocolate at the dining room table, my mother, a professional musician, played back that voice in her head. "I've got it," she said, slapping the table with the heel of her right hand. The mustard jar jumped. She laughed. "This Nepesov sounded remarkably like Pribanov." Then she fell thoughtful. "Assuming, of course, that Pribanov was Pribanov."

I called our man at the U.S. embassy in London back. "I'm afraid they've got Imant and me boxed in," I said, "and there's no way out."

"We're going to try to find a way out," he promised.

Nevertheless, I didn't see how, or where. How could I find a way "out" when I had no way of proving we were boxed "in"? I was living in a Kafkaesque world where the Soviets decided what was and what *wasn't*. And what was today, could vanish tomorrow, disinherited, gone without a trace. The Soviet authorities could pretend that Imant never sent any letters; they could lie about the application he had filed; they could say no cable was sent to Nepesov; they could say nothing had ever been real. Even Nepesov was not Nepesov. Pretty soon they'd be claiming Imant was a figment of my imagination. But if that was so, he was a most unhappy figment, who had very realistically called Russia "the biggest prison in the world."

He was locked in, and they were locking me out.

II

It was unfair.

Freud says women's chronic complaint about the world stems from their anatomical grievance—that life is "unfair" and has shortchanged them. That grievance stunts their moral development. If he had done his thinking about this subject a little later in life, he would have viewed it in a different light. Only a well-off pre-war white male might fail to see that the world is unfair to men *and* women. It is the stunted moral development of people in power that gives rise to women's grievance.

I used to ask myself what "fair" would be, in terms of a human society. I had in mind a kind of abstraction—justice—which would be instantly recognizable to everyone who experienced it, or the lack of it. (For it is possible to conceive of a just world in which the inhabitants, not appreciating the size of the pie or the number of partakers, merely *fancy* they are getting less than their share.) Lawyers, political theorists, and economists are wont to talk about distributive justice and retributive justice, and whether what one owns is rightfully his own, but setting up a world which is "just" according to any of these definitions means behaving in our present world in ways which will violate another definition of justice. For example, if I want to distribute the world's goods equally, I will have to take some from those who have more in order to give to those who have less, and if that "more" was rightfully earned, or perhaps if it was legally inherited, then according to an entitlement theory of justice, I am stealing. Or if I limit the amount that can be earned, then I must make all jobs equal, either before or after taxes; but somebody is bound to argue here that some jobs deserve to be higher paid than others, because they are more dangerous, more difficult, less steady, or more worthwhile. Even if you steer by that clever-seeming formulation—"From each according to his abilities, to each according to his needs"—you run into trouble. Who will judge my abilities? Who will judge my needs?

The kind of justice, or fairness, I hankered after was one which would satisfy all the members of the state, whether they were communists or capitalists or what have you. Now, this was only a question I thought about for the fun of thinking about it. I didn't expect to be leading any revolutions or counterrevolutions, so if it was a slightly silly question, the way I tackled it, at least my conclusions weren't going to destroy millions of lives.

Besides, the slightly silly question has a point, as in the Hasidic story about the Helmites who bought a barrel of justice.

Helm is in Poland, near Lublin, but "the wise men of Helm" live in legend, on the border between invention and truth. The living there is just as hard as anywhere, and one day it dawns on "the wise men of Helm" that each day the rich in their town get richer, and the poor . . . certainly not richer. There is no

justice anywhere in Helm. Well, think they, if there is no justice here, we will look for it elsewhere. They will go out into
the world, buy a barrelful, and bring it back.

A contingent sets off for Warsaw, and there they meet a man
who offers to sell them the Vistula Bridge. "No, thanks," they
say, "that's not what we came for."

So the man says, "A synagogue maybe?"

But they answer, "A synagogue we've got already."

"What, then?"

"Would you happen to have a barrel of justice?"

"A barrel of justice! Well," says the merchant, "why didn't
you say so in the first place?" And he gives them a barrel and
takes their money.

The Helmites load the barrel—it seems that justice is a very
weighty commodity—onto their wagon and return to Helm.
When they get there, the whole town turns out—mayor, rabbi,
beadle, the lot. And they pry the lid off the barrel, and what's
inside if not a catch of rotten fish?

"Look," the mayor cries, "this justice stinks!"

For my part, I'm not an unreconstructed capitalist—I don't
see how anyone could be who has no vested interests, and I
have lamentably few interests to vest—but Marxist communism has always struck me as the most naïve of political theories. I use the word *naïve* on purpose. What Marx did, it seems
to me, was to mistake his mind for the world—a classically
paranoid solipsism. Dialectic is an accurate description of one
way the *mind* works (analysis being another, and metaphor at
the root of both), but to say history proceeds by dialectic is to
confuse the observer with the thing observed. Look around,
or back.

But of course Marxism *would* appeal to Russia. Nations may
or may not have characteristic psychological types, but they do
seem to be subject to characteristic fallacies, and if the characteristic American fallacy, at least up until the present era of dis-
illusionment, has been a relentless optimism, the unexamined
belief that good ever triumphs over evil, as if the crucifixion
were, after all, only a temporary discomfort, like heartburn—
an optimism so staunch that we have had to produce a whole

tradition of prophets of pessimism, including, for example, Melville and Twain, to inveigh against it—then the peculiarly Russian mistake, czarist or Soviet, has always been solipsism, that egoistic reduction of the world to self. Russia has always been *philosophically* unresponsive to the complexities of real life, latching eagerly onto any scheme that is both comprehensive and simplistic: it's the very opposite of the pragmatic temperament.

The joke says: Under capitalism, man exploits man, but under communism, it's the other way around.

Theories of justice that assume that there is not enough to go around—enough of whatever—are lately out of fashion. These theories all say that whatever *is* available should go to those who most deserve it; merit can be determined on any number of bases.

Raw capitalists and Party bosses in fact operate according to some such theory, but even they generally have to pay lip service to the modern idea that everyone should and can get a "fair" share—whether it's food, job opportunities, energy supplies, living room, opportunities for education, or legal counsel and the protection of the law. Capitalists and Communists alike formally subscribe to a theory of justice that assumes that there *is* enough—enough of whatever—to go around.

Thus, I have a dispute with so-and-so, but the difference between us is assumed to center on how a *sufficient* such-and-such will be distributed between us. We hoof it to the nearest arbitrator, and if he's very wise or very lucky, he'll arrive at a decision that seems to both of us just. In practice, he's more likely to disappoint one or the other of us, but we agree to accept the case-by-case reality because we know that we are only one case among many and that the ideal of justice is meant to be realized in the interests of the majority.*

But suppose that there is *not* enough of Whatever to make

---

* Even the Soviet Union subscribes to some such ideal of justice, though their system makes it next to impossible for the majority to be served, since the Soviet individual has no real right of appeal *to* the majority against the abuse of power by the bureaucratic elite.

an equitable distribution of it, even if the means and the will for an equitable distribution exist. The time for such a supposition has come: if the population goes on exploding, or if our demands go on rising, we may indeed run out of sufficient Whatever before long. And perhaps it has always been, sadly, the right time for supposing this: all down the ages, people have suffered from an *effective* insufficiency. When the money goes toward a massive arms buildup, fringe benefits for secret agents, and hot rods for Brezhnev, the people reap the rewards in terms of meatless Thursdays. What would Marx say about Soviet Russia?

But Soviet Russia is too much to think about all at once—too much for me, anyway—so let's simplify the situation by limiting it to Siberia. Arctic Siberia. It is easier to think about, all that white waste. One snowflake does it; the rest is a simple exercise in multiplication.

Suppose that you are in Siberia, then. But why? You and a colleague—comrade?—are the sole survivors of a scientific expedition. Even the dogs are dead, or scattered in a final frenzy. The snow is blowing, and the flakes freeze on your face; you feel as though a hundred bits of glass have been embedded in your face. You couldn't weep—the tears have frozen in their ducts.

You are in Siberia, lost, and your colleague is giving you some pretty funny looks. Between you and him, or her, there is food enough for only one to live—enough food to fuel one of you to the nearest camp. If you *share* it, you will both die of starvation.

Right now, the single precious sliver of dried venison is sewn into the lining of your jacket, and why on earth should you give it to him?

If he takes the venison from you, he is a thief, and in *his* eyes, if not mine, if you withhold it from him, you might as well be a thief. In his eyes, you have robbed him of what is "justly"—by virtue of any measure he cares to adduce—his. What *I* think of you or him doesn't enter into this; there are only the two of you, and you are in Siberia, and it is snowing, and one of you is going to die.

There's only one way out of this dilemma. You have to

change one of the two horns. The two horns are labeled "Take," and one of them has to be changed to "Give." By definition, your companion is not about to give the venison to you: if he had the venison, he'd certainly keep it, and in any case, he doesn't have it. But you can choose to give it to him.

This will, of course, strike him as perfectly just (and it saves him the trouble of taking it from you by force). But the exhilarating paradox—which will escape his attention—is that you will think it's just, too—because you were the judge and decreed giving, justice. While there was still more than one avenue of acting open to you—you could resist, run, or eat fast—you acted. You actively elected to be acted upon. You gave up everything of value that you possess, except one thing—your authority.

Since in a world which has not got enough Whatever, someone must always have too little, each of us must—if we want justice for all—*act as if he has too much*; for if we act as if we have too little and take Whatever from someone else, we behave in his eyes unjustly, and if we only keep what we have, he will see it as taking, but if we act as if we have too much and give what we have to someone else, then we behave justly from every point of view.

Of course, if no one has anything at all—no venison—there is a problem, but it is not the problem of justice.

It has to be remembered that in this Siberia, as I've described it, there are only two points of view. *Every* means his and yours, or at most theirs and ours. It all changes the minute a third party is introduced. The logistics are different then. Your "colleague" may try to steal not from you but from the third party, or, stealing from you, will deprive the third party. But this, too, is not the problem of justice. It's the problem of *in*justice.

And again, you may find yourself ready enough to give up all you possess, but not knowing whether to hand it over to this person or that one, when there isn't enough for both. But this is not the problem of justice, and it is also not the problem of injustice. It's the problem of evil, though in an unfamiliar guise.

But we were fooling around with justice, thinking about how to achieve a justice that would seem just to everyone to whom it is meted, and the answer seems to be to create a world in which you, singular or plural, are *one* side, and there is *one other* side, and then you give yourself, singular or collective, up to the other self. It looks like another word for *justice* is *sacrifice*.

This kind of justice is not possible unless there are at least two personalities in the world; and if there are three, it is not possible unless two can act *as* one.

So if there were a God, and, being good, he wanted to be a just God, it would at least make sense for him to create a world and sacrifice himself for it. Abraham asked, "Shall not the Judge of all the earth do right?" Ages have passed, and Sodom and Gomorrah, which went up in smoke, have been blown away like smoke, but that question stays with us, like the earth under our feet. "Shall not the Judge of all the earth do right?" Often enough, the answer seems to be no—unless, like people laboriously deciphering a new and difficult language, we've mistaken "yes" for "no." Presumably, if there is a Judge of all the world, he wants justice for all, for One and the Other: and for him, that could mean, as it meant for you in Siberia, giving and giving up everything that he possesses, the world in the shape of his son. The "contradictions" in his character would be reconciled by voluntary renunciation, and the power to abstain from the use of power would be seen as the greatest power of all, coequal with infinite goodness. The world would be suffused with his sacrifice, and each little corner of it, irrigated by sacrifice, would bloom. There would be grass in the desert, roses in Siberia.

I could imagine how Pribanov would smirk if anyone ever asked him to define justice. My question *was* slightly silly, because whatever answer I arrived at was going to mean to the people in power about as much as if I decided to stand on my head in Trafalgar Square.

Sometimes, even now, I would try to tell myself that maybe the Soviet Union was not really hell-bent on treating people meanly—it only looked that way because the KGB was still fighting the Cold War. What used to be called cultural lag has become bureaucratic lag, and the world is being run by people who are always roughly about ten years behind it. They live on the other side of the looking glass, and to get anywhere, they have to run twice as fast as they can. I could only hope that someone would suddenly catch up with the times. Imant's and my situation would come to the notice of someone in the Kremlin who would instantly lament and condemn the short-sighted actions of his underlings. (Pribanov's head would roll.)

Someone would see that Imant and I were just two people, two nonpolitically active people, who wanted to marry each other and live together. Letting us live together in Latvia would say something attractive, however minor, for the Soviet government. But then, perhaps, someone would reconsider. Someone would lean back in his leather chair, sigh, fit the tips of his ten fingers one on one, take them apart and put them together again, and reconsider. And someone, reconsidering, might figure that Imant and I, by loving each other, *were* making a political statement. Put simply, it was this: our loyalty to each other came before our loyalty to *any* government. It could be that if enough people fall in love with each other, the state will indeed wither. In that case, my question might not be so silly after all—nor the answer to it irrelevant.

III

The U.S. embassy in Moscow came up with a new plan. They cabled my man at the embassy in London that if Imant could stroll casually past the embassy in Moscow at an appointed hour on a certain day, they would have an official stationed outside to meet him. The official would escort Imant past the Soviet militia guards into the embassy; there, they would take the letter of invitation from him.

I don't know how they were going to send the letter of invitation to me, since it would have been personal mail, ineligible for the diplomatic pouch. Maybe they were going to keep it there. They could point out to the Ministry of Foreign Affairs that if Imant was willing to deliver the letter in person, he obviously would have been willing to deliver it by mail—if it had been possible.

It was so simple—and so difficult. Did the KGB know of the plan as soon as the embassy in Moscow cabled it to the embassy in London? Could I get word of the plan to Imant? Would the KGB pick him up before he reached the embassy, and if he made it, would they arrest him afterward?

"We think our communism is fascism," Rudolf had said, his face gone white with shock at his own daring. People say, Yes, but they never had an Enlightenment over there. Or they point out that even in the West the individual has been respected only under special conditions, for brief periods. One woman actually said to me, "Maybe they have their reasons."

Yes, she actually said that and so, unwittingly, reminded me that Hannah Arendt had said that evil is banal. But though it is important to remember this, it is equally important to remember that evil is banal only when you're examining it dispassionately; close in, face to face with it, you see another aspect, its magnitude. It can daze you for life if it lets you live at all. It is a giant made of emptiness, with chasms for eyes and a whirlpool for a mouth, and its breath is death.

Does the giant recognize that the hurt it inflicts on us *is* hurt? I want to say it does, but I can't. The giant is blind and mute, and it doesn't know how it feels to *be*—hurt, or anything. How could it, when it is the absence of being? Even the hooded interrogator who calls the prisoner out for the fortieth time in a single night, shatters the man's kneecap with a blackjack and shouts obscenities in his ear—does he know? He may see that he is causing pain; he may be glad to be causing pain; but I don't think he *knows* what he sees, because he doesn't know what it means. He hasn't imagined what he would feel, sitting there in the prisoner's place.

I wanted to think that "they" were aware of the sadness and

anxiety they caused, that they could feel it themselves; then I could hate them absolutely, without hesitation. But it was clear at every turn that they themselves were locked in that same immense prison they'd constructed. Call it, without too much irony, *rampant* solipsism. If to know is to perceive, to grasp the sense or senses of, then the really scary and—there is the irony—the saving thing is, they *do* know not what they do. Whether I could forgive them was a separate question.

To get word of the Moscow embassy's plan to Imant, I sent a cable to Karl, who, still residing within the city limits of Riga, could sometimes be reached. In the cable, I asked Karl to call me. If he got the cable and was able to call, he would take my message out to the country to Imant. To be sure I omitted nothing, I slept with a sheet of paper on which my whole speech to Karl was typed, points numbered in order. All the next day I kept the paper in my pocket, and Wednesday night I went to bed with it again, but like a dope, when I took my glasses off, I put them on my desk. When the call came, at half past midnight, I found myself at the telephone with a piece of paper I couldn't read. The operator said she had Moscow on the line and I replied, "I can't see!"

She surely must've thought that whether I could hear was more to the point, but she went ahead with the linkup. I was trying to reach my desk with one hand while holding the receiver with the other, but I needed arms about three feet longer. "I can't see, I can't see," I repeated, hoping my mother—the upstairs phone was in her room—would find my glasses, but her reaction was to dash from bed, run downstairs, and put the cocoa on. My father, without his hearing aid, *couldn't* hear me say I couldn't see. Are similar crises going on in other households all over the world in the middle of the night?

Karl seemed calm enough at his end, though he was probably wondering, since I couldn't see, why I didn't turn the light on.

I tried to recite my message without the piece of paper. "The Soviet authorities are saying that Imant doesn't support my application for a private visit!" How I got that out, I don't know; I was so afraid that I wouldn't get everything said that the words crowded up; I felt as if I had a traffic jam in my throat.

And just suppose the Russians weren't lying, suppose Imant had changed his mind? I had been so long without a letter from him, without hearing his voice on the telephone. Besides, this was a hell of a thing to have to ask any man, even one in love: to travel some five hundred and fifty miles from Riga to Moscow, dodge the KGB, arrive for an assignation in front of a foreign embassy, and present to a foreign government the letter which his own government was trying to claim didn't exist. Would Imant do it? I asked Karl.

"Yes, I am sure," Karl said. "But he sent the cable and letter to the embassy in London, as you asked."

"The Soviets will not admit it," I said. "Karl, *everything* depends on this letter. Tell Imant that without it, we may never be able to see each other again." I picked a date out of the air. "Can Imant go to Moscow on December the seventh?" I asked.

"Yes, I think so," he said, "but why this day especially?"

There is a tone of voice that seems to me peculiar to East Europeans, which they use when they are puzzled but don't want to offend a Westerner by asking an intrusive question. They ask the question but in a voice that stands very slightly to one side, as it were, so that if the question does turn out to be troublesome, the voice can reach out and put handcuffs on it. Karl's voice was doing this now—policing his words.

I said, "They will have a man to meet him out front. I'll tell them that Imant will be there on the seventh." Then I gave Karl the telephone number of the Moscow embassy, which I'd gleaned somewhere along the line. I thought he might have a use for it. He had to search for a pencil, and in the interim I could hear my telegraphic heart again. It was beating in dots and dashes. I realized that I must have been shouting into the telephone, because I could also hear my voice echoing in my head.

"Okay," he said when he was ready. For some reason, I pictured him writing with the stub of one of those yellow half-size pencils, with no eraser and a worn point that would just barely produce an impression on paper. I gave the number to him, he read it back, and then the operator told us our time was up. "Tell Imant," I said, "that I love him very much and think about him all the time."

The operator separated us, and I went downstairs for a cup of cocoa. It was Thanksgiving morning.

Understandably, England wasn't going to celebrate the day. Neither would my parents, both of whom hated turkey. They had a concert to go to, and I stayed home with Beauregard. He joined me in the green chair, winding himself up into the smallest possible ball against my hip. If you tugged on his tail, he'd unwind and spin like a top. The U.S. embassy in London was closed, the postman had come early and bore no bad tidings, I couldn't reasonably start worrying about Imant until he'd had time to get my message from Karl. I had, in fact, that rare thing, an entire day free of fearfulness. I actually didn't have to spend the daylight hours in my usual mental crouch, tensed for blows. I could sit in the green chair, stretch out my legs, and relax. The Russian word for détente is *razryadka*, an easing or relaxing of tensions. If the world powers could feel the way I felt on Thanksgiving Day, they'd dismantle all their warheads, sack their spies, and break open a bottle of Cointreau. That's what I did, and for my money, it beats turkey anytime.

The scene framed in the bay window matched my mood, or maybe, for once, I matched it. My brain seemed to turn to bark. There were yellow leaves on the brown branches of the oak tree, all the green gone to glory. The skies were gray, a flat gray of unvarying value, the same quiet shade spread from pane to pane like a lead coating. Outside, in the fir tree, a blue tit was hanging upside down, like a Christmas ornament.

The next day a rising wind was ripping the last leaves from the oak and flinging them across the yard; they scattered like finches in a cloud of gold. I called our man at the embassy and relayed my conversation with Karl; I was worried because I hadn't thought to set an hour for the appointment on December seventh. He took Imant's address so the embassy in Moscow could send a wire to Imant in Vecpauleni, giving the details of the meeting.

But something was wrong, something was not going right, and I knew it. I had bad dreams at night and woke up worn out, and carried all day the sense of a confrontation to be resumed—with the interrogator who lives at the back of the brain and calls you in just when you think you're safely sleeping. The questions he asks are killing ones. This time he asked the same question over and over: Is Imant in Moscow?

And I knew Imant wasn't in Moscow. If Imant were in Moscow, I would feel it. I would feel the tug of those additional five hundred and fifty miles on my heart. I didn't feel it, so I knew Imant was still in Riga. Something was wrong, something was not going right, and I could hardly bear to hear the daily news, with all its tantalizing references to détente. I couldn't listen to it without experiencing sudden rushes of deep anger, like someone rejected. Could I sue the Soviet Union for breach of promise?

I had been sitting on the couch, gazing abstractedly at the telephone, when it occurred to me that it was going to ring; and then it rang.

Imant had not gone to Moscow. He was in Riga. But he had been able to telephone the U.S. embassy in Moscow on December seventh. It was now the ninth.

What he had told them was this: The authorities in Riga now said that he could not invite me to stay at the farmhouse, because the farmhouse was outside the area open to tourists. He would have to establish a residence in Riga. He would also have to become employed there.

These were evidently more *ad hoc* regulations designed to hassle us, and yet we had no recourse against them. Fulfilling them could take up to a year.

A year! *Another* year!

The Helsinki Accords said requests for entry permits from persons wanting to marry persons in another signing state would be examined "favorably and on the basis of humanitarian considerations." The Soviet Union said, in effect, we were fools for taking them at their word.

But Imant was already trying to do what the authorities said he had to do. He told the embassy he was in the process of moving back to Riga. Unfortunately, in the Soviet Union you can't just pack your bags and move. He had to file a formal request for living space inside the city limits, and then he had to wait for an answer. And we knew what it was like to wait for an answer from the Soviet Union.

Imant also said, to the U.S. embassy in Moscow, that he had sent me this information—he didn't say how—"but I am afraid she will not get my notice," and so he asked them to get it to me. This meant that, in our so-called era of détente, Imant, in order to get a message to me, had to telephone Moscow from Riga; the U.S. embassy in Moscow cabled the U.S. embassy in London; and the U.S. embassy in London telephoned me in Burghfield Common.

In fact, Imant was very carefully and obediently meeting every task the Soviet authorities set for him. Like the youngest prince in the fairy tale, he managed to accomplish every assignment. But how many tasks would they set, and how long would they make him labor?

In all of this, what Imant had asked for was simply the right to do what the law (not to mention the *ad hoc* regulations) required. Montesquieu defined liberty as "the right to do everything that the laws allow."

Justice can be realized only in freedom. If I met a Helmite who was looking for justice I would say, Go find freedom first. There is no such thing, it seems to me, as social rights without individual freedom: if justice is a kind of giving—even a kind of giving to the law—you have to be free to give. The State that simply confiscates what it wants—property or soul—works against itself, by denying its citizens *the right to behave justly;* it cuts the ground out from under its own version of law and order. That's why any tyranny creates its own opposition: the people rescue their souls by demanding the right to relinquish them how they will. The point is that moral obligations depend on freedom; without it, they aren't moral obligations. Legal obligations, maybe, social or economic or even religious obligations, but not moral. Moral obligations are those we legislate for ourselves. (In the same way, it's *because* it's possible to fall in love with many people that we pledge prior and lasting commitment to certain ones.)

IV

Brezhnev and I had birthdays. He got a czarist sword; I got a corkscrew. This seemed fair: I had very little use for a czarist sword.

It snowed in Burghfield Common, insulating the house from neighborhood sounds. From the upstairs, I could see a layer of snow like a rug on the flat garage roof. One wayward rose was blooming.

The morning of Christmas Eve dawned cold and clear; the snow had melted overnight. The mail was mostly cards—except for a letter addressed to me. The address had been typed, cut out, and pasted onto the envelope, and it was mailed, with no return address, from Crawley. There's an airport in Crawley.

Stunned, I opened it. *The letter of invitation.*

It was dated December fifth, and in it Imant said all the essential things: that we were to be married, that he invited me to stay at his place, that he had applied to the Ministry of Culture in Riga for living space inside the city limits, that he could support me. I hardly knew how to react—what to do, now that I was holding, by some incredible stroke of good fortune and timing, this letter. I did what I suppose any woman would have done. I went out and bought myself an engagement ring.

Sooner or later, the Soviet Union would have to let us get married, wouldn't they? I used my birthday present to open my Christmas present, and reflected that if I ever got to spend Christmas in my home with Imant in Latvia, I could send season's greetings to Messrs. Nepesov and Nepesov at the Soviet consulate in London.

Would I need one card or two?

CHAPTER 11

The American Connection

There'd been no answer to the letter in which I told Imant that I had received his. Recent refugee news from Latvia said that the Russians had installed computers to censor all mail. Incoming letters were said to be delicately numbered with a raised impression.

Does the computer recognize a love letter when it reads one? Do computers fall in love? "I love you," I would write to Imant—in FORTRAN. But Imant—Imant could answer in Chinese.

For that's exactly what he'd said in his last letter—that the language he was working on now was Chinese. "Could you look for some stuff concerning Chinese language," he wrote me, "some dictionaries." I started laughing all over again. If I could get it past the computer, I'd have to explain to him that Riga was one thing, but Peking was another. I draw the line at Peking. Didn't I draw the line at Peking?

I

Nepesov was Tarassof. At least one of the Nepesovs was. The true identity of the other Nepesov remained secret. For all I know, he may even have been Nepesov.

Tarassof's name was a piece of information I gleaned from the U.S. embassy, as a result of the Home Office's finally setting a date for my hearing.

The Home Office couldn't be sure that I wasn't just finagling a way to hang out in England indefinitely. I needed to be able to prove to the United Kingdom that I was making every effort to leave for Latvia—but all my days and nights of feeling the axis of my soul tilt toward Imant like "the Earth for the Sun," my hours of trying to trace my journey on a map that made some kind of moral sense, the letters I wrote trying to get there—all this was untranslatable into bureaucratese. Was there a dictionary that would help *me* out? Love is plaintext. I needed an interpreter.

My man at the embassy came through with one. On a Tuesday in March, I went to see him—my "interpreter"—at the U.S. consulate.

He had an office into which half a dozen of my "waiting" rooms would have fit very neatly. He also had stomach trouble. He was also a chain smoker. It was no wonder; the man was a worrier, and I liked him instantly for it. When I was a teenager, my father made me a box to keep pens and pencils in; on the lid he had pasted a label, to make it *my* box: WORLD'S GREATEST WORRIER.

My worries never have any effect on anything, and so can't be said to be consequential. This man, however, was clearly a man of just that: Consequence.

I explained that I was hoping for my visa to the Soviet Union to be granted any day, since the Soviet authorities now had—undeniably had—the letter of invitation. Could he help me to prove to the Home Office that I was only waiting for this visa?

The Man of Consequence immediately left the office and dictated a letter to his secretary in the anteroom; then he brought the draft back in. It confirmed that the U.S. government, including Vice-President Mondale, knew of my intention of marrying in Latvia, that the U.S. embassy had been assisting me in my efforts to go there, and that they would account it a courtesy if my United Kingdom visa were extended while I pursued this other visa. The U.S. consulate was under no obligation to do this kind of thing for me, and I was elated. Then the Man of Consequence—because he really did know how to make things happen—went a step farther. "The cables that have gone back and forth about your case," he said, more or less, "are classified. But there's nothing to stop me from dropping them casually on a desk in front of the right person while I lean over to pick up a book of matches, say." And he demonstrated the maneuver at his own desk. The stack of cables from my file landed on the blotter with a substantial thud.

"And nothing's to stop the right person from taking a look," he continued, lighting a cigarette with a match from the book he'd picked up as part of the demonstration, "at the papers in front of him. It's his job to read whatever crosses his desk."

"My goodness," I said. "I mean, my goodness." Which is not what George Smiley ever said.

Man of Consequence smiled. "I think there's something else we might try too. One of our fellows will be having lunch soon with one of the fellows from the Soviet consulate. It's possible that he can drop a hint or two, nudge things along a bit."

I was openmouthed. But I recovered quickly enough to ask if someone could telephone me after the lunch took place.

"Don't worry, we'll let you know everything that happens."

Ten days later, I received the phone call from the man who'd lunched with the Soviet representative. The Soviet representative's name was Tarassof, and Tarassof revealed that he was the man my parents and I had met. He also said that he would try to help Imant and me as soon as the consulate *received the letter of invitation*.

I was apoplectic. How long could they play this game? How many times could they change the rules?

I explained that the Soviet consulate had received this letter months ago from Imant; that they had received it again, forwarded by me, in January; and that I had a letter from Mr. *Nepesov* acknowledging receipt. Was the Soviet consulate really as incompetent as it appeared to be, or was one of the Nepesovs lying? There was no third alternative. I felt sick, realizing another two months, while I thought some progress was being made, had dropped into that great Soviet maw which swallows up all inconvenient realities. It ate whole lives.

II

My hearing had been scheduled, but suddenly I had a letter from the Home Office asking me to appear at Lunar House in advance.

Lunar House: I had visions of Commander Koenig counting down for lift-off. Eagle One on the launchpad. Moon Base Alpha hurtling through time warps. You think I wasn't in seventh heaven?

Lunar House is where aliens in England go who are hoping to stay in the U.K. for longer than their visas allow. It's a big building on a street with a sign that says: WARNING! TWO PEDESTRIANS DIED TRYING TO CROSS HERE LAST YEAR. The day I went, with my mother for company, the wind in that particular stretch of street was so cold it seemed to sweep in from outer space—an alien wind from the far side of Nowhere.

As for Nowhere itself—only my mother and I were there, in a large room with bucket chairs and ankle-high tables. We caught ourselves whispering. I asked my mother why we were whispering, and she said, in makeshift sign language, "Microphones."

"You're joking," I said.

"Probably," she agreed. "But why *do* they want to see you? They've obviously already made up their minds to extend your visa, or else they would have gone ahead with the hearing. If they merely wanted a final chance to reconsider the decision to make you leave, they could have done that at the hearing. It's what the hearing was supposed to be for."

A girl in trousers entered the room and asked for my passport. I gave it to her.

I half-thought the girl would simply bring the passport back, restamped, but instead, when she reappeared, it was to lead us into a smaller room at the end of the hall. The person she was taking us to turned out to be herself. She sat down behind the desk.

The desk top was entirely bare but for one file folder which she now laid upon it. There were no filing cabinets. There was no ashtray, as my mother discovered when she lit a cigarette. Two straight-backed chairs had been carefully placed on the suppliant side of the desk. A bare bulb strung from the ceiling forced us to blink. Obviously, no employee worked here; this was a room selected for the sole purpose of interrogation, a room where no one lived for any part of the day but where some people went to ask questions and others went to answer them.

My mother had an ash as long as the cap of a Bic ballpoint on her cigarette, and the girl in trousers went off to fetch an ashtray. We knew then that there was another room, with somebody in it, through the second door that led off from ours. This other person was not referred to in any way by the girl in trousers. I thought of the sour-faced bosomy blonde at the Soviet consulate and her ten-meter dashes to the other room. Who were these mysterious inhabitants of closed, cordoned, and curtained Other Rooms? Do they ride the subways with us in the evenings going home, do they stand beside us unrecognized at the frozen-food counter in the supermarket, buying meat pies?

She set the ashtray at my mother's elbow—we were both leaning forward as if to assume some degree of autonomy: we are here because we are interested in what you have to say, not merely because you summoned us—and opened the folder. "Now," she said, "tell me about yourself."

"What?"

"Education, employment . . ."

I glanced at the folder; it was not slim. "Well," I said, fumbling for the way in—there was an entrance to this conversation somewhere, but she wasn't handing out directions—"you know about Imant."

"How did you meet him?"

"I don't know how detailed you want me to be."

"I want to know," she said, opening a ruled notebook beside the folder and taking out a pen, "everything."

I told her everything. The café in the Metropol, the letter that came the week of the wedding. Periodically, I would become self-conscious, turn around inwardly to face myself across a mental desk, and smile awkwardly. "Do you really want to know all this?" I'd ask then, and then she quoth, like the raven croaking Nevermore, "Everything." Before she was through, the name of every job I'd ever held was inscribed in that notebook. She knew every college I'd ever attended. She knew my ex-husband's middle name and birth date, although I can't imagine what use this information might have had. Her right wrist had to be throbbing with pain, and she knew everything about me except one thing.

"All right," she said, "that should be sufficient."

"But you don't know—"

She looked at me.

"My books," I said, meekly. "Don't you want the titles of my books?"

"No."

"They're important," I said. "At least to me. They're the most important thing about me."

"I have enough data." She waved the folder, which now contained the lined sheets as well.

I was beginning to giggle. "Really," I protested, "I'd really appreciate it if you'd include the titles of my books. I'm sure they're significant *data*." For an instant, I considered sending autographed copies to the Home Office, the CIA, and the KGB.

"Not necessary," she said, firmly. She walked out of the room, her trouser-clad stride shadowed briefly on the bare wall by the bare bulb.

She had advised us to wait in the Nowhere Room again. We did—forever, it seemed. "She'll be back before one," my mother said. I asked how she knew. "Because the person she's reporting to will want to go to lunch." (My mother used to work for the government.)

At five to one, the girl returned. We stood up, towering over the tiny tables strewn around the room. (I would like to know what size the Home Office envisioned us aliens as being.) This time the girl had my passport with her. "Your lucky day," she said, suddenly expansive. The new stamp in my passport extended my visa for six months.

I tried to act surprised, although my mother and I had both noted, from a reference the girl had made to Mondale, that the Home Office had received the letter that the Man of Consequence had written on my behalf. Clearly, that letter had already swayed the Home Office toward letting me stay on. Why did they interrogate me? I suppose it was bureaucratic habit, force of a kind of thinking based on the intelligence-gathering assumption that More Information Is Always Better Than Less. But if so, why didn't they want to take down the titles of my books?

A writer could go to pieces, worrying about this.

III

I had six months—six months left in which I could try to get from England to Latvia—and the Soviet consulate was still managing not to act on my application. The Man Who Had Lunch had got back in touch with Tarassof about the letter of invitation. Tarassof told him that he had now written to Moscow and was "expecting a favorable reply soon." *A favorable reply!* Soon! I took up dancing—I waltzed around the living room—I sang to myself—until "soon" began to be "late." "Soon" was dragging its heels. Was "soon" ever going to arrive, could there ever be a "soon," was *soon* a word without any referent in reality? Come Back, Little Soon.

While waiting for "soon" to show up, I arranged for Vera, who was making another trip to Riga, to carry a letter and a copy of my new book of poems to Imant, or rather to a friend of hers who knew a friend of his. She carried the letter in an open envelope, as if it were a letter that had been sent to her *from* Latvia. The book of poems she carried like any book. Apparently, the KGB had not bothered to note the titles of my books any more than the Home Office had, because the customs official let her take it through, although he examined it closely first. I guess he was looking for trick bindings, lines between lines, penciled dots beside key page numbers.

Vera reported that the situation in Latvia had worsened considerably; she was followed everywhere, and her friends were afraid to be seen with her.

Vera's friends said the Soviet authorities were conducting a widespread crackdown: too many people had taken the Helsinki Accords at face value. The Iron Curtain had chinks and needed soldering. My man at the American embassy in London, my main man with the comforting voice, telephoned to say that the Soviet consulate was clearly stalling again. He would cable Moscow.

You wouldn't think it would be possible. How could the Soviet Union lie twice *in the same way?* Did they have no imagination? The U.S. embassy in Moscow answered my man's cable: the Soviet Ministry of Foreign Affairs said they "thought" the local authorities in Riga had told them Imant was no longer supporting my application.

It was exactly the same strategy the Soviet Union had employed before—halt all communication, allow time to elapse, and then claim that Imant had changed his mind.

I spoke with my man here; he cabled the U.S. embassy in Moscow; the U.S. embassy in Moscow cabled Imant; Imant telephoned the U.S. embassy in Moscow; the U.S. embassy in Moscow cabled the U.S. embassy in London; and my man at the U.S. embassy in London telephoned me. It went like clockwork, but why shouldn't it? We'd had practice.

IV

Imant confirmed to the U.S. embassy in Moscow that he *was* supporting my application. He also said that the authorities had promised him that he *would be* allowed to change his residence to Riga before the end of the year and that this would simplify the situation.

It was now July, a cold, damp July. The air smelled like wet laundry. No drought this year. And a weather report of my emotions would have said: thunderheads on the horizon. But my nerves were like tinder, ready to go up at the merest spark. For two years I had been waiting, hoping and waiting, working in my waiting room, hoping, waiting in my working room, waiting and working in my hoping room, waiting. I had forgotten how to be with people. I felt worn out, like the ribbon on my Smith-Corona.

I finished a new novel and traveled to London to give it to my agent's English representative.

Writing this new novel had been, in spite or because of the circumstances in which I was doing it, fun. I thought of it as my "happy" book. Each novel seemed to have a secret color. The manuscript of the first might appear to be black on white, but really it was red. The new one was yellow; it was golden, and all through that dark spring it'd glowed on my desk. All of the characters in it engaged me warmly, and I felt, constructing a world for them to move and have their being in, almost as if I were doing them a favor. I felt useful.

It was a novel in which I had taken the unhappy time with David and converted it into a joyful experience. This is partly why a fiction writer writes: with a scene here, a simile there, to rewrite the world. In this revised world, there are no KGB agents or laggard bureaucrats. There are, as it happens, an ex–arms smuggler and a stripper, a bellhop whose mother is not above blackmail, a "David" whose motives are comprehensible and generous and who is therefore likable in a way the real David had not been, and even someone rather like me except that she is happy. Except that I *was* happy when I was writing.

But that was only the fiction track of my brain running. There were also a poetry track and a nonfiction track, and these kept going too, absorbing, as the girl at the Home Office might say, data, working on Input even when the Output switch was on off. I suppose other writers work similarly. Certainly, critics love to talk about the "gestation" period, when a writer's work grows and develops internally, approaching at its instinctive speed the time of labor and delivery. Most of these critics are men, however; very few of them are mothers.

The process is really closer to the way a computer works. R2D2 knows. . . . So with the fiction track shut down, I began, I couldn't help but begin, to think about something else. This time it was forgiveness. I was thinking, actually, that it was the one thing I couldn't feel. Was it even a feeling?

For years I had thought the most important problem was solipsism: How do you progress beyond the perimeters of your own intelligence, how do you become conversant with other minds, how do you know that the voices you hear are real and not merely echoes of your own consciousness, hallucinations saying hello and good-bye with all the authority of a man in a bowler hat?

But as I grew older, another question was gathering urgency, accumulating ramifications as a tree accumulates branches. It is this: How do you forgive trespasses against you, which pile up like leaves in the fall? No answer now seems so vital or necessary as the one to this question which, as the former is the problem philosophically appropriate to the first half of life, is the great interrogative you must ask in the second.

Nothing in particular had happened to bring this question to the fore; or, rather, everything in particular had conspired to do just that. It is by experiencing things *in particular* that you discover the points at which metaphor is possible, the points even at which it is inescapable, for metaphor holds things apart precisely as it holds them together, so that the mind of poetry is not only a house but a house in a neighborhood of houses.

Everything in particular led me directly to the plural world in which, as we were saying last time around, a joyful martyrdom often seems the only just action. But the world itself remained and remains unjust. In other words, everything in particular forces us to ask how we can *live* in an unjust world. For example, how could I forgive Brezhnev, Nepesov, Tarassof, and Pribanov—that Soviet law firm, firm law—for keeping me from Imant? (I figured I didn't have the right to forgive them for anything they had done to anyone but me.)

It isn't true I had never asked this question before, or wondered in other contexts how you—I, we—achieve forgiveness, emptying the heart of all its psychological clutter, the defense mechanisms that get in the way and block the view, the ego's own knickknacks keeping the light out of the window that fronts on Redemption Drive; but I had never before realized how dark it was in the house.

How could we talk, say, about Christ's forgiving his murderers as he hung on the cross? Did he forgive and forget? Me, I never forget a rejection slip.

I try to imagine myself on a cross. It's not easy, this act of the imagination, what with bacon frying, and Beauregard loudly twitching his tail, responding to the smell of that sizzle with both ends of his body. In England, milk still comes in glass bottles—"pintas"—and I can hear the milkman down the street, clanking bottles as he swings the wire baskets off his truck. But Christ had his distractions too, three disciples who kept falling asleep and needing to be waked, until finally he said they might as well sleep on: "The hour is at hand." For an instant, I think of opening the door to the milkman and announcing, "The hour is at hand."

All right. I'm on a cross, my toes are pointing downward, and my knees, which appear to be bent from modesty, are skewed that way because the weight of my unsupported body has nowhere to go and falls forward onto itself; my head is as heavy as a planet. This is not the place of my choice; but on the other hand, for the thing I have to do, there is no better place in which to do it. What I am doing is trying to forgive the sons of bitches who nailed me here.

I cannot simply erase this event from my mind—how can I, when it is my mind that is being erased by the event?

No, you forget—if you can—*after* you forgive.

If you can't forgive via a convenient lapse of memory, how about ignorance as a basis? "They know not what they do"— but even if that's true, it isn't a sufficient excuse, to me. They damn well *ought* to know what they do. Someone else may have been ready to forgive on that account, but I'm up here only imaginarily; I've been hoisted by metaphor, not virtue; and I'm only tentatively trying out—in my mind—what it feels like to be suspended between heaven and earth, with some six hours to kill before it kills me.

I can say, legitimately, that I'm not worthy to judge them, and that a judgment would be implicit in any act of forgiveness. This sounds right; but it happens to be beside the point. In the first place, I reckon it's my duty—and anyone's—to judge that wrongdoing is wrong doing whether we're worthy or not; in fact, if we were worthy, probably we wouldn't do wrong, and being able to judge it would be an inessential talent, like being able to walk on one's hands. Second, judgment can't be the whole of forgiveness: if it were, we would be talking again about justice, repeating ourselves—and forgiveness at least appears to be something else, or something more. To the one on the receiving end, forgiveness may be, as it were, only just; but to the forgiver, it is surely an emotion as well as an act, a feeling as of discarding burdensome cargo, leaving him buoyant, raised and free.

So, what is it that gets thrown overboard, if it's neither the judgment itself nor the act of judging?

When you forgive somebody, I think (looking down at the curly heads of the soldiers), you don't mean nothing's changed—the world is forever altered by any event; the event by definition proceeds in time, and any reversal necessarily takes place in new time. And you clearly don't mean that nothing matters—if the difference between good and evil didn't matter, you couldn't judge that you weren't worthy to judge. What you must mean is that you have decided to remove yourself—literally, your self—from the court of judgment: you have decided that insult has not been added to the injury, whatever it is, which has been done to you. The injury remains—there's no putting the leg back the way it was before it was broken—but since you've dispensed with your pride, there is no insult—how could there be, if there is no ego there to be deflated?

At this point I quit; I quit to eat breakfast—buttered toast, orange juice; I hope rumination will somehow work mentally too. What I am mulling over is that David—do you remember David? do I?—would have been deeply angered by the preceding paragraph. (When David became angry, he became sarcastic. His words were like dry ice. They'd burn you if you let them touch you.) In David's eyes, egoism was the sine qua non of happiness—and he had at least the grace to say happiness and not, as they do now, shying away from their own meaning, self-fulfillment. Yet it seems to me that self-emptyfication is a more logical way to that state in which you are free of the constraints that straitjacket the soul, inhibiting the active stretch of the sensations and mind that would, if it could, range over the entire universe, lighting on and lighting up all facts, possibilities, and paradox.* If you could pour your self out from the pitcher of your body, you might be water anywhere. You could surface like an artesian spring in Afghanistan. You could be the Mississippi, the Thames, or the Daugava. You could be a well in Imant's backyard, a ripple on the lake beside his house. You could be a tear.

V

The telephone rang.

When the operator said "overseas," I was thinking Latvia, and for a moment I was wildly disoriented: Wisconsin? Where was Wisconsin?

They were offering me a job. Out of a clear blue sky—over where?

Where on earth *was* Wisconsin?

VI

I couldn't afford to turn it down. I needed the money and the opportunity, and my parents needed the house to themselves in their retirement, but all weekend I had flashes of panic, blinding reflections, as it were, when anxiety would suddenly

---

*No Nepesov anywhere in the world worries about whether I have forgiven him or not; his spiritual freedom does not depend on me. But mine does.

glint off the mirror in the mind and angle back against the self.
Wisconsin was in the wrong direction.

Time was running out (the four-mile minute). There were
ten thousand things to do and only two weeks to do them in.
First of all I sent a cable to Imant: PLEASE TELEPHONE IMME-
DIATELY STOP IMPORTANT NEWS. I waited and waited, but Imant
didn't call. He had always called within a few days of my
cables. I had typed a set speech twice, once in the first person
and once, for my folks, in the third, and made two copies of
each, one to go by the downstairs telephone and one by the
upstairs extension. I knew I would be too excited to remember
everything I had to say.

I was packing, reading my carbon of the new novel for close
corrections, writing a review, answering and filing correspondence, making travel arrangements, and waiting for an
answer to my cable.

On the ninth of August, I took the train into London to
meet, at last, my man at the American embassy.

He suited his voice very well: he was large and reassuring.
He said that the details of my case were known to U.S. officials
in London, Moscow, Leningrad, Belgrade, and Washington—
why not Madison, Wisconsin? He would continue to help
Imant and me and keep after the Soviet consulate in London;
and he would still be my contact with the U.S. embassy in
Moscow. We agreed that it was neither necessary nor advisable
for me to notify the Soviet consulate of my change of address;
it was, after all (I thought), a temporary address, and if the Soviets tried to make us start all over with a new application
from the States, they might prevent Imant from even receiving
the forms. My man also said he thought I should steer clear
of any publicity until I could discuss the question with a Certain Person—he gave me a name—in the State Department. I
wasn't to mention the word *publicity* in my telephone conversation with Imant, and, of course, I was now not to give
him my new address either, so my "speech," when I got
home, was whittled away to a few words. The IMPORTANT
NEWS had all been deleted; maybe it was lucky that Imant still
hadn't called.

VII

Later, I felt sad that I had said good-bye to my man at the embassy.

That night I had a dream about Imant. I was wandering around the world, calling for him. "*Kur ir Imants?*" I called, but there was no answer, except that the wind sounded like a voice. It had gotten dark, and I was in a forest, but I didn't know what country the forest was in. A whippoorwill was crying, a sound like night itself weeping for lost day.

I woke with a great sense of loneliness, a sense of having been divided from myself, or emptied, wiped bare, like a book from which all the words have been erased. We didn't have whippoorwills in Burghfield Common. Maybe I'd heard one of the mourning doves, in my sleep, sighing under the eaves. All day I felt slow, heavy and dim, as if my real business were elsewhere, in a forest in a foreign country, calling for Imant.

My plaid suitcase with wheels, which had carried my wedding dress to Riga, was going with me to Wisconsin. I packed manuscripts and Imant's picture in it, and zipped it up, and climbed into bed. In a few hours, it would be time to get up again. I would still be waiting, but no longer in my waiting room. The walls were bare—the map of the Soviet Union and the postcard of the Daugava were stowed in a footlocker. I had said my good-byes. Good-bye to England, to Burghfield Common. And bid a fond farewell to Latvia. But not to Imant, who hadn't called.

I fell asleep wondering what Wisconsin would be like. Were there forests in Wisconsin? Were there whippoorwills? Was it anything like Vecpauleni?

CHAPTER 12

Vecpauleni

You go where you have to, to live. You shape the walls of your house out of mud and thatch your roof with care: love lives there.

Utopia, the ideal society, is not supposed to exist. That's what the word means—"nowhere." Or "not-a-place." But it all depends on what you call ideal. What I call the Nowhere Room, that bleak cubicle in Lunar House about as homey as a crater, is not what I call Utopia. *My* Utopia exists approximately sixty kilometers outside the city of Riga. It is named Vecpauleni, and it is a farmhouse. It is my *māja*. Imant called it "exotic." I am not sure what is exotic to a Latvian, but I dreamed of low ceilings, shuttered windows, bare floors, wind in the eaves and frost on the panes. There would be snow on the ground, like a quilt; the planet turns in its sleep. At night, warm indoors, the moonlight and starlight making patterns on the frosted window glass, Imant and I would be miles from everyone—well, sixty kilometers, at any rate. We'd be blissfully alone.

Except, of course, for Princess, Imant's kitten. And the dog I would have. And the cow. And the alligators.

I had left some things behind me, in Latvia, which Imant

took to the farmhouse. Therefore, in this house there were also two hand-painted teacups, a Bechstein piano, a wedding dress, an oil portrait, a photograph of a window taken from the inside on a rainy day, some books, a curling iron and assorted cosmetics including several Rum Plum eyeshadows, a television set, music manuscript, and a black silk garter belt with tiny red satin bows which was my way of bringing a little friendly decadence into the Workers' Paradise.

As I say, I had stocked up on eyeshadow because I figured the Five-Year Plan wouldn't appreciate the strategic importance of Rum Plum.

Living in my *māja,* I would keep on writing books, even if the Soviet government prevented me from publishing them. I would publish my books for myself. I learned to do this in grade school. My teacher, Mrs. Wells, showed us how to write a title page and a table of contents, how to number the text and secure all the pages in a folder with brass pins. I liked the result so much that I wrote dozens of booklets, covering every subject I was interested in, including grammar, telescopes, and a history of the Soviet Union. (A few years later, I tackled the history of the world, but my teacher—it was no longer the patient Mrs. Wells—declined, understandably, to read it.)

But while I could "publish" my own books—and a quarter of a century later, I was still writing about the Soviet Union—Imant couldn't play his own symphonies. Utopia would have to include an orchestra. Imant and I would be blissfully alone except for the cat, the dog, the cow, the alligators, and the symphony orchestra.

In the early spring mornings, with the fresh air full of ascending larks apparently made buoyant by their trills (Latvians say larks fly skyward to sing to God*), Imant and I would go for long walks. He would teach me when and how to pick mushrooms—he knows how to do things like that. When the lake freezes over in wintertime, he goes ice-skating. He goes

---

*Shakespeare says this too. "Haply I think on thee, and then my state / (Like to the lark at break of day arising / From sullen earth) sings hymns at heaven's gate . . ." (Sonnet 29).

fishing in the summer, or writes music at a long picnic table out back, a finger of sun crossing the staves with a bar of light. I watch him do all these things. Certain abilities, which no one else gives a thought to, because, I suppose, everyone but me has them, fascinate me. He slices a loaf of bread by inserting the blade near the edge equidistant from two sides, twisting the knife in one smooth motion and turning the loaf against it in another. He knows the names of all kinds of things, and in several languages. He can chop wood and build a fire or play a piano or fix the roof. I don't know how to do any of these things.

I did learn to cook, sort of, after David and I were married. I bought a steak—we were going to eat dinner by candlelight when David got home from his day at Columbia. The steak had been in the oven for hours, and it was still raw. It turned out that I didn't have the steak in the broiler; I thought the pan at the bottom of the oven was for catching grease; I thought cooking something that close to the floor in our kitchen was like sending a dinner invitation to the cockroaches. I was baking the steak.

So much for cooking. Oh, I am incredibly incompetent, but at least I tried. Does Russia?

Doing is always a testing of limits, limits of space and time and energy. When defeat or rejection—failure—is too probable and too distasteful, what *can* you do? Nothing, or nothing much. You back away, you withdraw or stay away, you ring down an Iron Curtain, and sulk. You stick to what you can do. One easy thing to do is *tyrannize*. Tyranny is a relatively easy game to play because all the dice are loaded in your favor to begin with. You can call yourself a "great nation" and a "world power," and the only thing you will have to do is keep your citizens from testing your limits. *You* don't have to test your limits, because you won't recognize that you have any limits. A name for the refusal to recognize limits is solipsism. Another name for the same state, viewed from a different angle, is, as I had learned, paranoia. What I am getting at is this: The Soviet Union is paranoid, but it isn't crazy. It's just incredibly incompetent.

In other words, if the Soviet Union felt itself on a par with the rest of the industrialized nations, it mightn't be so fearful. It wouldn't be so uptight. It could relax, laugh at itself, and let its people go—and come and go.

Many people—Soviet officials among them—argue that the West must not, cannot, superimpose its own ideas of individual dignity onto Soviet Man, that to do so is to act contrary to hundreds of years of tradition. But "Soviet Man" is not very old; nor is he all-Slavic. A great many Soviet citizens are neither Slavs nor willing partners in the Soviet Communist enterprise. Even those who are, are just as human as anybody else. Soviet Man, at least insofar as I've been acquainted with him, doesn't naturally exemplify some specifically Soviet way of relating to the State—that relation is dictated by the Soviet State, not by the individual. And why does the Soviet State insist on this relation? Because it is afraid of being found out for what it is—incompetent.

When the Soviet Union achieves a Western standard of living—what the Soviet Union thinks of as a Western standard of living—it won't have to worry about losing its labor force. (Maybe we've got it backward, and instead of attaching restrictions to trade agreements, we should be airlifting T-shirts, rock records, and dishwashers behind the Wall. Not even Communists complain about manna.)

But Imant and I didn't want to wait for the Soviet Union to reach a level of competence corresponding to the West's. Who can wait that long? I remember the window that fell out of the Sovietskaya. We wanted to be married *now*. I didn't want to live out my days in a waiting room. My home was Vecpauleni.

There are red roses near the front door of Vecpauleni, because I asked Imant to plant them. I like roses to be red the way I like string quartets to be Beethoven: roses that are red manage the wonderful trick of being at one and the same time romantic and irreproachably classic. In summer, as Imant buckled down to work at the picnic table out back, I would step out the front door and smell roses on the air. In summer I would stand at the door and watch an early bird running across the lawn, poking his beak into the soft topsoil every three steps to pull out a worm. I'm no Audubon, but I know that this bird belongs to the species Early Bird, because he catches the worm. He opens his beak and the worm slithers into his gullet whole. How long does the worm live in that unexpected environment? Does it have time to look around, form an opinion? How long could I last, in the Soviet Union? But that's a mystery the world over, no more so there than anywhere, and no less. ". . . the great maw / Swallows all energy / And soon nothing will stay." I cut two roses for the table; in one of them, there is dew, like tea in a cup.

If this is Arcadia, it has death, like devil's fungus on the forest floor. If it is Eden, it has temptation, like hanging "moss" that suddenly moves, and winds itself around your head before you can get away. If it is the Workers' Paradise, it has despair, that brave, hopeless, lorn music in the wind, rising and falling, like clouds borne by currents of air. And if it is Utopia, it can have all these things—death, temptation, and despair—and still be the perfect place to live, while you live. The question here is not, How long? but, How?

How Imant and I would live here: Imant and I would live here blissfully, alone except for the cat, the dog, the cow, the alligators, the symphony orchestra, and the spies in the ditch.

That we would be alone was an important condition of Utopia, not because I'm painting a picture of simple togetherness—both of us would have our separate day's work to do—but because our privacy was one of the values we sought to protect when we elected in the first place to live in society; civilization was meant to ensure privacy. When the government comes crashing in on us like a bear, we might as well be living in a jungle. The first law of the jungle is, Nobody is entitled to privacy because everybody is entitled to invade it. So Imant and I would tend our own garden to some purpose, even if we didn't carry cabbages to the black market in Leningrad. The garden keeps the jungle, including the bureaucratic jungle, back. That proliferating snarl of weed and branch stops precisely at the point where we cultivate our privacy. Government qua government—as distinct from government qua jungle—exists only where it is limited.

Living in Utopia, Imant and I wouldn't claim to be self-sufficient, and we wouldn't even especially want to be, since being totally self-sufficient would take up too much of the time we need for our work. Music and poetry certainly rank, in the economic scale of things, somewhat lower than food, shelter, and clothing (although not necessarily lower than espionage: Shakespeare called singers and tellers of tales "God's spies"). But presumably, there are other houses not too far off—sixty kilometers—and some of their residents would be engineers rather than poets or composers. Ideally, I suppose, we would all have been brought up knowing how to perform a range of tasks, from cooking to construction. I wish I had been—but for my own sake, not society's. If I am thinking about the ideal me, I don't see myself contentedly fulfilling my role in society for *society's* sake. Who is Society? Nobody I ever met—or everybody, in which case I have not one role in respect to it but several. The ideal me knows how to do it all. But I am not talking about an ideal me—only about the ideal place in which an imperfect me might live happily enough.

A place in which you can be yourself is, obviously, a perfect place for you. I figure this is one definition of Utopia which assures diversity. You can be what you are, in your perfect place—though perhaps you can be fully that nowhere else. You live in your mind, and in your friends' minds.

You walk up, knock on the door, and enter the house of metaphor.

When a friend welcomes you in—or, to move this metaphor just a short way down the road, when he rolls up the barbed wire and throws open the Brandenburg Gate, and pitches a party on top of the Berlin Wall, when he pulls down the barriers and lets you into his mind—you feel at home. In the Workers' Paradise, as in any other paradise, admittance is gained by forgiveness; someone forgives you not for being what you *are,* but for *not* being what you're not—namely, perfect—and you go in, to a perfect place. Utopia isn't an anomaly, then; it's simply the world redeemed. It is the world after forgiveness. Here, in this new world, you are real, because your unreality is forgiven. It may even be forgotten.

More had a name for Utopia-actualized. "My name is Eu-
topie: a place of felicity," he wrote. In Vecpauleni, Imant and I
would be blissfully alone except for the cat, the dog, the cow,
the alligators, the symphony orchestra, the spies in the ditch—
and maybe, if we kept faith with each other, the Spirit of
truth, "for he dwelleth with you, and shall be in you."

Dear heart, a final note about the kitchen. Keep the teacups
Teodor painted on a safe shelf: one is for love, one is for faith's
long-enduring self.

CHAPTER 13

September in Wisconsin

From my office window, I can see Lake Mendota. Picnic Point thrusts itself from the center of the window into the upper right corner; Observatory Drive winds uphill across the left side of the single, broad pane. Already the leaves are turning.

I need this view. When I leave the office, I go home to a basement apartment. My neighbor, aged eighty-five, wears babydoll pajamas at night because the steam pipes that run along our ceilings—others' floors—never quit kicking out heat; I sleep in a T-shirt that says DELMORE SCHWARTZ.

I

Shortly after I got here, I had a letter from my mother: Imant had telephoned in response to my cable. Apparently he had just received the cable—one month after I sent it.

The pared-down note was still by the telephone in Burgh-field Common, and my mother read it to Imant. But Imant had his own message. "I want you to tell Kelly for me that I have been promised apartment in Riga *before year is out,*" he said. "You must tell Kelly that I have not given up, I wait for her, everything will be all right."

("All right" and "okay"—they were our favorite phrases. They allowed you to hope, but modestly, in a way calculated not to call the gods' attention to you. Of course, what we were guilty of was not exactly hubris, but on the other hand, the Kremlin was not exactly Olympus.)

"You haven't yet moved to Riga?" she asked. She had told him only that I was "away," not wanting to say more over the phone.

"That is right. But I will have apartment in Riga before the year is out."

He said he would inform me when he got the apartment. "You will forward the message to Kelly?" he asked.

"Of course."

"Then that is good, very good. Tell Kelly I wait."

II

My mother said he was so emphatic about his having been promised the apartment that it seemed to be not so much a communication to her as a warning to anyone listening in that he expected that promise to be kept.

Someone *was* listening in. At least, the State Department said so. The man my case had been referred to in Washington telephoned me one morning to advise me not to go for publicity quite yet or even to use the word *publicity* in any telephone conversation with Imant, since it would be overheard, and not with pleasure. "By the way," he said, startling me, "are you the Kelly Cherry who used to write for *Plume and Sword*?"

Who ever heard of *Plume and Sword*?

Plume and Sword is a now-defunct underground college literary magazine. I had published some poems in it, nearly my earliest published poems.

"How do you know about *Plume and Sword*?" It's nice to know our boys are thorough, but this was ridiculous.

"Hell, ever since these cables started crossing my desk, I've been wondering if you were the same Kelly Cherry."

"Were you at Charlottesville?"

"Yep. You didn't know me, though." He said, "I've been curious about what you've been writing since then."

"You have?" I asked.

"Sure. I wish you'd fill me in on what you've published."

"You do? Would you like titles?"

"Sure."

The poor guy couldn't know how funny this all was. In fact, he seemed so friendly and helpful that I decided against telling him about the Home Office and went on to ask him my favorite question: why couldn't the Soviets see that it was to their advantage, to everybody's advantage, to let Imant and me marry?

The State Department answered by saying, "They're convinced that whenever they let one of their citizens marry a Westerner, it will lead to his emigration."

"But we want to live there!"

"They'll never believe it," the State Department said, "not in a million years. I have yet to meet a Soviet diplomat or official who isn't convinced any Soviet citizen would come here in an instant."

"Why?"

"Two cars in the garage. Stereo sets. Dishwashers—"

As the State Department continued ticking off items on this list, I looked around my room.

It was early morning, and I had been asleep when he called. The telephone was by the bed. My apartment was a furnished apartment, and the bed had come furnished with bedbugs. The screened window at my right was half below ground level, and I could see spider webs strung over the screen. The pipes were clanking. I began to laugh. The State Department wanted to know why. "It's nothing," I said, thanking him and hanging up, "really." How do you explain bedbugs to the State Department?

The weather turned cold. *Tell Kelly I wait.*

Vera sent me clippings from Latvian newspapers: Imant photographed at the annual summer song festival; Imant interviewed; Imant solicited for comment as his opera, with text by Ziedonis, not me, went into production. My heart was hurting: he had a life I could only read about in newspapers; I had one in Wisconsin, and he didn't even know I was there. *Here.* I read student stories and wrote a poem.

At the suggestion of the Helsinki Commission, I asked several congressmen to write letters on my behalf to Ambassador Dobrynin, with carbons to Colonel Vladimir Obiden, head of the All-Union OVIR, the Soviet passport office. Two of them did. The others didn't acknowledge my request.

Meanwhile, The Editor Who Liked Hellmann's had sent information about my case to the U.S. delegation to the Belgrade conference. In Belgrade the question of the mails was being discussed. I tried to pretend to myself that newspaper clippings were as good as letters. The weather turned colder.

Whenever I looked out my office window, I saw a snowplow on Observatory Drive, going up or coming down. One day I put on long johns, sweaters, scarves, and walked to work in a sixty-five-below wind chill. The next day I put on long johns, sweaters, scarves, and called a cab.

And then I met a man.

III

I had a primary commitment elsewhere, to Imant; therefore I thought that if the man I "met" were himself married everything would balance out, like an equilateral triangle. The tensions would hold, and consequently the center.

That the flesh in general, and mine in particular, should turn out to be weak didn't surprise me; it had never been otherwise. But suppose the *spirit* was less than willing? Now my students could find me in my office any day of the week gazing out at Picnic Point and wondering: What's wrong with this? Why not stay right here, where every day feels so good I can't wait to get up in the morning and try it on, like a new dress? It was one thing to hold faithfully to an ideal and a vow in a time of adversity, but what about—oh, Imant, what about *versity?*

IV

(I like this wordcross between poetry and good fortune.)

I gave Patrick a key to the apartment, and sometimes he let himself in. Or he'd stay after I left for class, and lock the door behind him when he left. The first time he called my apartment "home," he was both surprised at himself and pleased, and, being a man, not unaware of the effect it had on me. He was home with me when the Helsinki Commission telephoned; it was around nine in the morning.

The coffee water was boiling; Patrick fixed me a cup and handed it to me while I paced the room with the telephone receiver. I wondered if there was a woman in the farmhouse in Latvia, waiting patiently while Imant finished talking with someone about me. *Tell Kelly I wait.*

"The State Department and I," said the Helsinki Commission, "were discussing what we might do to get certain stalled marriage cases moving again."

I registered this as: Imant and I are stalled.

After thirteen years, I might have deduced this; but for two years, countering and overcoming one Soviet obstacle after another had paradoxically allowed us to think we were making progress. Periodically, there were flurries of activity, moments of crisis, the psyche rallying to its own defense against the mob of feelings stirred by this occurrence or that; and where there could be no motion, there had been emotion, a going-out from oneself. It was like flying the Concorde to Bahrain. One moment you were in your own head, the next you were transported.

But now for months there had been only silence and stasis. It was as if Wisconsin and Latvia belonged to two different worlds: not even a cartographer of the heart could include them on the same map.

"Are there a lot of these stalled marriage cases?" I asked.

"You and Imant are now the longest stalled. There's another couple who've been waiting about a year. What we thought," the Helsinki Commission said, "is that I'd mention your case and this other one in the context of a broadcast about East-West marriages which the Voice of America is planning. If it's all right with you."

I said I'd be grateful. Then I remembered. "I'm not sure if Imant thinks he's still engaged to a woman in England. If you say I'm in America, he might wonder if there're two of me."

"Don't worry, the Soviet authorities will know who is meant."

"What will they do?"

"Well, ideally they'll give you a visa to get married." The Helsinki Commission sighed deeply. "But don't count on it."

I had to report to the commission that I'd had no letter from Imant. And then, to my amazement, I'd gotten one from Indra, addressed to England.

"In my life," she wrote, in Latvian, her handwriting sweeping across the page, "there are great changes. On the sixth of September I had a son. Now there are many new responsibilities." I thought about Indra and her baby. "When children come," she had said, in sign language, "love goes out the window." Did she find that true still? She didn't say whether she was married. It was not hard to imagine her having her child out of wedlock; but it was not hard either to imagine her not mentioning her husband because he simply wasn't germane to the given sentence. She did mention Imant—he was germane to me. She hadn't seen him in months. "He is living in the country," she explained. But thoughtfully she added, later in the letter, "Imant is waiting for you."

All these letters came during the Belgrade conference.

At the suggestion of the Helsinki Commission, I wrote again to various congresspersons. This time one of them answered tersely, to the effect that, as Dobrynin already knew how he felt about the Soviet Union's failure to give me a visa, he couldn't write again. It was clear to me that the higher-ups were getting tired of me. I was perhaps a reminder of their ineffectuality.

I wanted to say to him and to Dobrynin, to men: You think time is unlimited, but women know better. Indra knew. She had her baby.

The Voice of America broadcast was repeated several days in a row. They used my name but identified Imant only as "a Latvian composer." Briefly I thought I might suddenly receive word that my visa was being granted. Then what?

"Then you'll do what you would have done if you'd never met me," Patrick said. "Marry him."

But there was never any Soviet response to the VOA broadcast.

V

Vera—my roommate in Riga in 1975—sent me a newspaper article interviewing Imant. His new opera had been premiered and was a hit.

Karl wrote, via England. He included a minibook, a little story in English translation, but he was neither the author nor the translator. Why did he send it? The story was about a dog. Men have brutally maltreated this dog for most of his life, but one day he escapes. He lives on the fringes of society, an outsider, an outcast, barely surviving but always grateful just to be free. In the end his fate catches up with him, and he is shot. Executed. Then this is seen to be the dream of an old man who is dying; in death, the dog regains his humanity—he was treated as a beast by men who were worse than beasts. "Imant told, he is going to write you a letter," Karl said, but no letter came.

All this time, I was seeing Patrick. If it was foolish to think of making a life with a married man, it seemed not at all foolish to think that involvement with a married man would help ease the transition from thoughts of a life with a man who was even *less* accessible. But who said I wasn't foolish?

I had spent the school year coming to terms with "reality," the reality that Imant and I would never, I thought, see each other again. I was like Mrs. Brewster. In his twentieth year, my brother taught seventh grade at a county school outside Richmond. One of his students had been singularly slow-witted, and, ripe with a sense of his own newly achieved authority, he called the boy's mother in. "Face facts, Mrs. Brewster," he had told her; "your son is stupid." I hope Mrs. Brewster had the sense to disregard this; but ever since, it has served as a watchword in our family. If someone is not being realistic, he is told to "face facts, Mrs. Brewster."

But reality has a knack of sliding away, exactly when you think you're getting a line on it. The reality was, Patrick was in no position to take Imant's place, and in the beginning this was something I was cognizant of and did not find disagreeable. Now I saw that the center *was* going to hold—even if I wanted it to give way.

I was leaving for the summer. On my last day in Madison, Patrick came over in the morning. We said good-bye. Then we went to lunch and said good-bye. Later, we had drinks and said good-bye. I didn't think he could get out of the house that night, but around eight o'clock, I heard his voice through the window screen. It was a case of love coming *in* the window. We went out and came back and said good-bye some more. All of a sudden, it really *was* time to say good-bye. I didn't want him to go. But he had to, and he did. I finished packing. I was thinking that I hoped Imant had had something like that too. He deserved it. I thought also: Even if it was in spite of myself, I could say to the world, *Tell Imant I wait.*

VI

I half-figured that the State Department would tell me it was time to give up. What the State Department said was that I *couldn't* give up. "You're obliged to wait for him, indefinitely," the State Department said, "because there's no way he can get out of the engagement. He will always be tainted by his association with you."

Tainted. This word remains loud in my memory.

"You mean things could just stay like this forever?" I asked.

"We're doing what we can," he said. "You're the longest engagement case on our list, so you can think of yourselves as next in line. Or you could, if there was a line. Which there's not, exactly. When we first raised your case with the Soviet consulate here"—so I didn't need to pretend any longer that I was still in England—"they tried to say they couldn't become involved because you had filed your visa application through the consulate in London, but they couldn't really push that. You *are* a U.S. citizen."

"That's reassuring," I said.

(But Socrates had said: "I am a citizen, not of Athens or Greece, but of the world.")

"I think you can be quite hopeful, in fact."

I didn't feel hopeful.

"Although," the State Department went on, "personally I think you should mount a low-level publicity campaign. At this point it can't hurt."

We had swapped positions, and now I was the one who was reluctant to go public.

I demurred. "I haven't heard from Imant in months. Maybe he doesn't want to marry me anymore."

The State Department shook his head. "I don't think you understood. Imant *has* to want to marry you. He *can't* change his mind."

"He could write a letter saying he's decided I wouldn't be happy there. You know they'd let that letter out." This had long been a pet theory of mine.

"If you get such a letter," he said, "don't believe it. It won't be from Imant."

"That's ridiculous," I said. But I remembered Imant saying, "They may have photographs." I remembered the bowls of potato soup, the white tablecloth, that we were whispering.

The State Department shrugged. "At this point," he said, "a letter from Imant would be just as ridiculous."

Someone had had the idea of putting those of us with Soviet fiancés in touch with one another; this was supposed to result in a sense of mutual support. Instead, there was a scramble for attention: a reporter in Jack Anderson's office had told the Helsinki Commission that Christina Onassis' imminent marriage had generated fresh interest in cases like ours; Anderson wanted to do a column. The Helsinki Commission picked three cases to supply information on; Imant and I were one. I thought Anderson might write about all three—it would have been a stronger column that way—but in the end, for one reason and another, there were only a few lines about someone else. I didn't mind.

I wished the other women well, but I was older than they were, and had been at this a lot longer, and knew, as they didn't, just how tedious and time-consuming this battle they were so eager to enter would be. My own opinion of the whole matter was that it helped a lot, if you wanted to marry a Soviet citizen, to own an oil tanker or two.

Imant had never received the promised permission to live in Riga. One day the mail brought me Karl's book of poems, forwarded from England; at least Karl's interviewing me hadn't wrecked his own career. I didn't hear from Imant.

The State Department who had known of *Plume and Sword* had moved on to Thailand; there was now a new State Department, and this one said I should *not* aim for publicity. He was nice, they were all nice, if of differing opinions, but I was learning not to hope.

VII

At Christmastime, I went to England. It was a season of strikes and dissatisfaction. I was amazed by the two people who met me at the airport—they were tiny, thin, nervous, elderly people who seemed to have shrunk from being left too long in the English rain, as if they were dolls made out of cotton. The father-doll wore his tweed fisherman's hat and carried a cane; he kept patting the mother-doll on the shoulder. The mother-doll's eyes were a soft hazel, the brown lightened with flecks of gold-green, and she spoke with a southern accent in a voice that had never acquired an adult vibrato, a young girl's voice.

I got into the car with these agitated, loving parent-dolls, and we drove through countryside I had begun to forget to the house in Burghfield Common. I thought Beauregard would jump all over me, greeting me.

He was standing with his two front paws on the seat of his favorite chair, the green velvet wing chair—and simply standing there. "That's just asking too much, Beauregard," I said. "You can't expect us to start *lifting* you into it." It was the best chair in the room. "You'll have to get in by yourself."

His ears pricked up, and he turned his head toward me, but he still didn't move. Finally, he dropped his forepaws to the floor and curled up by the electric fire.

Beauregard had arthritis. The vet gave us some painkillers to slip into his food, but she said there was nothing else she could do: it was age, after all.

So! I had imagined his mourning me if I went to Latvia; but I would grieve for him in Wisconsin.

It was snowing. From the bay window, I watched it fall. By English standards it was a regular blizzard.

My mother was in the kitchen; she had to keep an eye on the stove to make sure the cocoa didn't boil over, since now, when it did, she couldn't run in to grab the pot off the burner. She no longer had breath enough for running. Her emphysema was worse.

One day my father and I made a trip into London to see a play. One day my mother and I made a trip into London to shop. Both times we passed the sign that said: FAR AWAY IS CLOSE AT HAND IN IMAGES OF ELSEWHERE. Some of the letters were fading.

Several times I thought of stopping in to visit my man at the American embassy, assuming he was still there, but I wasn't sure he'd want to have to deal with me again; I knew the top of his desk would be piled high with new problems by now. And I was afraid to find out that the Man of Consequence was no longer there; I wanted him to be alive and well and living in London forever. And I considered it advisable to keep a low profile where the Home Office was concerned.

There was always the Soviet consulate, of course. I could drop in unannounced—that being the only way you'd ever find anyone in—but did I really want to spend Christmas haggling with lobotomized bureaucrats for a visa that was never going to materialize? In all probability they would tell me I had to work through the consulate in Washington now. I wouldn't give them that chance.

I spent my days with my parents, and my nights writing. The two moons still shone, one stationary, one roving, in the windowful of black sky beyond the waiting room. Was I still waiting? Was I? Yes. No. I didn't know. Can you wait for something that's never going to happen? At four o'clock in the morning, when both moons began to dim, I crawled into bed.

Two hundred pages later, it was time to go back. One hour before my plane was scheduled to leave, the ground personnel decided to go on strike. After that, it was like trying to get a flight out of bedlam.

In the middle of the melee, I looked across the floor and saw Patrick. He was living in London for the year, setting up a branch office. (I loved the language he talked—getting the ball rolling, running it up the flagpole to see if anyone saluted, trying it on for size.) He had come to Heathrow to see his son off. Talk about a small world. From New York to Madison via Milwaukee, Patrick's son told me about his "mom" and "dad." Which goes to show: our consciences catch up with us, even when they have to fly standby.

VIII

Everything catches up. Take Peking, for instance. It would do no good anymore to refuse to go there—Peking had come to America, as part of a new era in politics.

Everything catches up. Even *bad* news from a far country.

"I'm afraid I have bad news for you," Vera wrote. "The last time I got together with A."—she named an unnameable friend—"she told me she had met with the poet Imant Ziedonis and some third person whose name I don't remember, and that at some point in the conversation the two had discussed Imant Kalnin's remarriage as a well-known fact."

Vera had always been trustworthy. I had no reason to doubt her information, other than the general possibility that the KGB might have planted this the way they had planted "disinformation" once before. But too much time had elapsed to imagine seriously that the KGB was still bothering with us. It was evident that Imant could have gotten some kind of message to me if he wanted to, so there was a reason he didn't want to.

Very carefully, I tried on the possibility that this information was accurate; it seemed to fit. I ran it up the flagpole. Very carefully, I waited to see how I would react.

By next morning, it was clear: I didn't feel in the least inclined to cry. Twenty-four hours had passed, and I still had not burst into tears. If the KGB interrogated me, I would have to admit I was dry-eyed.

Here it was, then. Imant *did* have a woman in the farmhouse. (Later, Vera sent a newspaper article that confirmed her report.)

My *māja* still existed, because it existed on my *mappa mundi*. Imant and I'd be blissfully alone there, except for the cat, the dog, the cow, the alligators, the orchestra—and his new wife.

And the more I thought about this, the more pleased I became. It must have been painfully lonely for Imant for a time, day after day unbroken except by the sound of his own voice or the Voice of America, or his fingers on the Bechstein keyboard. He needed someone. Imant had never liked living without a woman.

I wondered if she had worn my wedding dress for hers, or if she had given it away or if it hung in the closet because it had acquired a symbolic value she was afraid to tamper with. I hoped she used the curling iron and Rum Plum eyeshadow— they would be my wedding present to her.

I wondered what Frederika had had to say about this.

I put my diamond ring away.

I still wore the watch Imant had given me. It had kept time for both of us for exactly fifteen years.

The train of events, and of thought, that had left Amsterdam for Moscow in 1965, had ground to a halt, leaving me on my own again.

IX

I wrote to the State Department, but the man at the State Department wrote back that he couldn't close the file on the case unless his own sources confirmed my information. He sent an "emissary" to Riga. I imagined this emissary walking the cobbled streets of Old Riga, the back alleys. Did he stop at the medical school, to listen to the tape of a certain symphony? I imagined him stopping likely-looking people on the street (and here I saw the faces of my former dear little friends, Indra, Rudolf, Emil, Karl), to ask, "*Kur ir Imants?*"

X

I still received occasional letters from Karl. They said nothing meaningful about Imant. They were about writing, publishing, the frontiers of poetry.

He sent me a book of poems, which I received. I sent him a book of poems, which he did not receive.

"Imant," he wrote, "is up in the country."

CHAPTER 14

Journey into Heartland

I said, when I set out on what I called "a moral travelogue," that I couldn't start from any place I wasn't already in. I couldn't start from Watts or Wounded Knee; I had to begin at the beginning *for me,* or so I thought. In fact, it seems to me now, I began at the end. And I have come this long distance that I might understand where I was.

To imagine a beginning or an end, you must imagine change not-existing, and to do this you must somehow step outside the world.

Something like this is, I think, what happens in the image of the crucified Christ descending into hell. We tried to imagine Christ dead—now we must imagine him *dead.* He is outside time.

Now Christ walks out of his tomb as if he had only been catching forty winks, and though nothing appears any different—his nails need trimming, the grass in the garden needs cutting, but nothing is really *different*—*everything* is different, and nothing will ever again be as it was just last Thursday, less than a week ago.

Thus, metaphorically at least, love has power to convert

death into life, stasis into change, timelessness to time, despair into hope. Love is not time nor timeless, but greater than either, eternal; it is not still, yet it is not change itself—it *causes* change, it animates the creation. It makes, no kidding, the world go round. Evil would put an end to the world, but love makes the end a beginning, bringing into the world the possibility—the inevitability—of change.

I like these metaphors of love, like turning them over in my mind, trying them out this way and that, seeing where they take me, what meanings or messages they have for me.

Perhaps I read metaphors the way someone else reads a secret code: to learn what's hidden. Perhaps we are all cryptographers, deciphering the resurrection. And perhaps there are resurrections all around us, everywhere, but we fail to recognize them because we don't know how to see what we are looking for. Someone says, Let there be light—and lo and behold, the truth is revealed to us in the most cunning code of all: none. It is an epistle in plaintext that le Carré's "lamplighter" brings, titled "Incarnation," and you open it up and discover— what? A poem. A love poem.

"I am Alpha and Omega, the beginning and the end," saith the Poem. And you get out your book on code-breaking, and spend the rest of your life wrapping this obscure message around a pencil. How peculiar! you say, as the meaning begins to come clear. How original!

I went looking for my "meaning"—the right point, the whole reason for this autobiography's being written, the message, the moral. Like the Dubner *Maggid,* I was sure it would reveal itself, and it has. How could I have guessed that the process of revelation would have altered it, rendering it so different from itself that I might, with worse luck, have overlooked it? It could have walked beside me on the road to Emmaus, or Riga or even Peking, and I never have known it was there. I could have mistaken my meaning for the gardener.

"Woman, why weepest thou? whom seekest thou?"

The KGB only think they know the answer to that one; they couldn't be more wrong.

But luck *is* with me; I remember that things are transformed by metaphor to seem different from what they have been. Our politicians may need some coaching in this matter. Will the men in high places even *recognize* the new heaven and earth, and if not, how will they know where to draw boundaries, erect their barbed-wire fences?

Will they know that the view from the window changes, and that even the room in which you write, looking out the window, changes? Do they know that the wood of the tree, any tree, is the living side of the holy rood, and that they can't see the cross for looking at the forest?

Do they know that the journey into heartland is inward, that you walk down all the rooms of your mind and open the back door on that mysterious, broad plain, that pulsing plain, and that the map of the heart is all of a piece, and the one you find there *is* the one you were looking for, but transformed, changed, made other?

How far does that journey take you? It takes you far enough out of yourself so that you can discover the Other in you.

It takes you around the world in more or less than eighty days, depending, of course, on where you start, where the beginning is *for you*.

I started at the end, the back of the book, and have, it seems, worked my way around to the Table of *Content*. Well, it is a route.

Can I complain, if it gets me there?

I went in to my heart, which was like a tomb, and found the stone rolled away.

CHAPTER 15

Postscript: A Meeting in New York

I

On a day in May the telephone rang. It was Imant, calling from New York.

"You have a new book of poems," he said. "*Natural Theology.*"

Was the Home Office listening? The KGB? The State Department? *Put that in your files,* I thought, *and smoke it.*

I kept saying, "What? What?" Imant tried to explain: he had been issued a visa at the last minute, allowing him to accept an invitation to attend the premiere of his Fifth Symphony in Boston. The symphony in Boston had paid his way. He now had two days on his own in New York before he was to return to Moscow. He had been going crazy at the thought of having to leave the States without seeing me. He had not had any idea where I was; he had never received a single letter from me after I left England. In the ten years since the State Department had closed their file, Imant had had *no* news of me. In New York, with the help of a Latvian-American, he looked me up in *Books in Print* and called the publisher of my most recent book to get my home number in Wisconsin. He wanted me to come to New York. "Kelly," he said, "I cannot to leave without seeing you."

At La Guardia, I saw him a second before he saw me. His

head was bowed—a characteristic posture, I now realized, for someone who had learned it was safer not to antagonize people by appearing too proud. He was wearing a hat. In Indra's garden of orange nasturtiums, in 1975, we had clowned around with our respective hats, but in New York, in the late eighties, his hat seemed eccentric. His hair had receded to reveal a bulging forehead and at the sides and back hung to his shoulders. He wore wide-ankled gray slacks and a burgundy jacket that looked as if it had originated on Carnaby Street in London in 1969. He wore a very wide tie. He was shorter than I had remembered him—and I remembered having made this same discovery in 1975. He was no taller than I. He was hunched over his cigarette. He was carrying a small black clutch that contained his money and cigarettes and lighter.

He looked positively disreputable.

Then he looked up, and I looked into his eyes and realized, for the third time over the course of nearly twenty-five years, that this was the most remarkable man I had ever known.

His light gray eyes were still startling, and even more haunting. The dark pupils contrasted disconcertingly with the pale irises, which tended now toward blue, now toward green.

It was the complexity of character in those eyes, the depth of intelligence and range of emotion, that made him handsome.

He dropped his cigarette to the floor and put it out with his foot, and I took his hand. He was with the wife of the professor at whose apartment he was staying. Imant kept his head down while I talked with her. How American I must look to him, I was thinking, chatting away like this, blue-jeaned and Reebocked, a pink T-shirt to match my aerobic exercise shoes. Every so often he would turn to look at me, squeezing both eyes half shut for a quick second in a smile that denied its own existence at the same moment it came into being. It was clear—to me, probably to anyone who met him—that this was a man who knew what defeat was and had found a way to come to terms with it.

The professor's wife took my suitcase and dropped us off at the Metropolitan Museum of Art. "I do not want," Imant said, when she drove off and I suggested we go inside. I thought

I should show him the sights of New York. "I wish just to talk with you and feel what is like the city," he said. "Besides"—he gestured—"I have seen." He smiled ruefully: the banner hanging from the front of the great museum read PAINTINGS FROM THE HERMITAGE. I had probably seen them myself.

I was conscious of talking too loud—as if that would help him to understand me. In fact, he understood me just fine; but he had not had much practice in speaking English, and his accent was thick and I was finding it difficult, as it had been in the beginning, to understand him. "Kelly," he said, "soon it will be twenty-five years since we meet. Ai-yai-yai!" He slapped the side of his face. His beard had grayed.

He told me how things had been for him after I left Latvia. He had been alone in Vecpauleni—isolated. Almost no one would come to see him. Either his friends didn't have transportation, or they were afraid. For the first year, his father refused to acknowledge his existence. When at last his father did come out to the farmhouse in the second year, he said to Imant, "You realize that Kelly has broken your life and your career."

But Imant told me that he had answered his father, "No, you are wrong. No matter what happens, I will always be grateful to Kelly for helping me to change the life I was living at that time."

I was asking myself, Did I do that? Did I break his life and his career?

"You have made me who I am," Imant said.

They had made him a "nonperson." They had abrogated all his contracts (including the contract to write music for a movie in Bulgaria, so there never could have been a wedding in Bulgaria). Each week he would be called in by the KGB colonel, who would say, Do you know who is this woman you want to marry? Yes, he'd say. Well, the colonel would continue, she is a very bad woman. And then the colonel would tell "bad stories" about me, about my wild life. (Reading student manuscripts! Writing poetry!)

"Did you ever learn why they were so against our getting married?" I asked.

"No," he said. "I still do not know why they do all this to

261

us. They have known there was nothing political in our relationship. They knew all we are writing to each other for three or four years before you came, even. They knew we were in love. They were listening to all we said."

"You mean they had microphones?"

"Yes, and tapes for the telephone. And cameras—what you call them?—I think, infrared cameras. They take pictures of us together."

The colonel had told him our marriage would never be permitted under any circumstances. I told Imant that I had been told the same thing by the State Department. The colonel had gotten the letters I had sent to Imant. "But this woman," the colonel had said once, in confusion, "she is a Latvian!" The colonel must not have known Latvian any better than I did, or else my Latvian had been better than I thought. I asked Imant if his brother hadn't kept him informed about me—about where I was, what I was doing. "I think Karl did not often get your letters. I think Father took them." I had figured out for myself that whenever I referred to Imant in one of my letters to Karl, I didn't get a reply.

"Your father!" I said, with exasperation. "Your father sounds—" I searched futilely for a word that would sum up all I felt without hurting him but that would be a word he knew. "Mean," I said clumsily.

"Oh no," he said, laughing. "He is not mean. He is a good father. He is the *best* father. He is a father *star.*"

I asked after our old friends. Imant was not in touch with most of them. Indra had her son but was unmarried; she worked as a theater director. Rudolf had wandered into the homosexual underground. Karl had never remarried and still lived, at fifty, with his parents, writing and translating. Karl was bitter about his marriage, about the Russians, about life.

As for Imant, he had, he said, found a kind of peace. The isolation had been difficult, and for a time after that hard stretch he continued to be "very sad." About the Fifth Symphony, he said, "It is a very sad symphony. Is about all this." He had learned "what is a tragedy." Then at a still later point he had come to terms with his situation. He had stopped arguing with what could not be changed. What he wanted out of life now, he said, was just not to hurt anyone else. He felt that in his life he had harmed a great many people.

"I was a very long time learning what is a human soul," he said.

He said that, for example, when his first marriage had ended, his father had asked him if he didn't feel he was abandoning his responsibility to his infant daughter—and he had answered his father, "No." Sometimes he wondered who that young man—himself—had thought he was.

That first daughter was now twenty-six, married, and the mother of two children. She still kept the denim Beatles cap and vest I had brought over for her in 1975.

"Now," he said, "I have very good relations with all my children."

"And Frederika?"

He looked grim. "Not Frederika. We are enemies. She is still angry."

I asked if his current wife knew about me. He said she did and that she was "very jealous." I thought it was a good thing that I hadn't inscribed the copy of *Natural Theology* that he had asked me to bring for him. (This is your book, I wanted to say, written for you and about you. But surely the poems themselves would tell him that.) He described her as a "simple country woman." She had been his neighbor in the country. When he met her, she had been in the midst of divorcing her husband because he drank too much. After a while, she said to Imant that if he was going to keep on "visiting" her, he ought to marry her. "I thought she was right," Imant said, "so we got married." She had two children from her first marriage, teenagers, and she and Imant had an eight-year-old son. "He is taking piano lessons," he said. "I want him to have a good education." I knew that to get a good education for your children in the Soviet Union you had to play by the rules.

I felt that Imant saw himself in his son, wanted to see him become a musician too. Here is a man, I thought to myself, who is determined *not* to change his marital situation.

Our chance was gone. "But I tried," he said. "I knew I must

to see you, to say you I did everything I could, for we could get married."

Back at the apartment where he was being put up, we talked in the falling dark, in the living room that looked out over Morningside Heights and Harlem. The professor's wife wouldn't return until nine or so. I wished we had *A Little Night Music*.

He asked about my work. He had been glancing through *Natural Theology*. "What does *bribe* mean?" he asked, coming across it in one of the poems. I explained. *The life of a KGB agent is a hard one, / God knows. Paperwork all day, and at night— shadowing lovers to the cemetery. Oh, / it's work and no thanks, / except an occasional bribe. . . .* His face lighted up. "Is angry!" he said. "Good!"

He turned the page. "Kelly," he said, "no one writes like you." I knew that he was not an authority on contemporary American poetry, but it was still nice to have someone who believed in you. When I confessed I had thought of giving up on fiction, he said, "Kelly, you cannot quit. You have been touched by the finger of God."

And if I had not been, when he said that, I *felt* as if I had been. This must be what love is all about: helping the other to feel loved not only by oneself but also by God.

His own career was back on track. After the period of isolation, of being officially a "nonperson," when it was not permitted for his work to be played, the broken bones of his career began to knit. He wrote two successful operas. He had twice taken what I understood to be the top award for cinema music in the Soviet Union. He wrote and performed "classical rock" with a band that toured three or four days a week.

The rock band business worried me. Was he forgetting to write "real" music? And how long could he bear up under the strain of touring? He wasn't getting any younger, I pointed out. "I am looking for another keyboard player right now," he assured me. "When I find one, I will tour less. But I like these performances. The rest of the week, I work alone." I asked him what a typical day was like for him; I wanted to be able to picture him going about his life in Latvia. "I am going to bed very early," he said. "I do not watch telly much—some sports sometimes. Often I am in bed by eight-thirty or nine. Then I get up at four or five, and by six I am at my desk. I write music until noon. In the afternoon there are errands to do." His wife didn't work; she looked after the house and children. The "house" was an apartment in Riga now—an apartment that was not as large as the one he'd shared with Frederika but "large enough."

"I still have all," he said when I asked him about the wedding dress, the Rum Plum eyeshadow, the painting and photograph—all the items he had taken to "our" house. He still had the teacups Teodor had made. "I will ask when I get back," he said, "why they did not let us marry. I have friend in KGB now. He will tell me."

Even if the situation had altered so completely that he now had "friend in KGB," I wondered if it was wise for him to mention that he had seen me. But he thought it was better that he volunteer the information, in case word got back otherwise.

I thought of those weekly interrogations, all the hard things he had had to endure in his life. I wanted him to understand that what he had gone through had not gone *unknown*. "You are a good man," I said.

"No," he said, adamant. "In the Soviet Union we are all deformed. But I feel at peace now. I feel I have learned who I am. I think I can do something for my country. And that is something."

He had recently been made the first president of a new association of Latvian musicians. He believed that, under Mikhail Gorbachev, the Baltic States were steering in the direction of a much greater freedom. He dared to hope he might now be able to travel to the West frequently. After the professor and his wife had both come home and we'd all said good night, Imant smoked another cigarette and read a Latvian newspaper published over here. He wanted to know what Latvians outside of Latvia were writing about Gorbachev.

I was a little annoyed that he was reading Latvian newspapers instead of paying attention to me. I started spreading the bedspread over him, since the couch was also his bed for the night. "What are you doing?" he asked.

"I don't know," I said. "Tucking you in."

He leaned forward to light yet another cigarette. (It was a good thing we hadn't gotten married, I said. If we had, he would have divorced me for nagging him about his smoking.) I sat down next to him. Despite my lessons of a decade before, I could no longer make out enough Latvian words to follow an article very far.

I couldn't hold my eyes open anymore, and I said good night and returned to the makeshift cot in the dining room, on the other side of the pool table. The professor could not have played pool very often because the pool table was covered with a sheet and piled high with books.

In the morning, the sun was shining. We went to the Cathedral of St. John the Divine on Amsterdam Avenue and ate pastry at a café across the street—sitting at an outdoor café being one of the things Imant had most wanted to do in America. (I suppose Moscow is short on outdoor cafés.)

It was strange to be strolling in the brilliant sunshine on the upper West Side with Imant. This was where I had first lived with David.

"If we keep doing this," I said to Imant, "we'll be sixty years old the next time we meet."

He smiled. "It will not be so long, I think," he said. He was cooking up various schemes. He was going to come live in New York for six months. I explained that Wisconsin was not exactly next door to New York. "Yes, yes," he said, "I understand. So you will come to New York one week and I will come to Wisconsin the next week." The extravagance of this notion made him like it all the more. But he had no desire to live in the States. He thought, he said, that "it must be very hard to be an artist in this country." He had seen for himself what I had tried to tell him about the limitations that commerce imposed on art in the West.

I told him about the book I was writing about us. I mentioned that I had changed the names of all my Latvian friends, including his. He was amused by the names I had chosen for the others, but when I told him the name I'd assigned to him, he said, "I do not like." I said I would find another name, but he said, "No, use my name." I pointed out again that his wife might someday read this book—not to mention the KGB. "No, no, Kelly, I want you to use my name. It must be the truth."

This man, who, only a few years ago, had been subjected to weekly interrogations by a KGB colonel, was now carrying in his suitcase, along with all the presents for his family and friends, a Congressional Certificate of Recognition for Achievement in the Field of Music, signed by the young Joseph Kennedy, representative to the U.S. Congress. Every time he looked at it, he laughed again. He wondered what Customs in Moscow would make of it.

He was dazed, amazed. "Americans are eating a great lot of vegetables!" he had said in the restaurant where we ate dinner. "I like these WALK–DON'T WALK signs!" he had exclaimed at the curb. His mind was whirling.

He was standing in the luggage line at Kennedy. The Pan Am counters were a mess—everything was delayed. I had hoped to see him onto his plane but instead had to leave to catch mine. Here we were, once again saying good-bye—and it seemed to me that we had not yet quite figured out how to say hello. I hugged him and started to leave but then couldn't stand it and ran back to him and kissed him. "Take care of yourself," I whispered. And then I left him there, in that line, in that chaos, looking lost.

It would be the next night before he got to Moscow, Saturday before he was back in Riga.

II

I am sorry that I do not have more of a love story to tell. People like a love story.

I have written a love story now and then, and in it the narrator never frets over the nature of justice or wonders what

267

Utopia might be like. A meaningful love *story* may ask these questions, but not the narrator of it.

Here, I am the narrator, and I have asked these questions and others like them. I have asked them because this is not so much a love story, however meaningful, as a story *about* meaning. Girl meets boy, yes—but why? Why did I meet Imant in the Metropol in Moscow in 1965? What did it mean that our lives and careers had been violated by the intrusion of government? Did it mean anything? Often enough, at night, I thought it did not; I thought Imant and I had let the politicians of the world fool us into thinking it was somehow important to defy them. Maybe it had never been important at all.

And now even history had pulled the rug out from under our feet. All that time that had been Imant's and my long struggle—that was now "the period of stagnation." That was now "the Brezhnev Era." Time itself had been given a label and filed away, out of mind. For the time being, at least—but for how long?—there was the possibility of an open Soviet society, economic reform, greater freedom for minorities, and an end to the Cold War.

(But, at least for a time, after our meeting in New York, my letters to Imant would still not get through. At least for a time, I still would not be allowed into the Soviet Union. Imant would be harassed upon his return.)

Then I remember that meaning has never come without a struggle. It has always been necessary to decode the text. Language must be learned. It has always been necessary to describe a context for narrative—a circle around the arrow—before the center reveals itself as center.

God is not manifest until you open your eyes.

So that is why I tell my story, which is not entirely a love story. It has been a story in search of itself, a story that found its meaning in being told. Call it a history. This is what happened to me. I went to Moscow, and I met there a young man named Imant, and together we tried to make this mean something. And did.